The Prophets

The Prophets

by EMIL G. KRAELING

 RAND McNALLY & COMPANY

CONTENTS

FOREWORD

This book has been developed as a result of reader reaction to an article on the prophets written by this author for *Life* magazine's Special Double Issue on The Bible (December 25, 1964). There was an enthusiastic response to the article in many quarters and a desire on the part of some readers to hear more about these elect spirits of the Hebrew people. There seemed to be a need for an expanded version of the *Life* article, which would re-create the ministries of these men and utilize the new background information about their times that has recently become available.

In order to make such a book possible at an attractive price, it was necessary to limit major treatment to the best-known and most significant figures among the so-called "writing prophets," dealing with the others only lightly. The interested reader may refer to the author's *Commentary on the Prophets* for more information on these lesser figures.

I wish to thank those who encouraged me to undertake this work and bore with me in patience when completion of it took more time than had been foreseen. May the book help those who seek to understand the prophets, and enable them to feel something of the spirit that moved these men.

EMIL G. KRAELING

The Prophets

INTRODUCTION

The Historical Importance of the Hebrew Prophets

The influence of the Hebrew prophets on human history has been so vast that it is impossible to appraise or describe it. Without the prophets there would have been no Judaism, no Jesus called the Christ, no apostles and martyrs. Mohammed would have been merely an unknown camel driver. There would have been no Crusades, no Reformation. All history would have been different and far poorer. It is apparent then that these elect spirits of Israel demand attention not only from the religionist, but from all those who would understand our civilization.

To the Jewish synagogues of the last pre-Christian centuries—both within Palestine and outside, in the Hellenistic Roman world—belongs the credit for giving the ancient prophets of the Hebrew people their start toward world historical influence. This was because the synagogue admitted to reading, in addition to the basic Torah, or books of Moses, some historical books in which prophets played a role, and other books which consisted mainly of the words, or sayings, of prophets. These two bodies of material were called the "former prophets" and the "latter prophets" by the Palestinians, and soon came to be regarded as canonical, or sacred books, though in the view of their rabbis secondary to the Torah. Thus the prophets spoke anew to generation after generation, and the power inherent in their words was widely distributed. Through translation into Greek these books also became available to the Jews of the dispersion, and there, too, exerted their influence. Many pagan Greeks, dissatisfied with their own religion, were intrigued by the Jewish scriptures, and attended synagogue services to hear them read. Since the pagans had a special interest in divination, the reading of the prophets must have had a special attraction for them.

The prophets, however, would have failed to attain their potential in world influence had it not been for the birth of Christianity. This movement made much of the prophets, and saw in the events of the life of Jesus the fulfillment of a great number of their sayings. The Greek Bible translation contributed enormously to the expansion of Christianity in the Roman Empire. Although they were driven out of synagogue after synagogue, the Christian missionaries were often able to convert some Jews and especially some pagan listeners. When the Jewish war broke out in A.D. 68, a substantial number of Greek-speaking Christian congregations already existed in foreign lands. Though public sentiment in the Roman world turned against the Jews, these Greek-speaking Christians, thanks to the teachings of Paul of Tarsus, clung to the Jewish sacred books and looked upon them as having been written for the people of God of every race and color. Thus the prophets became part of the church's Bible, too. After the Jews sank into a ghetto existence, their prophets would otherwise have had no further effect outside their own circles; it was the Christian church that made the Jewish sacred books known to the western world and thereby extended the influence of the prophets throughout the world.

The Prophetic Consciousness

Before proceeding further we must ask: "What is a prophet?" The modern man will promptly reply: "One who can foretell the future." But this is too one-sided an answer to fit the great Hebrew prophets. Crystal gazing was not their special interest, though they showed a capacity for it at times. Broadly stated, a prophet in the Hebrew sense was a man who was subject to moments of inspiration in which he knew himself to be speaking with divine authority. The title Nabi, which is the one that is rendered "prophet" in our translations, is of uncertain meaning. It has been widely held to mean "speaker." Some scholars think it is a word borrowed from the "Akkadian" (or Assyro-Babylonian), in which nabi'u means a person "called" by the deity. But since there is no evidence of that word being a title for inspired men in Assyria or Babylonia, this explanation remains doubtful, too. Whatever Nabi meant at first is not as important as what function the title suggested to the great prophets themselves. And here we can hardly be in doubt. When addressing an individual or an audience spontaneously the Nabi regarded himself as being either a spokesman of his god, or, if prompted to go somewhere to deliver an oracle, as a messenger of his god. Perhaps the former situation was the more common one. No introductory words for oracles are used more frequently in the prophetic books than "Thus says the Lord"; this is the spokesman situation, in which the seizure of the prophet by the spirit of the Lord could be most clearly observed. When a prophet was sent elsewhere to carry a message, the inspiration in which he received it took place before he delivered it, in most cases no doubt in private and most often in the early morning hours. Witnessing a prophet's seizure of inspiration must have impressed people with particular awe. The prophet, they realized, was a "man of God," one whom the deity owned and controlled. But some worldly and sophisticated persons were skeptical, and regarded such a man as insane (meshugga').

How is it thinkable or possible that men should have this consciousness of being authorized to utter or carry communications revealed to them? This is a secret which we shall never be able to penetrate. Psychology, psychiatry, and psychoanalysis have been used in discussing the subject. But the remoteness of the times and the uncertainty and the incompleteness of the reporting are formidable barriers. The tests and interrogations that can be applied to living persons cannot be applied to the prophets. It is no wonder then that few valid results have emerged from such studies, and certainly none affecting the metaphysics of the matter. More fruitful is a broadening of the base of inquiry by analogy and comparison.

The Uniqueness of Hebrew Prophecy

Inspired men who have something in common with the Hebrew prophets can be found almost everywhere, in the East or West, in antiquity or in more recent times. It would be like carrying coals to Newcastle to enumerate examples here. Even the messenger idea has been found associated with such persons; for instance, in letters from the kingdom of Mari on the Euphrates (eighteenth century B.C.). In these letters we hear of a message given to an inspired man by a god at his temple in the city of Terqa, for forwarding to the king of Mari. But the similarity with the messenger consciousness of the Hebrew prophets is purely formal. The contents are what matter, and in this case they were merely a revelation that offerings should be brought to the spirit of a deceased former ruler of Mari. Neither this message nor any other one from the same quarter can compare intellectually, morally, or religiously with the oracles of Israel's prophets. One can range throughout Oriental antiquity and study Egyptian and Assyrian prophecy, but in the end one will not be any the wiser.

As far as one can determine at present, prophets of the status of those whose utterances are preserved in the Old Testament were possible only among the Hebrew people. If one asks why this should be so, it may be pointed out that nowhere else were circumstances so favorable to the rise of such personages. The ancient Oriental states, such as Babylonia or Assyria and Egypt, had existed for thousands of years and were bureaucratically and thoroughly organized. They had numerous great temples and powerful priesthoods; inspired men there immediately came under priestly control. Religious independents, driven by high moral impulse, would hardly have been tolerated. In the Greek states, a prophet of the Hebrew type is also unthinkable, but for a different reason. Here the civic organization was too firmly established to leave room for such persons. Actions like those of the Hebrew prophets would have been regarded as undignified or as indicative of diseased minds. While the "ecstatic" prophetic factor did exist, it was confined to certain oracle centers to which cities, rulers, and individuals submitted their inquiries.

Greek Prophecy

It will be useful to dwell for a moment on the Greek oracle practice. The most famous center was at Delphi. The Pythia, as the inspired person was called there, was a priestess who achieved an ecstatic state by sitting on a tripod set over a cleft in a rock. The fumes emanating from the rock were believed to enter into her. In addition she might chew the narcotic laurel and drink water from the sacred Cassotis Spring. The oracle produced by her in the ecstatic state was usually so incoherent that it required interpretation. It was the function of special men to do this interpreting and to put the oracle into the poetic form in which it was issued. Such men had the title *prophétes* (prophet), which meant "interpreter." But the credit for the substance of the oracle belonged not to them but to the Pythia. It was something aloof, however, and was not associated with an effort to persuade the public. The deity had given its dictum, and men could take it or leave it. As a matter of fact, the advice given by the oracle was often disregarded by those who sought it.

In his discussion of the different kinds of madness that could possess human beings, Plato links the "mantic," or prophetic, madness—such as that of the Pythia—with the poetic madness. The latter was able to develop more freely among the Greeks than the prophetic variety. There is a surprising parallelism between the call to the poetic office experienced by the Greek Hesiod (c. 700 B.C.) and the call to the prophetic office received by the slightly earlier Hebrew Amos. Both were shepherds. Hesiod states that he was taught noble songs by the gods when he was pasturing lambs at the foot of the Helicon mountain range, for there the goddesses known as the Muses began to speak with him. They breathed into his spirit a divine voice, able to sing of that which lay in the future, as well as of that which lay in the past, and commanded him to praise the eternal gods, but first and last, themselves, the Muses. Amos, on the other hand, speaks tersely of his call and with a mere hint of what happened (7:15). But the poets of Greece and the great prophets of Israel are indeed brothers under the skin. One may hold that the universal Spirit inspired each one according to the degree of light provided by his own time and environment.

The Crucial Problem for Prophecy

The great Hebrew prophets were public men, mainly concerned with political and social questions of the day. But the life of a people is inextricably bound up with that of other peoples. Israel was to learn that a land acquired by the sword had to be defended by the sword. Wars with peoples from Transjordan, with the Philistines of the coastal plain, and with the Aramaeans of Syria had to be fought. The early prophets before Amos generally played a patriotic role in these wars. But in the mists of the future lurked far greater perils, of which people generally were hardly aware. From the vantage point of modern historical knowledge we can see—more clearly than they could—the problem that would soon confront Israel and Israel's prophets.

In the ancient Near Eastern world there were two major power centers, one in Asia, in the Euphrates-Tigris countries, and one in

Africa, along the river Nile. If either of these was in an active imperialistic stage it had to strive to expand into the Syro-Palestinian area. Such
a move regularly called for counteraction by the other power center.

The Hebrew absorption of Palestine had begun in the late thirteenth
century b.c., in a period when the northern power center was inactive,
and the southern was allowing the despised Asiatics, who seem to have
been greatly reduced in numbers at this time, to stew in their own
juice. This disinterestedness of the great powers made possible not only
the gradual conquest of Palestine by the migrating Hebrew tribes, but
the whole upward thrust of early Hebrew history.

The Rise of the Lord

A peculiar religious development created a grave problem for the
prophets. The people called Israel, or a segment of it, during its early
migration had covenanted with a god of a sacred mountain, Sinai, or
Horeb. Like all gods he had a name. It was written in four consonants,
originally without accompanying vowels—Yhwh, probably pronounced
Yahweh. Israel credited this god with its deliverance out of Egyptian
captivity. His leading ordinance forbade the making of any image or
likeness of him. An "ark of the covenant," looked upon as his seat,
was carried along in the desert wanderings. The people thought of him
as "the LORD, the god of hosts" and fought the early successful wars
with his help.

In the ancient world a god grew in importance as his people increased
in numbers and influence. With the rise of the kingship in Israel the
Hebrew god became regarded as a king-god. The Judean David succeeded in getting possession of a real potential seat of power, the
Canaanite city of Jerusalem. He made this city the residence of his god
by bringing in the Israelite ark of the covenant that the northern tribes
had lost to the Philistines, and had failed to repossess. David's son
Solomon built a temple and palace with the aid of builders and craftsmen obtained from the king of Tyre. The Lord was now a great king-
god in Hebrew eyes. When a sacred procession was held with the ark
and the latter was brought back into the city, men sang, "The LORD
of hosts, he is the King of glory!" (Ps. 24:10). Imperialistic goals
beckoned. Even the secession of the northern tribes under Solomon's
son and successor did not change the status of the Lord previously

achieved. In both Israel and Judah, he was still the god of gods. This view was maintained in spite of the relatively light political weight of these kingdoms.

But what would happen when either of the major power centers burst their bounds and put the upstart kingdoms of Syria and Palestine in their place? Would the Lord be as strong as Ashur or Marduk, the chief gods of Assyria and Babylonia, or as Amon, the great god of Egypt? This question was going to be a desperate one for the Hebrew religion, and it was going to concern the prophets very much.

Seers and Prophets

Hebrew prophecy did not spring forth full-grown with the emergence of the people. It evolved, underwent change, attained maturity, declined, and was metamorphosed in the end into something else.

At what period the prophetic process began is uncertain. True, some strata of material in the Pentateuch represent Abraham and Moses as "prophets." But this is generally regarded as a projection of the later prophetic ideal into the past. According to a remark in an ancient narrative in 1 Sam. 9-10, the term "prophet" had come up only in the course of time.

> (Formerly in Israel, when a man went to inquire of God, he said, "Come, let us go to the seer"; for he who is now called a prophet was formerly called a seer.) (1 Sam. 9:9)

"Seer" (Hebrew, ro'eh), thus, was the early Israelite term for an inspired person. This agrees well with the fact that we do not hear of prophets, but only of seers, among the pre-Islamic Arabs, whose milieu corresponds most closely to that of the early Hebrews. We must assume then that other narratives calling Samuel a "prophet" are using the later terminology and viewpoints.

The story of 1 Sam. 9, however, presupposes that prophets already existed in Israel in Saul's time. For Samuel, in telling Saul what will happen on the way home to Gibeah, says:

> "... you will meet a band of prophets coming down from the high place with harp, tambourine, flute, and lyre before them, prophesying. Then the spirit of the LORD will come mightily upon you, and you shall prophesy with them and be turned into another man." (1 Sam. 10:5-6)

It is unlikely that "prophets" here is a substitute for "seers." Conduct of this kind is not characteristic of the latter. The seer had clairvoyant ability. If he had to seek inspiration his ecstasy was attained in a more passive manner, typically described in the case of Balaam (Num. 24:4), and his function was completed when he gave his oracle. The early "prophet," on the other hand, felt seized by the spirit and was then to "do something," convinced that the Lord was with him.

Israel then had only seers when it came into Palestine. The probability is that the Hebrews became acquainted with a new type of inspired person, called a *Nabi*, through the Canaanites. We hear of 450 prophets of Baal whom the Phoenician-born queen Jezebel subsidized (1 Kings 18:19). The Phoenicians certainly did not derive the institution of prophet from the Hebrews. The Phoenicians, too, were Canaanites, and their settlements extended far into Asia Minor. Indeed, the latter region may be the ultimate home of the kind of "prophesying" described in the passage quoted. For the Dionysian mysteries were marked by a similar abandon. There is even a surprising parallel to the story of Saul among the prophets in an account of the Scythian king Scyles among the devotees of Dionysus (Herodotus, 4, 79).

The Change in the Ways of the Prophets

Whatever the origin of the prophet as distinct from the seer, the two classes eventually merged and the terms became synonymous. The conduct of the prophet became more like that of the seer, but the prophet title replaced that of the seer.

The change also applied to the role in public affairs. The early prophets during the upward thrust of national history had at the same time been activists who sometimes felt inspired to take action of far-reaching consequences. A Deborah urged going to war against a Canaanite oppressor (Judg. 4–5). Samuel, according to sources that think of him as a prophet rather than as seer, undermined the position of Israel's first king, the Benjaminite Saul (1 Sam. 15). An Ahijah of Shiloh sparked the secession of the northern tribes from Judah (1 Kings 11:29 ff.), thus inflicting a grievous blow on the national unity. An Elisha instigated the overthrow of the northern kingdom's most able dynasty, the house of Omri (2 Kings 9:1 ff.).

We have not the space to enter into early prophetic history in this volume. This does not mean that we do not recognize its importance. What is told of some of its heroes, notably of Samuel, of Nathan, of Elijah and Elisha, has had a powerful impact on Christian history. Not all of the repercussions have been beneficial. Some of the Elijah and Elisha stories encouraged religious fanaticism and provided pretexts for the persecution of heretics; they even led to the horrors of the religious wars of the sixteenth and seventeenth centuries.

The classical prophets of the eighth century and their successors, however, were not political activists. For their mission they relied mainly on the spoken word.

It is not necessary to suppose that every utterance of an Old Testament prophet proceeded from a special revelation. Where the attitude of his God is well known to a prophet only the prompting to speak was necessary. Even in the special revelatory message the poetic figures and thoughts in which it is couched are contributed by the prophet's own imagination. Still more is this the case with the description of current evils. The prophet did not need to be told by the Lord what they were. He saw them with his own eyes by virtue of his own moral and religious sensitivity, and spoke accordingly.

The Prophets and the Historical Process

The period of grace for Israel and the other new peoples that had arisen in the Syro-Palestinian area in the thirteenth century B.C. came to an end in the ninth and eighth centuries. This was when the kings of Assyria turned their eyes westward and began to subject the kingdoms of Syria one by one. As those birds called the petrels, of which the albatross is the greatest, were said to appear to mariners in the storms at sea, so prophets emerged at the time when the tempests of war were approaching: Amos, Hosea, Isaiah, Micah. The kingdom of Israel was destroyed, along with its old rival "Syria," or Aram, centering at Damascus. Egypt, called forth to the scene, sought to rally Judah, the Philistine city states, the Phoenicians, and the Transjordan states for a shield. In this fighting Judah was overwhelmed by the Assyrians, though its royal house was allowed to continue.

In the latter part of the sixth century, when the fall of Assyria loomed on the horizon, the storm-birds flew again: Zephaniah, the young Jeremiah, Nahum. Once more there was a mighty historical change.

When Assyria had been crushed in 612–605 B.C. between Medes from the north and the "Chaldeans," or Babylonians, from the south, the latter, after defeating the Egyptians in 605 B.C., became the successors to Assyria's title of empire in Syria and Palestine. The petrels of the Chaldean ascendancy were Jeremiah and Habakkuk. Judah, which had fallen under Egyptian control, finally accepted Chaldean sovereignty. Subsequent rebellion, aided or incited by Egypt, became Judah's undoing. In 597, the Chaldeans took Jerusalem for the first time and deported the upper classes to Babylonia. Among these exiles the prophet Ezekiel carried on a ministry of warning, while Jeremiah continued to the end of Judah, powerless to avert the second rebellion that led to Jerusalem's destruction in 587.

But the days of the Neo-Babylonian empire were brief. The petrels of the age were prophets who wrote anonymously. Above all others, the author of fifteen chapters appended to the book of Isaiah 1–39, whom we call Deutero-Isaiah, saw its end coming, and prophesied of a new future for his people. In 539 B.C. Cyrus of Persia captured Babylon and soon gave permission to the Jews to return and reconstruct their homeland under Persian rule. New prophet-petrels attended various crises, notably Haggai and Zechariah, Obadiah, Joel, and Malachi. But they are of lesser interest, since they were living in a period when the Jews could not participate in world affairs.

When the Persian empire fell under the blows of Alexander the Great in 333 the Jews came under Greek rule. In this period there were only anonymous literary prophet-petrels, whose productions were worked into the existing books. The canon of the prophets was probably complete and immune from further interpolations by 200 B.C. The author of Daniel issued his work in a great religious crisis (165 B.C.), but too late to get into the Hebrew prophetic canon.

The Prophetic Situation

What manner of men were the prophets beginning with Amos? By their words we must know them, for biographical information concerning them is slight. But is it much different with Plato or with Shakespeare? One must be struck first of all by the fact that we have before us in most cases men torn apart inwardly by a tremendous devotion to their people and an even greater devotion to their god. Fortunate

were the few for whom these two factors were in accord. Most of them
saw a situation of complete discord. In the minds of some of them
lived an impression of an ideal relationship that had existed between
God and his people in the beginning, and a longing to see this relationship restored. We smile at their belief in the good old days. The
early historical narratives make it abundantly clear that human beings
were just as wicked and willful then as later. But a deeply satisfying
historical illusion is like a strung bowstring that can speed an arrow
to its mark—in this case the arrow of moral worth and spiritual religion.
The imaginary past produced by the moral mind begets the imagined
future, and the latter has in it the potential of lifting men into a higher
sphere.

CHRONOLOGY OF THE PROPHETS

Prophets of the Assyrian Era

Amos c. 760 b.c.
Hosea c. 750
Isaiah c. 736–700
Micah c. 725
Zephaniah c. 627
Jeremiah c. 625–
Nahum c. 612

Prophets of the Chaldean Era

Habakkuk c. 600
Jeremiah –586
Ezekiel 593–571
Deutero-Isaiah (Isa. 40–55) c. 547–539

Prophets of the Persian Era

Haggai 520–515
Zechariah 519–515
Trito-Isaiah (Isa. 56–66) c. 495
Obadiah c. 480
Malachi c. 460
Joel c. 400

Prophets of the Greek Era

Deutero-Zechariah (Zech. 9–11) c. 330–
Trito-Zechariah (Zech. 12–14) c. 285
Isaiah Apocalypse (Isa. 24–27) c. 275
Author of Jonah c. 250
Daniel 164

PART 1

PROPHETS OF THE ASSYRIAN ERA

1 AMOS, HARBINGER OF JUDGMENT

OUT OF THE MIST that shrouds Hebrew history of the early eighth century there steps forth the figure of a man named Amos. He marks a new age in the development of religion. With him creative individualism enters Israel's spiritual and intellectual life. In that respect he has a parallel in Hesiod (c. 700 B.C.), who had a similar importance for the Greeks. History remembered Hesiod, as shown by the remark of Herodotus who ranks him next to Homer. But Hebrew historians omitted any mention of Amos's name, though speaking of the slightly earlier Jonah (2 Kings 14:25). If Providence had not preserved a book containing collected oracles of Amos we would not know that he had existed. The editorial introduction of that book preserves information about him.

The Time of Amos. One may suspect that the original title of the book was "The words of Amos of Tekoa which he saw concerning Israel two years before the earthquake." The first editors thus resorted to a method much used in early Babylonia—the dating by an important event. It seems likely that it was the earthquake mentioned which led to the publication of Amos's oracles, as that calamity had substantiated some of his predictions. Since the book reveals that Amos prophesied at the time of King Jeroboam II of Israel (c. 787–747), who was a contemporary of King "Uzziah" (Azariah) of Judah (c. 787–736), later editors could easily expand the title by adding reference to these rulers. They knew also that an earthquake had occurred in the days of Uzziah from its mention in a late prophetic book (Zech. 14:5). The quake, according to that allusion, had caused a panic in Jerusalem, and may have done far more serious damage in central and northern Palestine.

While it is not possible, therefore, to say just when Amos carried on
his brief mission, a probable dating of 760 B.C. is generally accepted.
This is because the great military successes of Jeroboam II (2 Kings
14:25, 28) must have been achieved prior to Amos's appearance on the
scene, since he refers to some of them (6:13).

The Home of Amos. The home town of Amos was Tekoa, some five
miles south of Bethlehem. It lay on the eastern rim of the high plateau
country, from which the land drops off into the "wilderness of Judah."
"Wilderness" in this phrase does not mean "forest," but rather rough
country, unfit for agriculture. Here canyons and gorges descend three
thousand feet to the Dead Sea. Portions of that great salt lake, with
the high country of Moab on the eastern shore, are visible from where
Tekoa lay. The very name of the ancient city has lingered at its site
to this day in slightly Arabicised form. The town, however, was not on
the main route leading south from Jerusalem via Bethlehem to Hebron,
but rather near one leading from Bethlehem down to the oasis of
Engedi, near the Dead Sea. Two centuries earlier king Rehoboam of
Judah had fortified Tekoa, when he established a defense line against
inroads from the south (2 Chron. 11:5 ff.). For here on the very
edge of cultivation there was always the peril of raids by nomads.

But Tekoa was not wholly agricultural. A remark about Amos in the
title states that he "was among the shepherds of Tekoa." This suggests
that much grazing was carried on there. In this region the nineteenth
century explorer Edward Robinson found that the towns were only inhabited in fall and winter. When spring came the population went
forth and lived in tents to watch over their crops and flocks. It seems
probable that the same sort of life was lived here in Amos's day. The
acreage where grain and vegetables and fruit trees could be grown was
limited. But the opportunity for grazing was extensive, especially in the
springtime. For then the adjacent wilderness blossomed with sparse grass
and flowers. But when the hot weather came, shepherds and sheep had
to get out of the sunbaked region near the Dead Sea and roam in upland
areas. The various towns had their bailiwicks, and trespassing on another's grazing grounds, except by arrangement or treaty, led to feuds
and warfare. Invasion by outsiders was also possible. Life was never
wholly safe in antiquity. The story of how the nomadic tribes Simeon
and Levi treacherously attacked and overcame the people of Shechem,

butchering the male inhabitants (Gen. 34:25), is typical of what happened innumerable times in all lands of the ancient world.

The Occupation of Amos. In a biographical fragment interpolated into the book of Amos (7:10–17), the prophet calls himself a *herdsman,* yet then speaks of his following the *flock.* The word "herdsman" is not certain, for the Greek Bible translation has "goatherd." Still, the more difficult text is often the more original, and it may well be so in this case. Robinson found the natives in this region having some cattle as well as sheep. It would not be unnatural for a shepherd whose family also owned a cow to emphasize his higher rank in the social scale by calling himself a "herdsman." The cow could be taken care of nearer home, but sheep rove widely, as anyone who has ever followed a sheep trail will know.

But Amos also had a subsidiary occupation. He calls himself "a dresser of sycamore trees" (7:14). Thereby hangs a twofold problem. What was this activity, and how could he combine it with his tending of sheep?

The sycamore (also called "sycamine tree," Luke 17:6) which is meant here must not be imagined as like our American sycamore. W. M. Thomson (writing in the last century) tells of a missionary in the American West who was puzzled how Zacchaeus could climb a sycamore beside the Jericho-Jerusalem road to get a better view of Jesus (Luke 19:4). The sycamores the missionary was acquainted with were "tall as a steeple and smooth as hypocrisy." The sycamore of the Near East is very different. It has powerful roots, and develops outspreading branches only a few feet up from the ground. Jesus could well think of it as almost impossible to uproot, and Zacchaeus could easily climb out on a limb. The sycamore, however, is a tree of the low altitudes, and the important fact here is that it does not grow in the high region around Tekoa. A sharp frost will kill it, as a psalmist remarks (Ps. 78:47). Whatever Amos had to do with sycamores would have been at a distance. Certainly some other member of his family or clan must have tended his sheep when he was busying himself with the sycamores.

Just what Amos did with the sycamores is expressed in a word that only occurs this once in the Old Testament and is rendered as "dresser." The modern translators here are guided by the rendering "scraper" of the old Greek translation. As the sycamore was raised in Egypt, where its lumber was much used, the Greek translators may have drawn on their knowledge of what was done there with sycamore figs: They were nipped with a nail or knife to hasten their ripening.

The sycamore fig is at best an insipid fruit, and Thomson, though providing a picture of a seller of sycamore fruit, says that these figs were generally given to the poor. It thus is not clear whether Amos lived on sycamore figs, as did a rabbi of Lydda of much later times, or whether he raised them for marketing. Dalman holds it possible that Amos gathered them for cattle fodder, and cites Jewish tradition that he even owned property on the coastal plain, where this tree thrives particularly. As the sycamore produces several crops of figs in a season it could well have been an important aid in keeping a cow or two. In view of these various possibilities one cannot be positive about Amos's economic status. The point Amos was trying to make in the connection in which he alludes to this tending of sycamores was that he did not have to prophesy in his native Judah to "eat his bread." He had his livelihood and was only taking time out from it to execute a divinely given task.

The Education of Amos. The oracles of Amos show the influence of intellectual culture. Where such a man of the border encountered it is hard to say. If there still was a garrison at the fortress of Tekoa in his time there must have been a scribe or two to send reports and keep accounts. The men of this profession were the cultivators of the Wisdom Literature, which particularly developed in Egypt but was also nurtured in Edom and at Arabian courts. By contact with scribes Amos may have become familiar with literary devices such as meter, stanza, and rhetorical expression. A "wise woman" of Tekoa is already mentioned in the time of David (2 Sam. 14:2), so wisdom may have flourished there earlier. It is conceivable, too, that Amos sometimes went to Bethlehem or Hebron and that his horizon was enriched and broadened by what he saw and heard there. Natural ability, with which he obviously was endowed, finds its way surely as water does underground, and bubbles forth unexpectedly in an out-of-the-way place.

The Call

The all-important event in Amos's life was his call to become a prophet. He has given no detailed account of it, but the biographical fragment already mentioned quotes him:

"I am no prophet, nor a prophet's son; . . . the LORD took me from following the flock, and the LORD said to me, 'Go, prophesy to my people Israel.'"
(7:14–15)

We can see from the first statement that there was a professional prophetism, attaching itself to leading prophets (cf. 2 Kings 4:38, 6:1). But Amos was not of such an occupation. He reports that his call to the prophetic function came directly and unexpectedly from the Lord. It was as irregular as was the call of Jesus to quit his carpenter's bench and start preaching the kingdom of God.

We may think of the young shepherd, seated on a hilltop, near his grazing flock, and practicing on his reed pipe, like many a shepherd lad of that region in more recent times, or as following his sheep through dark canyons to a fresh grazing area. Somewhere in that jumble of hills and ravines upon which one looks down from Tekoa there came an hour in which Amos heard the voice of the Lord. Apparently Amos's initial revelatory experience was one of hearing words only, unaccompanied by a vision. Was it in the reverberations of thunder that he heard the voice, or in a narrow escape from a bolt of lightning? "The voice of the LORD flashes forth flames of fire. The voice of the LORD shakes the wilderness," says a psalmist (Ps. 29:8). Or was it in the roar of the lion on a ghostly, moonlit night, as his sheep huddled in fear about their shepherd? Amos himself says in explaining the necessity that lies upon him,

"The lion has roared; who will not fear?
The Lord GOD has spoken; who can but prophesy?" (3:8)

But who can penetrate into that moment of mystery when a man of an age long past became convinced of a divine call?

The commission given Amos—"Go prophesy to my people Israel"—involved a journey. For Amos did not live in Israel. "Israel" in that period meant the northern kingdom which had seceded from Judah after Solomon's time. If we are told in Genesis 38 that Judah "went down from his brothers" and married a Canaanite woman and even begot sons by a Canaanite daughter-in-law, this reflects the mixed nature of the population of Judah. The northern tribes were proud of being the true and only Israel. The time was to come when the people of Judah would appropriate the name "Israel," but in Amos's day that still lay in the future. His commission did not include prophesying to or about Judah, and for this reason we suspect that allusions to Judah in his words were inserted by editors. He was to prophesy to the northern kingdom. Even the title of the book "The words of Amos ... which he saw concerning Israel" suggests the limited nature of his task.

Was there then no prophet in Israel itself, that the Lord had to send a shepherd from Tekoa to his chosen people? This is a question that nobody seems to ask, but that needs to be asked. Amos gives a hint that prophecy—at any rate of the ominous kind he brought—was suppressed (2:12) in the northern kingdom. Even long before that, as the story of Micaiah shows, such prophets were at times clapped into prison with scant fare of bread and water (1 Kings 22:27). But a prophet coming from the outside might at least be able to make a few pronouncements for the Lord in Israel, before being arrested or driven out. There may have been, too, some special reason for officialdom to exercise patience in the case of a man from southern Judah. Jehu, founder of the dynasty now reigning, had owed much to the Rechabite chieftain, Jehonadab, who had come here from there (2 Kings 10:15 ff., 23). Jehonadab and his followers had provided support in his revolution. They were nomads, related to the Kenites, and with ascetic principles (1 Chron. 2:55; Jer. 35). Amos, as his friendly allusion to the Nazirites (2:11) suggests, must have had sympathy with such a group as the Rechabites.

The Visions of Amos

Soon after his call Amos, we must suppose, had a series of four or five visions in which the message he was to carry was disclosed to him (7:1–9; 8:1–3; 9:1). The commission to prophesy was hazy as to what he was to say. We shall find a somewhat similar pattern—visions after the call—prevailing in the case of Jeremiah. The first three visions of Amos are reported in quick succession, but the fourth has been separated from them by interpolation of the biographical piece about Amos already mentioned. The fifth vision, as preserved, is not styled like the others and is separated from the fourth by intervening oracles.

The Locust Plague, 7:1–3. It seems likely that days or weeks intervened between the first four visions. The time of the first presumably was that which he indicates in the account of what he saw. It was the season of the "latter growth," which developed after "the king's mowing." The allusion is to barley, the early growth of which is still used sometimes for fodder in Palestine. We can assume, though it is otherwise not attested, that the kings of Israel exercised a right to claim the first growth of barley for their horses. Since King Ahab was able to put two thousand chariots into battle in 845, according to the inscription of the Assyrian ruler Shalmaneser III, the rearmament under Jeroboam II must have reached a high figure too. Hence a great amount of fodder had to be gathered to support all these animals. This left the common people with only the second growth for a food crop. Its development depended on the "latter rain," or spring rain, for which the people of Palestine always prayed earnestly and hopefully. The time reflected in the vision thus would have been about the end of April. Dry and hot weather, without any rain, posed hazards enough. But Amos in his vision saw the absolutely disastrous event of an impending locust plague. What a scourge this could be is made vivid by the book of Joel and by reports of modern locust plagues. How much greater was the danger in Amos's day than in modern times, when communication, transport, and charitable concern make help available to the starving. Who cared then whether man and beast starved to death?

The Lord has taken Amos into his counsel. Filled with his new prophetic consciousness the man rises heroically to the role of intercessor:

> "O Lord God, forgive, I beseech thee!
> How can Jacob stand?
> He is so small!" (7:2)

He bases his appeal for clemency on the small size of Israel. Certainly the extent of central and northern Palestine and the number of people it could support in those days was small by comparison with countries like Egypt, Assyria, Babylonia, and western lands. In any case as intercessor Amos seeks to arouse pity.

The prophet's appeal finds a hearing. He reports that:

> The Lord repented concerning this;
> "It shall not be," said the Lord. (7:3)

Amos had influenced the course of events by prayer. He had forestalled this drastic action of the Lord. He would not have to carry that message of disaster to Israel.

The Flame from Heaven, 7:4-6. But soon he had another vision. He saw a flame of fire come down from heaven. "It devoured the great deep and was eating up the land." The language is highly mythological. "The great deep" includes the waters supposedly encircling the earth and couching beneath it (Gen. 49:25), according to the Oriental cosmology that the Hebrews shared. Thus when the deluge came it not only rained from heaven but "the fountains of the great deep burst forth" and swamped everything (Gen. 7:11). But Amos is hardly thinking of a coming cosmic catastrophe—a flood of fire, counterpart to the ancient deluge of water—such as late apocalypticism thought about (2 Peter 3:5-13). That would have affected the whole world of his horizon and destroyed life. A limited use of fire is enough. Thus fire from heaven was rained down very locally on Sodom (Gen. 19:24). Whether the idea was suggested by lightning or by knowledge of volcanic eruptions, such means were imagined as at the disposal of the Lord when he was bent on punishment. A broader sweep of activity is implied by Amos than was the case with the cities of the plain. The question here is, however, whether the fire and the devouring of the deep are not just a mythical figure for heat and drought. That assumption has much in its favor. For the next reaction of Amos is much like the first:

> "O Lord GOD, cease, I beseech thee!
> How can Jacob stand?
> He is so small!" (7:5)

The catastrophe now planned by the Lord and brought about by a bolt from heaven, while not as horrible as a locust plague, is still serious enough. When there no longer is groundwater; when the cisterns are dry and the hot wind from the Arabian desert, the sirocco, makes life miserable, then sheep and cattle can die and crops wither. The time for the sirocco is the month of May, and since Amos asks for "cessation" the calamity is already developing. But his intercession is again successful. "This also shall not be," said the Lord.

The Plumb Line, 7:7 ff. But a third vision comes to Amos. He sees a figure standing on a wall and demonstrating with a plumb line and its lead (or tin?) "bob" that the wall is leaning, and hence should be torn down. Perhaps the wall was suggested to Amos's mind by the fortress wall built at Tekoa two hundred years earlier by Rehoboam. Some parts of it may no longer have been in good condition after so long a time. The message attending the vision interprets it as follows:

> "Behold, I am setting a plumb line
>   in the midst of my people Israel;
> I will never again pass by them;" (7:8)

Twice the Lord has "passed by them." But he cuts off any further intercession by the prophet.

The account of this vision is now followed by a prediction of the desolation of Israel's sanctuaries and of revolution against the house of Jeroboam (7:9). This, however, could be a separate fragment put there editorially to establish a transition to the biographical passage, which contains this saying, perhaps in more original form. The verse goes beyond anything that would flow naturally from the vision itself.

The Basket of Summer Fruit, 8:1–2. A fourth vision is put after the biographical piece. Since the form of this vision is the same at the beginning, it may once have followed the third directly, and, as it were, clinched and confirmed it. In this vision the Lord showed Amos a basket of summer fruit. This might have consisted of early figs, available about the beginning of June. All four visions, then, were probably seen at separate occasions between April 1 and June 1. The Lord interprets this vision as meaning: "The end has come upon my people Israel; I will never again pass by them." There is a pun here, not easily reproduced in English, for the Hebrew word "summer" (qayis, pronounced with a dipthong as qais in Amos's time) suggested the word qes, "end." This vision, too, is followed by a saying which likewise does not flow from the vision itself and must be suspected of having been put here editorially (8:3).

Whether the fifth vision (9:1), which again is separated from its predecessors by other material, was received at this time is uncertain. It has the appearance of a mere fragment and differs in form from the others. It thus seems to stand outside the collection of the four. We will assume that it was received during Amos's mission and refer to it again later.

Amos in Israel

So the shepherd left his flock, quit Tekoa, and went to Israel. A man with so grim a message on his mind would not have lingered on the way. To prophesy Amos needed firsthand observation. For while the Lord had revealed his intention to his chosen messenger he had not explained what warranted such drastic actions as he was contemplating. It was left to Amos himself to see what was going on in Israel and to supply the charges, partly by observation and partly by inspiration that would come to him on the spur of the moment. And where could he observe what was going on in Israel better than at the capital, Samaria, where king and aristocracy resided? It seems clear that he went there, though it is not expressly stated.

What Amos, the man of the simple and ascetic life, saw at Samaria was to him unbelievable. Think how some seventeenth-century Puritan would react could he visit New York today, and you will appreciate the reaction of Amos to Samaria.

Here were men who hardly had a rag with which to cover their nakedness. Their garments had been seized by creditors (2:6–8) who were using the garments as spreads to lie on in the special reclining places in the temple, where they were feasting from sacrifices they had brought. Connected with the temple was a brothel, Canaanite fashion, and one might see father and son enter it. There were judges who always sided with the rich and influential and collected fines from the farmer, usually in the form of products such as the wine from his vats or the grain from his threshing floor. The upper-class women were notorious for their love of wine, demanding of their men, "Bring, that we may drink!" (4:1). The merchant class was particularly greedy— impatient to have the religious holidays, new moon and Sabbath, over with so that they could carry on business, operating with false balances and bent on plunging the poor into debt slavery (8:4–6). The aristo-crats were living in luxury and idleness. Amos heard that the rich lay on beds of ivory, ate lambs from the flock and calves from the stall, sang idle songs to the sound of the harp, drank wine not from cups but bowls, and anointed themselves with the finest perfumed oils (6:4 ff.). He speaks of houses of ivory (3:15), evidently based on a mistaken report, or just meaning houses full of objects inlaid with ivory. The rich had summer and winter houses—the former no doubt in the countryside. Some—the winter ones naturally—were of hewn stone. But these men were patriotic. They thought that by their people's own strength they had defeated the Aramaeans of Damascus and regained the cities of Transjordan that had been lost to them (6:13).

All this was brought about by social and economic changes in Israel. The rise of urban life and of a large idle class that held control is typical of what took place almost everywhere in emerging nations. In the beginning the clans and tribes acted individually or in federation. When settled and active in farming, the farmers might go forth to the defense of their country. But with the rise of a monarchy a bureaucratization takes place. The monarch depends on the more vigorous and successful individuals, whose clans then get rich through his favors. They can live in the cities only by reducing the farmers to serfdom. Since these patricians get hold of the judicial powers, the impoverishment of the agrarian population is the inevitable result. Warfare now requires armament—armor for the warrior, and horses and chariots with the necessary maintenance men. The patrician group (*gibborim*) was composed of those who could supply and maintain their own military equipment and who stood ready to go forth to war. Warlike undertakings were almost a necessity to keep this class satisfied and to provide spoils and luxuries.

These conditions mark the passing of the patriarchal society, in which all are embraced and protected in the clan or tribe, and where all live on a humble level, without craving for luxuries. This ideal of the simple life was shared by Amos. What he saw in Samaria demonstrated to him the departure from the kind of society in which his religion had arisen. The fact that social change, inevitable with an increase of population, necessitated defense against rising neighboring powers was something he could not appreciate. It is inevitable, too, that where the pursuits of power and pleasure flourish, as they will in an urbanized civilization, the evil side of human nature will assert itself far more obviously than in a nomadic or seminomadic society. A few more sheep, goats, or cattle and a few more wives and more children are virtually the only luxuries obtainable on the earlier level. The pessimistic observation of the ancient narrator, "The LORD saw that the wickedness of man was great in the earth, and that every imagination of the thoughts of his heart was only evil continually" (Gen. 6:5), was drawn from urban life.

The state of affairs at Samaria must have been startlingly different
from anything Amos could have seen in Hebron or Bethlehem or even
at Jerusalem. Austerity probably prevailed at the capital of Judah and
in the whole southern kingdom after the defeat of Amaziah of Judah
by Jehoash of Israel (2 Kings 14:11–14). Part of Jerusalem's walls had
been dismantled and all its treasures given up. True, under Azariah, in
whose reign Amos lived, there was recovery. But there the priestly class
still held the dominant position gained with the overthrow of Athaliah
(2 Kings 11), and this no doubt curbed excesses.

Amos's Message

Amos is sure that God has determined Israel's destruction. It must
have been at some public occasion that he arose with the announcement:

> Hear this word that the LORD has spoken against you, O people of Israel,
> against the whole family which I brought up out of the land of Egypt:
> "You only have I known of all the families of the earth;
> therefore I will punish you for all your iniquities." (3:1–2)

He calls the aggregate of tribes composing a people a "family." The
Israelite family was chosen by the Lord and experienced his favor in its
migration from Egypt to Canaan, where, as he adds in another connection, God destroyed the Amorite before them, fruit and root (2:9).
Amos must have believed in "the iniquity of the Amorites" (Gen.
15:16) which made them deserve destruction. God expected the new
family he brought into Palestine to live up to his commandments and
thus receive his blessing. His special favor involved special accountability. He will punish them for all their iniquities. One might think
that the downtrodden part of the people, with which Amos has so
much sympathy, would be spared. But Amos had not yet arrived at the
point where he could entertain such an idea. He believed in collective
guilt; the majority share in the fate which the actions of the dominant
element cause. That was the harsh rule governing life in the ancient
communities.

Past and Future Punishment. Israel has been in its land a long while
now, and the sins Amos sees are not new. He reminds his hearers that

God has sent punishments previously, in the hope of bringing about betterment. This is set forth in a piece of five stanzas (4:6–12). The punishments were 1) starvation; 2) lack of rain or irregular distribution of it; 3) blight, mildew, and locust plagues; 4) pestilence, and calamity to the armed forces; 5) earthquakes and narrow escapes. Each stanza ends in the refrain, "Yet you did not return to me, says the LORD." Something more decisive is called for now. According to the present text the Lord said in closing, "prepare to meet your God, O Israel!" Had it not been revealed to Amos in a vision that "The end has come upon my people Israel" (8:2)?

Amos thus does not hesitate to utter a lamentation, as at a funeral:

> Hear this word which I take up over you in lamentation, O house of Israel:
>> "Fallen, no more to rise, is the virgin Israel;
>>> forsaken on her land, with none to raise her up." (5:1–2)

The death of a maiden always has a particular pathos, as the story of Jephthah's daughter who went down on the mountains to bewail her virginity (Judg. 11:37), or the incident of the Jairus in the Gospels show. It is a sad spectacle he foresees—beloved Israel dead and past revival, prostrate on her land. Equally emphatic is an ironical comparison drawn from his shepherd life:

> Thus says the LORD: "As the shepherd rescues from the mouth of the lion two legs, or a piece of an ear, so shall the people of Israel who dwell in Samaria be rescued . . ." (3:12)

In other words there is no rescue at all. The animal is dead and gone, and so it will be with Israel.

Preceding or following or entwined with Amos's invective there are declarations giving detailed glimpses of the sort of calamity he expects. It is not possible to combine these into a lucid picture, and some indeed are not fully clear in meaning—probably because of corruption or damage suffered by the Hebrew text. There is, however, much military symbolism; it suggests that the terror which Assyrian arms have spread for a century or more fills the prophet. That he is thinking of the Assyrians is fully clear in at least one passage:

> "For behold, I will raise up against you a nation . . . and they shall oppress you from the entrance of Hamath to the Brook of the Arabah." (6:14)

The points mentioned are the northern and southeast limits of Israel.
But Egypt is also a possible agent of punishment, since both it and
Assyria are invited to come and see what evil goes on in Samaria
(3:9–10); the prediction then states:

> Therefore thus says the Lord GOD:
> "An adversary shall surround the land,
>   and bring down your defenses from you
>   and your strongholds shall be plundered." (3:11)

Only those two states were able to surround Israel's territory. Amos
may have heard that Egypt was making preparations to prevent Assyria
from gaining or holding the approaches to the Nile.

One gets glimpses of specific moments in the tragic events of the
future: decimation of the citizenry in battle, or more generally of the
falling by the sword; destruction of cities and of the sanctuaries; seeking
out of the hiding women; wailing in the sacred precincts; exile of the
people. But there is also allusion to hunger and thirst (spiritualized by
a later editor by interpolating "for the words of the LORD") that will
cause the fair virgins and the young men to perish (8:11–14). Pestilence
too is brought in, notably in a passage that lacks meter and therefore
may have been supplied by a traditioner who could not reproduce it
in the exact form in which it had been spoken. A lone survivor in a
house cautions against mentioning the name of the Lord for fear of
bringing discovery and destruction on himself (6:9–10).

Basically all this is only more of the same thing already described in
the survey of past calamities (4:6 ff.). It was difficult, one must admit,
to intensify the descriptions of such scourges. But the intention to do
so must be assumed; the fourth vision with its decree of the "end" of
the people gives the basic guideline (8:2).

Against Optimism and Reliance on Cult or Pilgrimage. But there
was resistance to Amos's fearful message of doom for Israel. Popular
religious optimism was founded on two pillars of support. One was
provided by the active interest in the cult of the Lord. It was by no
means a time when the worship of the Lord was neglected. The priests
must have been well satisfied with all the sacrifices brought to the
sanctuaries of the land. But Amos dismisses reliance on such external

observances. More than that—his God loathes them because men think
they have a control over him by such means:

> "I hate, I despise your feasts,
>> and I take no delight in your solemn assemblies.
> Even though you offer me your burnt offerings and cereal offerings
>> I will not accept them,
> and the peace offerings of your fatted beasts
>> I will not look upon.
> Take away from me the noise of your songs;
>> to the melody of your harps I will not listen.
> But let justice roll down like waters,
>> and righteousness like an ever-flowing stream." (5:21–24)

Amos even adduces a rational argument against sacrifice by asking an
audience:

> "Did you bring to me sacrifices and offerings the forty years in the wilder-
> ness, O house of Israel?" (5:25)

The answer, he implies, is "no." Hence, according to the traditions
known to Amos, ritual sacrifice cannot have been considered essential
by the Lord. But the thought raised by this rhetorical question is not
followed out, and indeed is obscured by the puzzling reference to the
taking up of Babylonian star gods, Sakkuth and Kaiwan (perhaps a
later addition, made with an eye to the Babylonian settlers, 2 Kings
17:24 ff.), and the threat of exile beyond Damascus (5:26–27).

There was, too, a great amount of pilgrimage to Bethel, one of the
two national temples established by Jeroboam I two centuries earlier,
to Gilgal near Jericho, and even to distant Beersheba. In the case of
Gilgal and Beersheba one may posit a desire to maintain a link with
holy places of earliest Israelite memory. It must have been considered
to be meritorious to go there and bring sacrifice. Presumably special
favors or remission of special sins were obtainable there. Amos, however, sees no benefit in going to those places, but points to the thing
that God desires and that still could save:

> For thus says the LORD to the house of Israel:
> "Seek me and live;
>> but do not seek Bethel,

and do not enter into Gilgal
   or cross over to Beer-sheba;*
for Gilgal shall surely go into exile
   and Bethel shall come to nought."

Seek the LORD and live,
   lest he break out like fire in the house of Joseph
   and it devour, with none to quench it . . . (5:4–6)

He castigates the zeal for pilgrimage and sacrifice at two of these places
with bitter irony:

"Come to Bethel, and transgress;
   to Gilgal, and multiply transgression;
bring your sacrifices every morning,
   your tithes every three days;
offer a sacrifice of thanksgiving of that which is leavened,
   and proclaim freewill offerings, publish them;
   for so you love to do, O people of Israel!"
Says the Lord GOD. (4:4–5)

Really seeking the Lord is the same thing to him as seeking the good.

Seek good, and not evil,
   that you may live;
and so the LORD, the God of hosts,
   will be with you,
      as you have said.
Hate evil, and love good,
   and establish justice in the gate;
it may be that the LORD, the God of hosts,
   will be gracious to the remnant of Joseph. (5:14–15)

Significantly he introduces the "remnant" idea here, but only half-
heartedly.

A second pillar supporting popular optimism was the belief in a
coming "day of the LORD," a day of salvation for Israel and of annihilation for its foes. The theological nature of this belief shows that it
did not arise among the secularly inclined classes, or even among the
aristocrats who boasted of having taken Lodebar and Karnaim—Transjordanian fortresses—"by our own strength" (6:13). It may have been
a dogma of the nationalistic prophets who spoke what was agreeable to

* Spellings in all biblical quotations appear as they do in the Revised Standard
Version.

kings and leadership (1 Kings 22:13). It is difficult for us to understand
how men could yield to such an illusory idea. Yet, have we not seen
or heard how the Gallic temperament could be thrilled at the words
of the *Marseillaise*, "le jour de gloire est arrivé"? The Near Eastern one
was and is even more fiery. Israel's God had been a god of war, with
supplementary attributes of storm god, god of fire, god of pestilence.
Legend told how he had intervened in behalf of his people in its early
struggles. The more such stories were repeated—and they may well have
been much beloved of the yeoman, whose ancestors had fought in "the
wars of the LORD"—the more they will have furnished a basis for the
belief in the Lord's future use of his terrible arsenal on Israel's behalf
at a climactic occasion. Given the notion that Israel was deserving of
the aid of its god, faith in him had to reach up and cling to some such
idea. The desperate process of destruction of states and peoples that
was going on made that necessary.

The Real Day of the Lord.   But Amos presents a very different picture
of the day of the Lord—one which was to be greatly elaborated—as
other "critical" prophets in Judah took up the theme, and at the
threshold of New Testament times would end in apocalypticism.

> Woe to you who desire the day of the LORD!
> Why would you have the day of the LORD?
> It is darkness, and not light;
>   as if a man fled from a lion,
>   and a bear met him;
> Or went into the house and leaned with his hand against the wall,
>   and a serpent bit him.
> Is not the day of the LORD darkness, and not light,
>   And gloom with no brightness in it? (5:18-20)

For Amos the day is a day of inescapable nemesis. He develops the
same idea in even greater vividness, though without reference to the
term "day of the LORD," in a piece now appended to the fifth vision:

> "and what are left of them I will slay with the sword;
>   not one of them shall flee away,
>   not one of them shall escape.
>
> "Though they dig into Sheol [= Hades],
>   from there shall my hand take them;
> though they climb up to heaven,

from there I will bring them down.
Though they hide themselves on the top of Carmel,
    from there I will search out and take them;
and though they hide from my sight at the bottom of the sea,
    there I will command the serpent, and it shall bite them.
And though they go into captivity before their enemies,
    there I will command the sword, and it shall slay them;
and I will set my eyes upon them for evil and not for good." (9:1b–4)

Much of this of course is poetic—rooted in mythological thinking—but in the hiding on Carmel and in the march into captivity realistic possibilities appear. These show that Amos is thinking of a "historical" rather than an apocalyptic day of the Lord.

The Great Reckoning. But Amos planted a seed that was to bear fruit for the later expansion of the idea of the "day of the LORD" to one of world scope. This was done through an elaborate poem in which he dwells first on retribution that will come upon the heads of Israel's immediate neighbors, and then on Israel itself (1:3 ff.).

One must, however, note the geographical limitation of the poem. The greater powers that lurk in the background—Assyria and Egypt—are not dealt with, but the former is perhaps thought of as the instrument of divine punishment. Amos, in an oracle already mentioned 3:9 ff.), calls on Assyria and Egypt to come and see what was going on in Samaria. This was like summoning the eagles to inspect their prey. These states, however, were not vivid to him, except as possessing tremendous power. But the near neighbors were vivid. He was reminded of them all the time. When he roved with his flock he came to points where he could see their habitats. Moab lay in sight of Tekoa itself, on the other side of the Dead Sea. If he stood on the height of the Frank Mountain, southeast of Bethlehem, his eye on a clear day could see Mount Hermon, at the foot of which lay Damascus. Across the great Jordan valley rift lay the whole country of Gilead and the lands of the Ammonites and Moabites. In the far southeast dwelt the Edomites. From points some miles west of Tekoa one could look toward the coast of the Philistines and north toward Mount Carmel, behind which lay Phoenicia. These regions were all knit together in a common fate and, indeed, had banded together in alliance to resist the southward progress of Assyrian imperialism. But just as the day of the Lord will be one of doom for Israel, so Amos also foresees doom for all these states. The Lord has determined it on what we would call "ethical" grounds. The sins of these neighboring peoples demand such an outcome. Each stanza of this poem begins with a pattern derived from Wisdom Literature (cf. Prov. 30:29),

> "For three transgressions of . . .
> and for four, I will not revoke the punishment.

Actually, however, Amos confines himself to less than three or four transgressions in his charges.

The prophet begins with Damascus (1:3–5), which has been Israel's chief rival and adversary in the past century. The grievance is that they ground to pieces the Hebrew population of Gilead. This was done by Hazael, and Elisha the prophet is said to have wept in foreseeing it (2 Kings 8:12, 10:32 ff.). The people of Aram are to go into exile in Kir—clearly a northern region, since elsewhere it is mentioned with Elam (Isa. 22:6). Amos refers to it later as the original home of the Aramaeans (9:7). Only the Assyrians could be the agents of their punishment.

The Philistine city of Gaza comes next (1:6–8). It was the strongest of the Philistine cities, evidently holding sovereignty over the other three that are mentioned. It is accused of carrying into exile a whole people (better "whole communities") to deliver them up to Edom. This is an accusation on which history has not yet shed any light. Some group or groups, whether Hebrews or others, must have been deported to the last man. There must thus have been some kind of international agreement or moral consensus of opinion not to remove a population completely. Amos regards this kind of deportation as an atrocity, for which Gaza and other Philistine cities are to be punished. A similar charge appears in the oracle against Tyre (1:9–10), which therefore may not be authentic in its present form. Deportations to Edom from either quarter do not seem very probable, though in the case of Tyre, "Edom" could be emended to "Aram."

The stanza against Edom (1:11–12) is suspect because it fits the postexilic situation much better and because Edom is victim rather than aggressor in a succeeding stanza.

The charge against the Ammonites (1:13–15) is for attacking Gilead

from the south and destroying its Hebrew population, even brutally
ripping up women with child. Destruction of the Ammonite capital
"Rabbah" (Rabbath Ammon) and exile of its leaders is foreseen.

More surprising is the charge against Moab (2:1–3). It is accused
of burning to lime the bones of the king of Edom. This presupposes a
Moabite invasion of Edom. The tomb of some particularly hated king
may thus have been violated and his remains destroyed. It is quite
possible that the allusion originally was to the "kings" of Edom and
that a whole series of royal sepulchers was emptied. Whatever was done,
Amos regards it as a crime for which Moab should be punished by the
Lord. There must have been an understanding among the anti-Assyrian
allies or a moral consensus not to do such a thing to each other's
royalty. Amos's God thus is a guardian of international law and morality.

The poem also contains a stanza against Judah (2:4–5). It was probably added (or revised?) later, for the charge reminds one of the "Deuteronomic" strictures found in some of the historical books. Amos
would have singled out some particular act of wrongdoing. It would
not have been hard to find one (cf. 2 Sam. 8:2; 1 Kings 11:15).

But the climactic charge to which Amos was leading up is directed
against Israel (2:6 ff.). This we have already considered. It is surprising
that it differs in form from the other charges by not remaining on the
foreign political plane and by not ending with a threat to Samaria and
the palaces of Omri. That may have been the case originally. In the
received form of the text, however, it is the social abuses on which
Amos bases the coming punishment.

The Axe at the Root of the Tree. In proclaiming God's judgment
over the neighboring states for their violations of what he considers
right, Amos is preparing the way for a new stage in religion. He already
presupposed that the Lord was concerned about other peoples as well
as with Israel, when he asked:

> "Are you not like the Ethiopians to me,
>   O people of Israel?" says the LORD.
> "Did I not bring up Israel from the land of Egypt,
>   and the Philistines from Caphtor
>   and the Syrians from Kir?" (9:7)

The most remote folk Amos knows of, the "Ethiopians" (really the
"Cushites," or Nubians, living south of Egypt) are just the same to

the Lord as Israel. The Lord, furthermore, not only guided Israel's wanderings to Palestine but the migration of the Philistines from their earlier home in Caphtor (i.e., Crete) and of the Aramaeans from Kir to their present ones in the coastal plain and in Syria. And this is the silent implication: The Lord can select some other people to replace Israel.

Thus Amos is striking a blow at counting on the idea of the "chosen people" as a secure asset. Being such a people is a responsibility which can turn into a liability. The ethical nature of Amos's conception of God becomes vivid here. It is the force that topples other gods from their thrones, peoples from their seats of power, individuals from their possessions and prerogatives. God's righteousness must rule everywhere. Whether Amos understood the logical consequences of the insights given him we cannot say, but they had to work themselves out in time to a full universalism, in which all men are equally the object of God's interest and care.

Amos was commissioned to proclaim the end of Israel. But national end or death does not mean absolute extermination of the population, or preclude a later revival of some sort. The pattern of the old narratives about Noah and Lot (Gen. 6:13; 7:1 ff.; Gen. 19:29) shows how difficult it was to entertain the idea of extinction. Amos had not yet arrived at the point reached by John the Baptist, who declared that God could raise children for Abraham "from these stones." It remains doubtful, however, whether the concluding prophecy of the book of Amos—in which the Lord promises to raise up "the booth of David that is fallen" and supplements that with predictions of a new golden age and restoration of Israel—lay within the scope of Amos's thinking. The phrase cited suggests that the house of David was no longer reigning when this was formulated. It is contrary to the "actuality" of prophecy, furthermore, to reflect on things not immediately relevant. This sort of thinking becomes the burden of prophecy when disaster has taken its course and left men hopeless.

Amos at Bethel

We have only assumed that Amos went to Samaria, since his direct address to the aristocrats there is best understood when based on observation and confrontation. But it is certain that he went to Bethel. It seems probable that he arrived there around the time of the autumnal festival, which was the old Hebrew and Canaanite season of the new year. That was the time when people streamed to this highly important sanctuary to celebrate. Did Amos have a special message for Bethel? It would seem possible that he had there his fifth vision, which survives only in fragmentary form in the words:

> I saw the LORD standing beside the altar, and he said:
> "Smite the capitals until the thresholds shake,
>   and shatter them upon the heads of all the people;" (9:1)

It is not clear whether the Lord is addressing aides or is soliloquizing. In the latter case one would expect mention of his holding a hammer in his hand, and saying "I will smite." Smiting the capitals of the pillars will have the same effect as Samson's leaning against the pillars in the house of Dagon—the building will collapse. The original vision, whether seen at Tekoa and altered in form or seen at Bethel, certainly applied to the Bethel sanctuary. The allusion is to an earthquake. The words of the Lord that then follow (9:1b–4) have already been cited and are hardly the original continuation of that threat of the Lord, but are the torso of a different oracle.

The biographical fragment, however, singles out something other than the temple vision in relating what Amos said at Bethel:

> "Jeroboam shall die by the sword,
>   and Israel must go into exile
>   away from his land." (7:11)

At Samaria Amos had apparently refrained from saying anything about the king. At the safer distance of Bethel he took the risk. The responsible priest Amaziah sent the king a report, describing the words of the "seer" as treasonable and as unbearable for the kingdom. He did not explain who Amos was—he could assume that the king had heard about him. But he showed Amos remarkable consideration—perhaps more out of superstitious fear of the inspired man than out of kindness. He did not clap him into jail pending arrival of the king's orders, but simply told him,

> "O seer, go, flee away to the land of Judah, and eat bread there, and prophesy there; but never again prophesy at Bethel, for it is the king's sanctuary, and it is a temple of the kingdom." (7:12–13)

We have already considered Amos's response and the information he gave about himself. But he follows this with an oracle for Amaziah:

"Now therefore hear the word of the LORD.
You say, 'Do not prophesy against Israel,
   and do not preach against the house of Isaac.'
Therefore thus says the LORD:
'Your wife shall be a harlot in the city,
      and your sons and your daughters shall fall by the sword,
      and your land shall be parceled out by line;
   you yourself shall die in an unclean land,
      and Israel shall surely go into exile away from its land.'" (7:16-17)

As this is reported in a narrative (which presumably is later than the oracle collection), it seems likely that what actually happened to Amaziah, his family, and his property, has colored the formulation of the prediction. But that Amos foretold misfortune for the high official seems certain. One might think that it was rather ungrateful of Amos, in view of what the chief priest could have done to him. But it is not the response to his being told to flee that aroused the prophet's ire, but rather to his being silenced, though a messenger of the Lord.

We must imagine that Amos returned to Tekoa—his commission being fulfilled. His expulsion from Bethel and the boldness of his words must have become a matter of public knowledge. He may have been asked to repeat his oracles or even to write some of them down.

Two years after his mission to Israel a terrible earthquake visited Palestine (1:1). The havoc wrought in the northern kingdom must have been very great. It is reasonable to assume that the temple at Bethel collapsed, thus vindicating the fifth vision of the prophet. This may have led to the high esteem placed on Amos's words, a collection of which already seems to have been available to Isaiah (c. 735 B.C.). The actual end of the kingdom of Israel in 721 B.C.—only forty years after Amos had prophesied—must certainly have enhanced his status still more and led to an abiding interest in his sayings. Thanks to synagogue and church we still have them. They have had a considerable influence in modern times in awakening the social conscience of Christendom. In spite of all the vast difference existing between Amos's world and ours, this prophet must be regarded as one of the pioneers of higher religion.

2 HOSEA, WITNESS OF ISRAEL'S DECLINE

SOON A PROPHET AROSE in Israel itself—Hosea, son of Beeri. He was the last of a great series of holy men that included such mighty figures as Elijah and Elisha. He was also the only prophet of the northern kingdom whose collected utterances were to find a place in the Old Testament.

We have seen, through the eyes of Amos, what conditions prevailed in Israel at the height of the successful reign of King Jeroboam II (c. 760). Hosea's beginnings can be put no later than the last year of that ruler (c. 747). What Amos saw in the course of his visit and what Hosea beheld are so different as to occasion surprise. According to the former there was great zeal in worship of the Lord, but he regarded it as vitiated by disregard of certain ethical requirements of his God. Hosea, on the other hand, pays scant attention to what Amos denounces, but is horrified because the land is flooded with a religious syncretism that directly violates the basic cultic law requiring sole worship of the Lord. One must wonder how to account for this difference between these two observers. Had a demoralization in religion taken place in the interim between Amos's visit and Hosea's beginnings? Or were there regional diversities, so that Amos did not happen to see at Samaria and Bethel what Hosea saw in the part of the country in which he lived?

Hosea's Home. But where did Hosea live? Unfortunately we have no remark about the prophet's home town in the title of the book of Hosea, as we have in that of Amos. His birthplace may no longer have been known when his book came into the hands of scribes. Arab tradition, presumably derived from Jews or Christians, points out a supposed tomb of Hosea on a mountain in Gilead, on the other side of the

Jordan. The height is called in Arabic *Jebel Osha*, or "Hosea's mountain." It is nearly a thousand feet higher than the more southerly Mount Nebo, from which Moses viewed the Promised Land. At Hosea's mountain the whole Jordan valley from the Sea of Galilee to the Dead Sea lies 4,500 feet below at one's feet. Central Palestine, the heart of the old kingdom of Israel, is directly opposite, with a fine view of Mount Ebal and Mount Gerizim. If one notes that Hosea is best informed about what occurred in places lying in Transjordan or in that part of western Palestine lying near the Jordan valley, one may reason that he was at home somewhere in the area directly commanded by Jebel Osha. His frequent use of "Ephraim" for "Israel" indicates that the former region was all-important to him. In one passage he even calls himself "the watchman of Ephraim," if the rendering can be trusted. This could indicate that he lived in that tribal area. During the first century A.D., his home and supposed burial place were thought to be at Ibleam, north of Samaria. That was old Manassite territory (Judg. 1:27), controlled by Ephraim. But this report may have been merely a guess—made, perhaps, because Canaanite heathenism lingered there until very late. Some modern scholars think he was a Benjaminite, primarily because Benjamin is addressed in one passage (5:8). Certain identification of his home thus seems to be unobtainable.

Hosea's Occupation. There is no direct report about Hosea's occupation. He clearly belongs to an intellectual stratum of the population. He is well informed in the history of his people and in the religious and moral teaching (including the decalogue) dispensed by the priesthood. He has a high regard for prophets, and is himself called one in a quoted saying (9:7), so he was probably a member of a prophetic group, or of a family in which a prophetic gift was hereditary. He was not, however, a public figure in the same sense as Amos. Perhaps it was impossible for him to speak openly at first, since, as we have seen in dealing with Amos, prophecy of the critical sort must have been suppressed in Israel under Jeroboam II. This may explain why Hosea had to present his initial message in a symbolical act. Later, when political control was weakened by successive revolutions, he may have been able to speak more freely. Hence several of his utterances are in the nature of public addresses, cast in the rhythmic form customary with prophets. Most of his effusions, however, are monologues.

The Young Prophet (Hos. 1-3)

Conditions Leading to Hosea's Prophetic Mission. Hosea apparently did not experience visions as did Amos and other prophets. But he received messages. They may have taken shape in his mind as unsought thoughts or impulses. But he knew, with the same certainty we find characteristic of other prophets, that the Lord was speaking to him. A "biographical" report, probably written by someone else, makes this plain at the outset.

According to this report the first message the young Hosea received was a command to marry. It would be difficult to persuade anyone that a decision to marry had any symbolic value. It was the unusual kind of marriage called for that made the act significant. He was told to take "a wife" (better, "a woman") of harlotry. The specific word for "harlot" is avoided. The Hebrew phrase used means "a harlotrous woman," just as in Hebrew phraseology "a woman of grace" (Prov. 11:10) means "a gracious woman," or "a woman of worth" (Ruth 3:11) means "a worthy woman." We may note that Hosea was not told to "love" the woman (cf. 3:1), but simply to "take" one of the specified type, with the explanation "for the land commits great harlotry by forsaking the LORD."

Many scholars hold that the command of the Lord has been refashioned in the light of later insight. According to this view Hosea loved and married a wife who was virtuous to begin with but became harlotrous, and it was only through the painful discovery of this fact that he came to realize how the Lord was grieved by Israel's disloyalty to him. While this explanation would create a more perfect allegory, it involves an undue weakening of what is stated. If we accept the words as recorded, they seem well suited for launching Hosea on a prophetic career. The taking of a woman of loose morals could have been intended to shock people and make them ask: What does this mean? Hosea could readily give the authoritative answer: The Lord hereby is showing you that the people of his covenant are harlotrous. It was in this way, we hold, that the Lord first spoke through Hosea (1:2).

Everyone knew that the Lord was Israel's God. "Thou shalt have no other gods beside me" was the ancient ordinance. But the truth was that Israel in those days did have other gods. It would seem that the term "harlotry" for the additional worship of pagan divinities already existed in the days of Elisha, for Jehu said to King Joram, "What peace can there be, so long as the harlotries and the sorceries of your mother Jezebel are so many?" (2 Kings 9:22). In Elijah's and Elisha's time, it was a definite god, the Tyrian Baal, whose worship was being promoted. Hosea, however, speaks of both *Baal* and *Baals*. That raises the question: Does this mean a single god (the storm-god?) in all his local manifestations? Or is it a general designation for diverse pagan gods? The latter seems the more probable (cf. 3:1).

It is easy to understand how such a trend toward paganism could arise. Many people of Canaanite extraction had been absorbed into Israel, and the survival of Canaanite heathen ideas in such families was natural enough. One need only think of how elements of paganism linger tenaciously to this day in European communities; how sites and rites once sacred to heathen divinities are still continuing through transfer to some Christian saint. The Hebrew "high places," too, usually occupied the sites of the old local pagan shrines. While the Lord was now worshiped there, there must have been constant pressure to tolerate worship of the old gods, and certainly to continue certain customs, such as sacred prostitution (4:13b). Hosea clearly belonged to a conservative element in Israel that was uncompromisingly committed to the covenant religion. It was the meaning of his life and ministry to denounce departure from the faith of the fathers. Apostasy must bring in its wake divine punishment—this was his basic belief, and history was to prove him right.

Hosea's Marriage and Children. A woman of the kind indicated by the divine message must have been known to Hosea, but the biographical report merely says: "He went and took Gomer, daughter of Diblaim." This sounds like marriage to a free man's daughter, but the words do not permit any certain inference as to the person's status, whether unwed, widowed, or divorced. It is even doubtful whether Diblaim is a personal name and not a town name, and this makes it uncertain whether she was born free.

The story of chapter one does not dwell further on the matter of Gomer's morals but hastens to its point, which obviously is to tell of the three children who were born to Gomer and given ominous names, predictive of what was going to happen to Israel. At the birth of the first child Hosea receives the message, "Call his name *Jezreel*; for yet a little while, and I will punish the house of Jehu for the blood of Jezreel." The blood of Jezreel can only be that shed at the town of Jezreel by Jeroboam's ancestor Jehu, when he made his revolution and murdered kings and princes, as related in 2 Kings 9–10. The prophet Elisha had had a hand in fomenting this revolution, and the storyteller in 2 Kings seems to regard Jehu as executing God's will. The command of the Lord to Hosea, however, shows that there were some thoughtful people who did not approve of Jehu's acts of violence, but regarded them as constituting bloodguilt for which atonement would have to be made.

At the birth of the second child, a daughter, Hosea is told, "Call her name Not pitied (Lo-ruhamah), for I will no more have pity on the house of Israel, to forgive them at all.

At the birth of the third child he receives the message, "Call his name Not my people (Lo-ammi), for you are not my people and I am not your God."

There is finality in this third ominous name. It should be noted, too, that the interpretation given by the Lord is put in the second-person plural. It thus was intended to be communicated to the public. In the cases of Jezreel and Lo-ruhamah the interpretation may have been for Hosea alone; people were left to guess what those names signified. With Lo-ammi no guessing was necessary: The Lord was going to disown Israel.

The naming of the children was hardly occasioned by mere personal experience of unfaithfulness of a wife. It seems far more likely that it was dictated by prophetic considerations of the times, as were the names of Isaiah's children. The child Jezreel was certainly born before the death of King Jeroboam II (c. 747), and perhaps several years prior to that event. The predicted punishment of the house of Jehu materialized when Jeroboam's son and successor Zechariah was assassinated after a reign of six months. Therewith the judgment over the house of Jehu was consummated, and a later historian found it significant that Zechariah was a fourth generation descendant of Jehu (2 Kings 15:12; Exod. 34:7). The usurper Shallum was in turn slain after one month and replaced by Menahem (c. 746–737). Perhaps it was under the impression of Menahem's ruthless seizure of power that Lo-ruhamah was named. For it is reported that in his revolution he "sacked Tappuah and all who were in it and its territory from Tirzah on ... and he ripped up all the women in it who were with child" (2 Kings 15:16). Here was the beginning of pitiless judgment that could well occasion such a name as "Not pitied." What led to the naming of Lo-ammi is not discernible. The birth may have taken place around the time of the beginning of the Assyrian King Tiglathpileser's campaign in the west in 743. But it was probably the renewed religious apostasy encouraged by Menahem (2 Kings 15:18) that provided the real occasion for the child's name.

The third person narrative breaks off with the birth and naming of Gomer's third child. Therewith the account has apparently reached its objective: complete rejection of Israel by the Lord.

An Autobiographical Report. In chapter 3 we find a first person narrative, which therefore was clearly written by Hosea himself or given orally by him to someone who handed it down. According to this narrative Hosea is told

> "Go again, love a woman who is beloved of a paramour and is an adulteress; even as the LORD loves the people of Israel, though they turn to other gods and love cakes of raisins."

This, too, is to be a symbolical act, surprisingly similar to 1:2. In both cases the woman represents Israel. In the first instance she is vaguely called a "harlotrous woman," whereas here she has a paramour and is called an "adulteress." In the one case the sin of Israel is characterized as forsaking the Lord, in the second instance as turning to other gods and notably to the goddess to whom cakes of raisins were offered (Jer. 7:18; 44:17 ff.).

Hosea relates that he bought the designated woman for a price paid partly in silver and partly in grain (3:2). The total amounted to a slave price of thirty shekels (Exod. 21:32). She was thus a handmaiden, and could be sold by her owner.

Having acquired the woman Hosea sets up a further symbolism. Without direct instruction from the Lord, but acting out of his own prophetic consciousness, he imposes a quarantine on her. She must dwell for many days without being able to play the harlot, or to belong to another man (namely, the paramour of verse 1) nor will Hosea himself have sexual relations with her. This confirms the woman's slave status, for Hosea could not have dealt in this manner with a lawful wife. It also shows how completely Hosea is dedicated to his national mission.

As he loves the woman, he is inflicting torture on himself, therewith symbolizing the grief the Lord feels over what he is going to do to Israel. The period of quarantine is to symbolize the suspension of relations between the Lord and the Israelites: "For the children of Israel shall dwell many days without king or prince, without sacrifice or pillar, without ephod or teraphim." Hosea thus implies the fall of the kingdom, and even goes beyond that, hinting at deportation. For if the Israelites remained in their own land they would not be without the things mentioned. No mere oppressor would have deprived them of their religion; he would only have superimposed some element of his own cult on the conquered people. But when a nation was carried off into exile its own worship was interrupted. Foreign soil is "unclean land" (Amos 7:17; 2 Kings 5:18) because it is defiled by heathen religion.

Inherent, however, in Hosea's words is the prospect that the woman will be accepted after a long period of discipline, and this is to symbolize the future renewed acceptance of Israel into God's favor. That remains a certainty even if the concluding verse of the chapter, or at least the phrase, "and David their king," is discounted as of later origin.

The Riddle of Hosea's Marital History. What is the relation between the two reports? This is one of the most controversial questions of Old Testament study. There are three main solutions. The first of these takes the slave woman of chapter 3 as a different woman. Since the average Palestinian farmer of recent times still had two wives there can be no serious objection to the idea of Hosea's having had at least a handmaiden. The second solution views the story of the slave woman as a fuller and more exact version of the "taking" of Gomer. Since chapter one was evidently written by someone who was chiefly interested in the portents established by the names of the children he might have passed over the details of how Hosea acquired Gomer. At the original occasion the prophet might have been more optimistic about Israel's future than he was later, and the author of the third-person report would have taken his final pessimistic standpoint. This theory requires the assumption that the word "again" in 3:1 is not to be stressed. It could refer to some previous oracle of the Lord in the account from which the piece was derived, or it could be an editorial addition to establish a connection of some sort. The third solution holds that chapter 3 is the account of the recovery of Gomer, who—it is supposed—had been divorced or had run away and been sold into slavery, perhaps as a temple prostitute. This interpretation enjoys the favor of many leading scholars, perhaps because it is more satisfying to imagine Hosea as having a single redeeming love that would form a counterpart to God's love for Israel.

To discuss these views in detail would be tedious, with small profit in the end. We must bear in mind that what may have happened in Hosea's life is not the primary matter. It is the significance attributed to what is actually reported that matters and in that respect each narrative is clear enough.

Hosea's Message As Based on His Experience. Those who have been deeply wounded by life's experiences are best fitted to speak or write in words full of depth and power. Hosea was such a man.

In chapter 2 we find collected a few of his utterances that deal with Israel's unfaithfulness and punishment plus some others about a future restoration (though three of these are later additions—2:16–17, 18, 19). To what extent the former may be exploited in favor of theories about Hosea's marital history is questionable.

The opening poem (2:2–3) may be partly responsible for the theory that Gomer became harlotrous (or else continued her harlotry) after marriage.

> "Plead with your mother, plead— . . .
> that she put away her harlotry from her face,
>   and her adultery from between her breasts;
> lest I strip her naked
>   and make her as in the day she was born." (2:2–3)

The Hebrew word rendered "plead" means "contend with" as a plaintiff would in bringing a lawsuit. It would be unrealistic to suppose that Hosea is addressing Gomer's small children, who were not of an age to bring charges. He is addressing the children of Israel (i.e., those of them loyal to the Lord) to bring accusation against their mother (i.e., their country or people) so as to induce her to put aside her idolatrous practices. The allusion to what is on the face and between the breasts is probably to jewelry. Women decked themselves for the Baal festivals (cf. 2:13), and of course did so too when going forth for amorous

adventure (Prov. 7:10). The threat of what will happen to Israel's land
if this contention does not avail is that the Lord will make it like a
wilderness or a parched land (2:3). Figuratively this is like shaming a
woman by public exposure of nakedness. Not only will the Lord have
no pity on the land but he will have no pity on its children of today
or tomorrow because they are children of harlotry.

> For their mother has played the harlot;
>   she that conceived them has acted shamefully.
> For she said, "I will go after my lovers,
>   who give me my bread and my water,
>   my wool and my flax, my oil and my drink." (2:5)

The theme of the judgment over the adulteress, but without reference
to the children, is taken up again in a subsequent piece (2:9–13). Here
the purpose of the "stripping" of verse 3 is made clear.

> Now I will uncover her lewdness
>   in the sight of her lovers,
>   and no one shall rescue her out of my hand. (2:10)

The stripping referred to was apparently done in connection with the
judging of a woman convicted of adultery (cf. also Ezek. 16:37 ff.),
though we have no explicit report of such a custom. The interpretation
is more elaborate than in 2:3.

> "And I will put an end to all her mirth,
>   her feasts, her new moons, her sabbaths,
>   and all her appointed feasts.
> And I will lay waste her vines and her fig trees,
>   of which she said, 'These are my hire,
>   which my lovers have given me.'
> I will make them a forest,
>   and the beasts of the field shall devour them.
> And I will punish her for the feast days of the Baals
>   when she burned incense to them
> and decked herself with her ring and jewelry,
>   and went after her lovers, and forgot me, says the LORD." (2:11–13)

Deprivation of certain religious institutions and desolation of the land
will be the punishment for the Baal worship. The wilderness and
parched land, or the future return to forest, are the result of laying
waste the vines and fig trees. These Israel wrongly regarded as gifts of

the Baals, whereas in reality they were given by the Lord (2:8).
In another piece there is a different symbolism.

> "Therefore I will hedge up her way with thorns;
>   and I will build a wall against her,
>   so that she cannot find her paths.
> She shall pursue her lovers,
>   but not overtake them;
> and she shall seek them,
>   but shall not find them.
> Then she shall say, 'I will go
>   and return to my first husband,
>   for it was better with me then than now.' " (2:6–9)

This in part seems to reflect the treatment of the bought woman of
chapter 3. Does this give us a decisive clue for reconstructing Hosea's
marital history? Does it not indicate that he took back Gomer? Many
hold that to be the case. But the thought of the first husband and the
better days only fits the ideal relation of the Lord and Israel in the
Exodus era and has no counterpart in Hosea's marriage. The latter was
under a cloud to begin with (unless one accepts the theory that the
report of 1:2 is unreliable). However, the closing lines predict the success of the disciplinary measures against Israel and therein correspond
to what is implied in 3:4.

Similar idealistic thinking about the future renewal of Israel's relation to the Lord appears in another eloquent passage (2:14–15). But
here it is not a case of repentance, but rather of a renewed wooing, with
the Lord taking the initiative. It thus belongs to a variant line of
thought.

> "Therefore, behold, I will allure her,
>   and bring her into the wilderness,
>   and speak tenderly to her.
> And there I will give her her vineyards,
>   and make the Valley of Achor a door of hope.
> And there she shall answer as in the days of her youth,
>   as at the time when she came out of the land of Egypt." (2:14–15)

This "alluring" hardly seems figurative for foreign captivity, but rather
of voluntary migration or flight. The Lord will bring Israel back again
into the wilderness out of which the people had come. There he will
woo her and she will be responsive as of yore to his speaking tenderly.

If he says he will give her her vineyards there and make the vale of Achor
(cf. Josh. 7:24 ff.) a door of hope, what does this mean? Is Hosea
saying that the Lord will permanently separate Israel from Canaan,
make the desert bloom, and reestablish life even in the desolate vale
of Achor (cf. Isa. 65:10)? Or is the author thinking of a renewed gift
of Palestine to God's people after they have been won over to his love
in the wilderness? Mention of the vale of Achor as a gate of hope would
seem to suit a reentry into the land better than an exit from it. Even
the sixth century Deutero-Isaiah thinks of the desert as being made to
bloom only for the purpose of easing the homeward journey of the
Hebrews from their land of exile (Isa. 41:18 ff.). Certainly whoever
added the supplementary materials that follow this passage (vv. 16–23)
understood this to refer to a future in Palestine. The thought, then, is:
Life will begin anew with return to the Holy Land, and develop according to the prophetic ideal.

The Mature Prophet (Hos. 4-14)

Hosea as Poet. In this second and larger part of the book, which
may represent a separate collection of his oracles, Hosea reveals himself
as a man of poetic ability. All his utterances in this section are in rhythmic diction, well suited to the enthusiastic state of one seized by a
deity. What impresses the reader most, however, is the depth of Hosea's
feeling. Jeremiah alone among the preexilic prophets is his equal in
this respect.

Hosea's imaginative power is displayed in his striking figures of
speech. Some of them have received wide circulation through the English Bible. Such are "sowing the wind and reaping the whirlwind"
(8:7), "plowing iniquity and reaping injustice" (10:13). Several vivid
sayings of Hosea are quoted or utilized with powerful effect at high
points in the New Testament. His prediction that "they shall say to
the mountains, Cover us, and to the hills, Fall upon us" (10:8) adds
depth to Luke's passion narrative (Luke 23:30). His cry "O Death,
where are your plagues? O Sheol, where is your destruction?" (13:14),
taken in a new and different sense, contributes vastly to one of Paul's
most eloquent flights of thought and speech (1 Cor. 15:55).

Hosea, like all true poets, draws on the sphere of nature and of life
as it presented itself to him in his own environment. He apparently
lived in a farming country, yet fairly close to desert areas, which in the

northern kingdom lay toward the east. He has seen the morning mist (13:3), as one sees it over the Jordan valley. He has seen the flourishing reed plant near a fountain of water wither as the sirocco, "the east wind, the wind of the LORD," comes rising from the wilderness (13:15). He has observed a chip swept away on the waters (10:7), in one of those sudden freshets that follow a cloudburst. He has known the surprise of finding some grapes growing in the wilderness (9:10). He knows the luxuriant vine that yields its fruit in the regular vineyards (10:1), and the first fruits of the fig tree "in its first season" (9:10). He is familiar with poisonous weeds in the furrows of the field (10:4), with the stricken plant whose root is dried up (9:16). Cattle are more in his range of observation than sheep, though he mentions "a lamb in a broad pasture" (4:16). While acquainted with the stubborn heifer (4:16) he also knows the trained heifer that loves to thresh, and whose fair neck the owner spares (10:11) by not imposing a yoke. He has observed the farmer easing the yoke on his oxen and bending down to them to feed them (11:4). He can think of animals gently led with cords or bands (11:4). With a bold figure he can describe Ephraim as herding the wind, yea pursuing the east wind all day long (12:1). He knows that the dove—much raised for offerings of the poor (Lev. 5:7; cf. Luke 2:24)—is silly and without sense (7:11).

Wild animals, too, have come to his attention, if only from hearsay. He knows of the wild ass wandering alone (8:9). He knows how the leopard lurks by the way; how a she-bear, when robbed of her cubs, may fall upon someone, tearing open the breast; how the lion rends and devours (13:7–8). He knows how the fowler lays his snare in the ways (9:8) for birds like the tasty sand partridge. He has seen how the net is spread for "birds of the air" and, in effect, will "bring them down" (7:12) permanently out of their element.

The household also furnishes Hosea with imagery. The useless vessel (8:8) offers a ready comparison. Moths and dry rot are familiar (5:12). He has observed the smoke coming out of a window (13:3)—presumably from a brazier used to warm a room in the cold, damp season (Jer. 36:22). He is acquainted, too, with the outdoor baking oven that is left to smolder all night, but blazes up in the morning (7:6). He knows that a cake not turned is useless, because it is charred (7:8); that there is no point to stirring the fire until the dough is leavened (7:4). He is well aware of how a papyrus roll—perhaps containing a contract of purchase of one's house or a marriage contract—is stored (13:12). He has heard of a situation that can arise at childbirth when the babe ready to be born does not present itself normally at the mouth of the womb, and calls such a one an "unwise son" for his seeming perversity (13:13). He knows the love one feels for a child (11:1). With all such homely means, drawn from the life of his time and environment, Hosea made his prophetic poetry vivid.

The Lord's Controversy with Israel.   At the head of the second collection of Hosea's sayings stands one of the few that clearly are in the nature of public addresses. It brings in ethical charges, apparently based on the decalogue.

> Hear the word of the LORD, O people of Israel;
>   for the LORD has a controversy with the inhabitants of the land.
> There is no faithfulness or kindness,
>   and no knowledge of God in the land;
> there is swearing [falsely, i.e., perjury], lying, killing,
>   stealing, and committing adultery;
> they break all bounds and murder follows murder. (4:1–2)

But he swiftly passes to an attack on the priests, as the ones chiefly responsible for the lack of knowledge of the Lord's will.

> They feed on the sin of my people;
>   they are greedy for their iniquity
> [i.e., the income from the cult]. (4:8)

The faithfulness and kindness Hosea misses is the "dealing loyally and truly" with another (cf. Gen. 24:12). When "knowledge of God" dies out, how can one expect anything else to prevail but the law of the jungle? And where the priests fail in their most essential task of conveying that knowledge what can one expect of the people? It is this knowledge of God, the insight into his will and requirements, that is of paramount importance to Hosea.

Hosea and History

Hosea shows himself familiar with the history of his people from patriarchal times on. It is Jacob who stands before his mind as the nation's ancestor; Abraham and Isaac are not mentioned. In alluding to incidents of Jacob's life Hosea is not dependent on the narratives of Genesis, but rather on traditions parallel to those reported there and not yet placed into the familiar sequence. He also has knowledge of the Exodus period and of the desert wanderings, and considers Moses to have been a prophet. There are allusions to happenings of the early days which are too uncertain to linger over (cf. 1–2; 6:7; 9:15; 10:9). But when he refers to the guilt incurred through worship of Baal and its ruinous effect on Ephraim (13:1) he is clearly thinking of the time of King Ahab (13:1). He knows that the Lord did not leave his people without prophetic voices to warn them by inspired visions and "parables" (12:10).

This prophet makes many allusions to internal affairs or events of his own time, but we lack the necessary information to understand them. The account in 2 Kings 15:8–27 reports the succession of rulers and a few items of importance, but that is all. It was a dreary period of unrest and decline. Each new revolution must have involved much bloodletting. The widespread idea that Hosea was antimonarchical in principle (like the author of 1 Sam. 8), however, is not vindicated by his words. Even such a statement as

> They made kings, but not through me.
> They set up princes, but without my knowledge. (8:4)

need imply no more than that the regular manner of appointing rulers was ignored in these actions. Nor does his grim prediction that when the Lord makes an end to their diplomacy they will cease for a while from anointing king and princes (8:10) mean anything more than disapproval of frequent change.

Hosea as Observer of the International Scene. We gain from Hosea passing information of the foreign political situation. It was a time of terrible dilemma. On the one hand there was Assyria, with its expansionist policy which had already laid low the states of northern and central Syria. On the other hand there was Egypt, which felt itself threatened by the Assyrian advance and sought by its wealth and its diplomacy to organize resistance on the part of the remaining Near Eastern states. The first line of such resistance would now necessarily be "Syria," or Aram, and Israel. No doubt opinion was sharply divided in Israel itself as to what should be done. There was vacillation of policy at times:

> they make a bargain with Assyria,
>   and oil is carried to Egypt. (12:1)

Hosea describes as silly and senseless the "calling to Egypt, and going to Assyria" (7:11). "Already they are among the nations as a useless vessel," with their hiring of allies, first on one side and then on the other (8:8–10). It is evident that Hosea was an isolationist. He condemned, too, the reliance on military power (10:13), such as Israel may again have acquired in the decade of Menahem's reign.

Assyria Acts. The final disastrous period of Israel's history was brought on by the revolution of Pekah (c. 735–732). It was a military revolt that must have been sparked by the belief that an anti-Assyrian policy was now required. Direct support by King Rezin of Damascus can be assumed, as Pekah of Israel now appears as his ally and subordinate. But a larger coalition was in the making, no doubt with the support of Egypt, which must have felt menaced by the specter of Assyrian domination of Western Asia. The young king Ahaz of Judah, who had succeeded his father Jotham, had evidently refused to join, and Rezin and Pekah were bent on overthrowing him and to that end marched on Jerusalem in 735. Ahaz, terrified by this powerful alliance, placed himself under the protection of Tiglathpileser (2 Kings 16:7). The latter thus had a welcome cause of war against Israel and Damascus, and swiftly proceeded against them.

It is from this situation that at least one of the utterances of the fifth chapter of Hosea can perhaps be explained:

> Blow the horn in Gibeah,
>   the trumpet in Ramah.
> Sound the alarm at Beth-aven;
>   tremble, O Benjamin!
> Ephraim shall become a desolation
>   in the day of punishment. (5:8 ff.)

The towns mentioned lying on the road to Ephraim, three, five, and eleven miles north of Jerusalem, are apparently facing attack from the south (judging from the order of their mention). All three are counted as Benjaminite in Josh. 18:21 ff. While Bethel (Beth-aven) already belonged to the northern kingdom at the time of Jeroboam I, Ramah and Gibeah were taken away from Judah (along with Mizpah, three miles north of Ramah) c. 900 B.C. (1 Kings 15:16–22). Recently scholars have been led to believe that the order of mention of these towns reflects a pursuit of the retreating Rezin and Pekah by Ahaz. But no invasion of Benjamin by Ahaz is recorded. Judah, furthermore, was hardly the chosen instrument of the Lord for punishing Ephraim. The exact sequence of military events is not known, but it is a fact that Tiglathpileser went down to Philistia already in 734. To do so he had to cross Israel's territory. A new fragmentary Assyrian account of that campaign shows that he annexed sections of Israel's coastland at that time.

It thus was perfectly possible for Hosea to anticipate Tiglathpileser's planning to invade Israel from the coastal plain, coming up from Beth-horon to Gibeah. Whether the expectation was realized or not, the peril of an attack on Ephraim from the south was certainly present. Rezin and Pekah must have retreated hastily from their undertaking against Jerusalem.

The next piece in this chapter may, in our opinion, come from a somewhat later juncture:

> When Ephraim saw his sickness,
>   and Judah his wound,
> then Ephraim went to Assyria,
>   and sent to the great king.
> But he is not able to cure you
>   or heal your wound.
> For I will be like a lion to Ephraim,
>   and like a young lion to the house of Judah.
> I, even I, will rend and go away,
>   I will carry off, and none shall rescue. (5:13–14)

The theory that this is to be explained from the situation of the war of Pekah and Rezin against Ahaz fails to convince. We know of no wound suffered by Judah at the time. Indeed, it seems very probable that "Judah" has been secondarily substituted for Israel—the appropriate parallel word for Ephraim. Furthermore it was Judah, not Ephraim, who went to Assyria at the time of Pekah and Rezin's invasion. The incurable wound of Ephraim suggests that the blow dealt the northern kingdom in 733–732 by Tiglathpileser, as related in 2 Kings 15:29, had already taken place. Ephraim "went to Assyria" when Pekah was murdered. At that time Hoshea became king of Israel (2 Kings 15:30; 17:3) and was recognized by Tiglathpileser (who says that he appointed him).

An Interesting Allusion.   There is one reference in Hosea's oracles that may perhaps refer to a historical event of the previous century (10:13–15). The prophet predicts calamity for Israel's fortresses because of its trust in military power and compares that coming disaster to an event of the past in the words:

> as Shalman destroyed Beth-arbel on the day of battle;
>   mothers were dashed in pieces with their children. (10:14)

Beth-arbel is no doubt the city in northern Transjordan, not the one in Galilee, known only in late times. The site with which it is usually identified, *Irbid*, is an old Bronze Age mound. In its original state of fortification it may have been a suitable scene for the "dashing to pieces" that took place at Beth-arbel. The city must have gotten its name from the Assyrians, for it is clearly a new "Arbela." Shalman is certainly the name of a king, and a likely candidate for his identity is Shalmaneser III (858–824), who in 841 carried his campaign against Hazael of Damascus as far as the Hauran region (east of *Irbid*), and campaigned against Damascus a second time in 838. That the city named Beth-arbel was colonized with Assyrians from Arbela and renamed in the course of these events seems possible. Hosea may not have known the name it had prior to its siege. The passing manner in which he refers to the tragedy suggests that it was not a very recent one.

Hosea and the Coming Punishment of Israel

This prophet, unlike Amos and Isaiah, remains entirely within the natural order in his thinking about the retribution in store for Israel. What he has to say about this is sometimes put in figurative speech. Once he borrows imagery of mythological origin when he says:

> O Death, where are your plagues?
>   O Sheol, where is your destruction?
>   Compassion is hid from my eyes. (13:14)

In other words the most terrible forces, personified Death and Netherworld, are to be brought against them by the Lord. Hosea can invoke too the idea of a divinely caused barrenness of women (9:11, 14; cf. Gen. 20:18). But he thinks chiefly of military invasion and attendant horrors (as in 10:13 ff.), or of exile, and consequent desolation of the land. He knows that the Assyrian kings had a retinue of tributary kings and their forces with them on their campaigns and hence can speak of "nations" being gathered against Israel (10:10). Apparently he foresees a twofold fate for the latter:

> They shall not remain in the land of the LORD;
>> but Ephraim shall return to Egypt,
>> and they shall eat unclean food in Assyria. (9:3, cf. 11:5)

Flight to Egypt by all those involved in a policy of reliance on Egypt and exile of the rest to Assyria was certainly foreseeable at the time of King Hoshea's treachery (2 Kings 17:4). For those going to Egypt the prophet apparently has no hope:

> Egypt shall gather them,
>> Memphis shall bury them. (9:6)

He no doubt knew of Hebrews already living at Memphis, since fugitives from Israel's revolutions had long made Egypt a haven of refuge, and he expected great numbers to flee there in the coming crisis. He describes what their feeling of deprivation will be when in captivity without their cultic institutions (3:4).

> They shall not pour libations of wine to the LORD
>> and they shall not please him with their sacrifices.
> Their bread shall be like mourners' bread;
>> all who eat of it shall be defiled
> for their bread shall be for their hunger only,
>> it shall not come to the house of the LORD. (9:4)

This is not to say that Hosea himself placed any value on the rites so dear to them.

As in 2:14 there is also the conception of a return to the wilderness out of which Israel had come. In both cases this seems to be meant realistically and is not just figurative for deportation:

> I am the LORD your God
>> from the land of Egypt;

> I will again make you dwell in tents,
>> as in the days of the appointed feast. (12:9)

This is not necessarily at variance with Hosea's other views. The prophet may be thinking of escapees to North Arabia, who had a much better prospect of returning to the promised land than any carried off to Assyria or fleeing to Egypt. The "wilderness" is the Lord's true baili-wick; there he had found Israel. There he could reorganize it and lead it once more to his land.

The Possibility of Repentance.   The possibility of a return to the Lord after deprivation of political and religious institutions was in Hosea's mind when he confined the bought slave-woman to symbolize Israel's captivity (3:1-4). In chapters 4-14 Hosea speaks a number of times of a repentant mood of Israel, apparently in a time of peril but before the utter desolation that will follow defeat and exile. In these cases he imagines the Lord as having departed from his land to permit history to take its course. For he once says "Woe to them when I depart from them!" (9:12) and hints that in that interval Ephraim's sons will be led to slaughter. Such calamity naturally will produce a repentant mood:

> With their flocks and herds they shall go
>> to seek the LORD
> but they will not find him;
>> he has withdrawn from them. (5:6)

In a great passage, to which passing reference has already been made, the Lord himself predicts such repentance:

> I will return again to my place,
>> until they acknowledge their guilt and seek my face,
>> and in their distress they seek me, saying,
> "Come, let us return to the LORD;
>> for he has torn, that he may heal us;
>> he has stricken, and he will bind us up.
> After two days he will revive us;
>> on the third day he will raise us up,
>> that we may live before him.
> Let us know, let us press on to know the LORD;
>> his going forth is sure as the dawn;
> he will come to us as the showers,
>> as the spring rains that water the earth." (5:15-6:3)

While there is no definite assurance of the Lord's return from "his place" (Mount Horeb? cf. 1 Kings 19:8), it may be assumed that such faith in his power to reanimate a wounded—yea dead—nation will move him to act mercifully. The resolve to cultivate knowledge of the Lord is implied, and therewith the way is opened for his renewed favor. But seeking him with sacrificial offerings (as 5:6 suggests they will do) is dismissed as valueless:

> For I desire steadfast love and not sacrifice,
> The knowledge of God, rather than burnt offerings. (6:6)

Elsewhere Hosea indicates that if Israel had proper religious and moral attitude it would experience divine help:

> Sow for yourselves righteousness,
>   reap the fruit of steadfast love;
>   break up your fallow ground,
> for it is the time to seek the LORD,
>   that he may come and rain salvation upon you. (10:12)

Renewed Faith and Restoration. In a piece full of pathos (14:1–8) Hosea once more urges Israel to return to its God. The situation in which the poem was composed apparently is one after a great calamity, for Israel has "stumbled" (and fallen) because of its sins. Some of the people are placing hope in Assyrian help, and in furnishing Assyria with auxiliaries. The nation is urged to pray and give assurance to God of its faith in him alone. It then makes both prayer and promise to the Lord:

> "Take away all iniquity;
> accept that which is good
>   and we will render the fruit of our lips.
> Assyria shall not save us,
>   we will not ride upon horses;
> and we will say no more 'Our God,'
>   to the work of our hands.
> In thee the orphan finds mercy." (14:2b–3)

The appeal for the orphans would be particularly understandable after a calamitous war. The allusion to Assyria indicates that this nation is still in existence and political choices are possible.

The response to the prayer is a prophecy of restoration:

I will heal their faithlessness;
  I will love them freely,
  for my anger has turned from them.
I will be as the dew to Israel;
  he shall blossom as the lily,
  he shall strike root as the poplar;
his shoots shall spread out;
  his beauty shall be like the olive,
  and his fragrance like Lebanon.
They shall return and dwell beneath my shadow,
  they shall flourish as a garden;
they shall blossom as the vine,
  their fragrance shall be like the wine of Lebanon.

O Ephraim, what have I to do with idols?
  it is I who answer and look after you.
I am like an evergreen cypress,
  from me comes your fruit. (14:4–8)

The ideal of the future for Israel is expressed in terms drawn from the sight of a lovely countryside with flowers, shade and fruit trees, and vineyards. The people is to return from its exile and be under divine protection. The idolatry of the past is no longer remembered. God himself will look after them (or, with emendation, "restore" them) and be like a fresh green cypress tree of Palestinian gardens, or like a fruit tree from which the people will receive its fruit. In these allusions there is apparently a slight influence from the idea of the garden of Eden and its tree of life. In Milton's phrase, there will be a "paradise regained."

Whether the prophet himself composed this description of future blessedness is debatable. The idea of the Lord's anger having turned from the Israelites (14:4) seems to imply that the national tragedy has run its full course and thus to presuppose that Hosea lived to see that happen. There is, however, no evidence of his having witnessed the last desperate struggle. But the defenders of authenticity meet the objection by simply eliminating the line about the Lord's anger as a later addition. Whatever the truth of the matter, the future is seen in purely materialistic terms. The passage, even if authentic, cannot enhance the prophetic stature of Hosea.

The final verse of chapter 14, however, has nothing to do with what precedes, and clearly is not by Hosea. It is an exhortation by a scribe to the wise to understand and take to heart the lessons of the book, and an affirmation of the justice of God as experienced in individual life.

The Prophet in Retrospect

In Hosea we encounter one of the great figures of the prophetic movement in Israel. He was a sensitive man, on whose soul painful experiences left deep scars. He was capable of loving, and eager to be loved. He carried in his heart an ideal of virtuous Hebrew womanhood, marital happiness, and love of children, but in the service of his God was condemned to find no realization. He was not to live "unto himself." The drama of his life was intended to serve a high symbolical purpose, not only for his contemporaries but for the ages. Though he had courage and firmness and was capable of passion and even of ferocity, he was a sufferer more than a doer. He was not at the center of things, where policy and history were made, and if he had been or had gone there he could not have prevailed. When a godless spirit seizes leaders and people, and movement in the direction of anarchy and demoralization starts, there is no halting the trend by appeal to higher motives or reminders of a noble past. A great patriot like Hosea could only warn and hope against hope that through God's grace his people would not be utterly lost.

Hosea introduced the love and marriage symbolism into the Old Testament religion. Jeremiah seems to have been much influenced by him in this respect, though how this influence was transmitted we do not know. But the acceptance of the idea by others paved the way for the allegorization of the Song of Songs, followed by the extension of the bridegroom symbolism to the Messiah, as is handled so beautifully in the Gospels. Thus religious language took on new warmth and depth of feeling. Truly, Hosea, too, deserves a place among the pioneers of higher religious life. He excellently supplements Amos, the exponent of the divine righteousness.

3 THE EARLY ISAIAH AND MICAH: JUDAH'S WARNERS

THE SAME AGE that saw Amos and Hosea prophesy in the northern kingdom was also to see two prophets speak up in Judah: Isaiah and Micah. Thus the whole four-leaf clover of the so-called "classical prophets" flourished within a period of fifty years. Samaria, the capital of the northern kingdom, was still in existence when the last two of these men began to prophesy, but their activity extended for a generation after its fall.

Isaiah, Citizen of Jerusalem

Isaiah is the most "classic" of these prophets in the Hebrew he spoke and in the thoughts behind his words. He does not address just Judah, but speaks to "Jerusalem and Judah." The city is the dominating entity, and indeed had a distinctive status politically, for it had been taken by David and his personal following (2 Sam. 5:6 ff.). "Zion," or "the fortress of Zion" evidently was the acropolis portion of the city. The latter originally occupied only the spur of the eastern ridge. To later ages it seemed incredible that this tract of a few acres had been Zion, and so tradition came to seek the latter on the more impressive western ridge. But modern excavations have proven that the old city was in the east near its water supply. It had a more impressive location in Isaiah's time than it has now, for during the long ages the level of valleys on either side and below the spur of the ridge has been raised far above that of antiquity. Josephus in the first century A.D. could still describe the situation as very elevated, though perhaps he exaggerated to impress his Hellenistic-Roman readers. It seems likely that in Isaiah's time the northern part of the western ridge was already within Jerusalem's walls, but improbable that the wall enclosed the whole western ridge. Isaiah was proud of his city's historic importance, and his thinking centers on what he saw there.

Isaiah was a freeman's son; his father's name is given. There is no report of what the prophet did before his call. Some think that he was a "wisdom teacher." As a prophet he no doubt enjoyed the backing of the kind of intelligent people who were loyal to the ancient religion of the Davidic era, and were opposed to any compromise with foreign cults or with "modern" ways of life. Much about him must remain a mystery. What matters is how he became a prophet.

Isaiah's Call

Isaiah was probably young when he received his call to the prophetic office. He dates the event in the year of King Uzziah's death. Uzziah (or Azariah) had become leprous and thus had as coregent his son Jotham and then the latter's son Ahaz. The year of Uzziah's death was probably 736.

The account of Isaiah's call (chapter 6) is unique, because it comes directly from him and because of its quality. The accounts of Jeremiah's and Ezekiel's calls are not on a par with it. Nor have we a comparable first person account of the call of any of the great personages of religious history—not even of Jesus or of Paul, of Zoroaster or of Buddha. It is thus a most significant document.

It is unlikely, however, that Isaiah wrote his memoir of this event soon after it occurred; probably he wrote it at some subsequent time —perhaps at the occasion of a temporary retirement (8:16). In view of the frailty of human life that would have been an appropriate moment for a prophet to set down something for the record. What the visionary saw must have been so overwhelming that it was difficult to describe. He must have meditated a great deal on the experience in the course of the years, and it would be natural for him to be unable to differentiate between his original standpoint before the call and his reflections in the fullness of his prophetic power. The possibility of slight additions by other hands, too, cannot be discounted. It may even be that two visions (following each other closely) have been contracted into a single narrative, for there is a seeming break between his experience of being shriven of sin (6:7) and his presence at a council meeting (6:8). The latter requires a heavenly scene, at which the deity is attended by other celestial beings besides the seraphim; for

these were imagined as serpentlike six-winged creatures (though probably with human heads), whose function was not that of councillors
but of lesser attending genii.

The sort of thing presupposed for this second part of the narrative
is described by Micaiah ben Imla when he says, "I saw the LORD sitting
on his throne, and all the host of heaven standing beside him on his
right hand and on his left" (1 Kings 22:19 ff.). The Lord then ques-
tioned the council as to what he should do to lead King Ahab to his
destruction. Thereupon a spirit came forward to volunteer his advice
and services.

Similarly, we might think, Isaiah saw such a heavenly council meeting
and felt that he was admitted to it and thus able to hear the Lord's
question to the gathering, "Whom will I send and who will go for us?"
Like the spirit in Micaiah's vision, he volunteers, declaring, "Here
I am, send me." The Lord without further comment thereupon gives
Isaiah his commission:

> "Go, and say to this people:
> 'Hear and hear, but do not understand;
> see and see, but do not perceive.'
> Make the heart of this people fat,
>   and their ears heavy,
>   and shut their eyes;
> lest they see with their eyes,
>   and hear with their ears,
> and understand with their hearts,
>   and turn and be healed." (6:9b–10)

It is a terrible task, which an evangelist centuries later saw repeated
in the case of Jesus (Mark 4:11). It is a ministry of making matters
worse—of increasing resistance to God by assailing the sins, evils, and
hypocrisies of the people.

Appalled at this prospect Isaiah asks how long this obdurate condition
of the people will last, for it seems incredible that God's anger could
go to the uttermost extreme. But he receives the grim reply:

> "Until cities lie waste
>   without inhabitant,
> and houses without men,
>   and the land is utterly desolate,
> and the LORD removes men far away,
>   and the forsaken places are many in the midst of the land." (6:11b–12)

Therewith the account fades out, for verse 13, modifying these words, cannot have been spoken at this time. Isaiah did not report his reaction to the commission given him. Clothed with authority from on high he went forth obediently to carry out what he had been told to do.

Significance of Isaiah's Vision. This account reveals a great deal about the young Isaiah's character and thinking. His nature was not that of a dreamer and sufferer like Hosea. He was ready to speak up to God and to volunteer for a service, the true nature of which was not yet disclosed. His idea of God had been schooled by what he saw in the world of his time. He lived under a monarchic system, in which a kind of mysticism enveloped the kingly office. True, the king of Judah was only a little king, but there were great kings in the world, notably in Assyria and Egypt, and it was that kind of monarch who stimulated the prophet's imagination. He could conceive of the world above only as peopled by beings that were minions of a kingly god. Indeed, his God is the king of gods, the God of gods, whose glory fills the earth. But above all he is "holy." Holiness was not, as we might think, ethical perfection, but rather a quality that set the deity apart from "unclean" or sinful man.

The Basic Message of Isaiah

For the early message of Isaiah we are thrust back solely on his oracles, which come from a ministry of forty years and were not edited in chronological order. There are no certain criteria for dating many of them. Only where foreign political background enters in can one attempt more definite assignments of dates. Perhaps those are among the earliest in which there are no side-glances on national or international affairs, but where the prophet is concerned purely with social and moral conditions, or speaks of catastrophe in mythical terms. We will dwell first on some characteristic utterances of this more general nature in order to understand the mind of Isaiah.

The "Soft Sell." Knowing that he would meet bitter opposition Isaiah may first have tried to bring his message in sugar-coated form. With such an approach would fit the parable of the divinely taught farmer (28:23–29). It makes one think of a man getting up at an

agricultural fair and giving a discourse. The knowledgeable farmer, he
points out, carried on his work intelligently, not in helter-skelter fashion.
Indeed, the complicated rules of agricultural practice, Isaiah believes,
were first revealed to men by the Lord, who "is wonderful in counsel, and excellent in wisdom." No further application is made. The
wisdom teacher—if Isaiah was that—was continuing in the vein of his
earlier rational, rather than emotional, teaching. But he is laying a
foundation. He believes in a God who is the possessor of all wisdom
—not only in agriculture, but in governing the world.

Another example is given by the vineyard parable. It is really a song
modeled on a girl's song about her "beloved" (samples of which are to
be found in the Song of Songs). It may have been recited by Isaiah
with female intonation. The "friend" of whom it speaks is revealed at
the end to be the Lord, and his "vineyard" is the Hebrew people—
Israel and Judah—the latter viewed as his "pleasant (i.e., favorite)
planting."

> Let me sing for my beloved
>   a love song concerning his vineyard:
> My beloved had a vineyard
>   on a very fertile hill.
> He digged it and cleared it of stones,
>   and planted it with choice vines;
> he built a watchtower in the midst of it,
>   and hewed out a wine vat in it;
> and he looked for it to yield grapes,
>   but it yielded wild grapes.
> And now, O inhabitants of Jerusalem
>   and men of Judah,
> judge, I pray you, between me
>   and my vineyard.
> What more was there to do for my vineyard,
>   that I have not done in it?
> When I looked for it to yield grapes,
>   why did it yield wild grapes?
> And now I will tell you
>   what I will do to my vineyard.
> I will remove its hedge,
>   and it shall be devoured;
> I will break down its wall,
>   and it shall be trampled down.
> I will make it a waste;
>   it shall not be pruned or hoed,

> and briers and thorns shall grow up;
> I will also command the clouds
> that they rain no rain upon it.

At this point the prophet unmasked himself.

> For the vineyard of the LORD of hosts
> is the house of Israel,
> and the men of Judah
> are his pleasant planting;
> and he looked for justice,
> but behold, bloodshed;
> for righteousness,
> but behold, a cry! (5:1–7)

This parable, which stimulated the thinking of Jesus (Mark 12:1–12 and parallels), sets forth what the Lord did for his people, asks the local group why the result has been disappointing, predicts the removal of the vineyard's hedge or "wall" (i.e., the land's defenses) and its devastation and return to wilderness. What the Lord looked for in choosing the Hebrew people was "justice" and "righteousness." What he got instead was "bloodshed" and "cry" (i.e., complaint by the afflicted persons or families). The contrasting words are near-rhymes in Hebrew. The finish thus is like the crack of a whip.

The optimistic belief that men will follow law if it is laid down with divine authorization is here attributed to the Lord. He has been proven wrong by events, however, and hence is bitterly disappointed thereby. Obviously this is extremely anthropomorphic thinking on Isaiah's part, but the Hebrew mind was not trained to see the intellectual difficulties involved in assuming such lack of foreknowledge on the part of God. As to the implied charge, we must bear in mind that Isaiah is addressing an aristocratic society. The influential and the powerful were the judiciary; they interpreted and administered the laws (which were already formulated to favor them) and often rendered the decisions to suit their advantage. What happened in the case of Naboth (1 Kings 21)—expropriation with the help of false witnesses—went on constantly in the land on the lower as well as on the higher levels.

It may have been on the occasion of a public day of penance during one of the several national crises through which Isaiah lived that he spoke the words that are so full of divine mercy, yet firmness also:

> "Come now, let us reason together,
>   says the LORD:
> though your sins are like scarlet,
>   they shall be as white as snow;
> though they are red like crimson,
>   they shall become like wool." (1:18)

Even the scarlet of sinfulness (perhaps reminding of innocent blood that has been shed) can be made white. But willing obedience to the Lord's requirements is a prerequisite. Isaiah thereupon offers a choice (vv. 9–20): either obedience and the consequent enjoyment of the good of the land, or continuation of a rebellious attitude toward God and death by the sword.

Criticism of Society: The Seven Woes. But sharper means were necessary, and Isaiah advanced to a more elaborate criticism of contemporary society. He once uttered a series of "woes" on its various classes (5:8–24). Each "woe" hinted at retribution that was in store for those characterized with mention of some distinctive trait. He leads off appropriately with an attack on the big landholders.

> Woe to those who join house to house,
>   who add field to field,
> until there is no more room,
>   and you are made to dwell alone
>   in the midst of the land. (5:8)

Second, he assails the revelers. Third come the scoffers who taunt the prophet by saying of God "Let him make haste, let him speed his work that we may see it." We observe here that atheism of a practical kind existed in Israel. Isaiah calls this drawing "iniquity with cords of falsehood" (better "of oxen"?) or drawing "sin as with cart ropes." Fourth, he attacks those "who call evil good and good evil"—hence those who are frivolous in their attitude toward right and wrong. Fifth, he assails the self-satisfied. Sixth, those bent on proving they can drink more than others. The seventh woe may have been verse 23, which in the Greek version has "Woe to those" before it. It is directed against those who have the privilege to act as judges but accept bribes and deprive the innocent man of his right.

Criticism of the Authorities. This picture of society is supplemented by another poem of woe, dealing with men higher up:

> Woe to those who decree iniquitous decrees,
>> and the writers who keep writing oppression,
> to turn aside the needy from justice
>> and to rob the poor of my people of their right,
> that widows may be their spoil,
>> and that they may make the fatherless their prey! (10:1–2)

Here Isaiah must be hitting at the officials who prepare the legislative measures issued in the name of the king. They are framing laws that work to their private advantage by enabling them to confiscate property of those unable to work or manage it.

Once he even assails a very high official of the government named Shebna, who was "over the house"—apparently the prime minister. The man had made himself a rock tomb (which may recently have been identified). Isaiah predicts his downfall and recommends a certain Eliakim, who would be a father to the people, as worthy successor (22:15–23). But in the case of the latter individual the prophet's judgment of character was mistaken. A supplementary piece (vv. 24–25) remarks sourly that Eliakim would practice nepotism of the worst kind. It may have been added by a later reader. Eliakim, indeed, appears as "over the house" in 701, while Shebna is mentioned as secretary (36:3 ff.). Shebna thus was still entrusted with a high office, and so did not fall very far.

As Amos criticized the aristocratic women of Samaria so Isaiah criticized those of Zion, and prophesied what would befall them (3:16–24). We need cite here only the charges he brings:

> Because the daughters of Zion are haughty
>> and walk with outstretched necks,
>> glancing wantonly with their eyes,
> mincing along as they go,
>> tinkling with their feet . . . (3:16)

This was later supplemented by addition of a prose description of a fine lady's clothing, jewelry, and other accessories (vv. 18–23). In the prediction (vv. 17, 24) the prophet sees these women reduced to poverty and neglect.

Perhaps the height of Isaiah's sorrow over this social scene of his time is reached in his lament over Jerusalem:

> How the faithful city
>> has become a harlot,

> she that was full of justice!
> Righteousness lodged in her,
>   but now murderers.
> Your silver has become dross,
>   your wine mixed with water.
> Your princes are rebels
>   and companions of thieves.
> Every one loves a bribe
>   and runs after gifts.
> They do not defend the fatherless,
>   and the widow's cause does not come to them. (1:21–23)

He has a nostalgic picture of the "once faithful city" in mind and on the basis of it imagines its future revival.

All in all, then, this is a picture of a society in which avarice was given free rein, in which justice was thwarted, in which the poor and defenseless were exploited. It is a city society, in which numerous individuals no longer enjoyed the protection of a clan. We get a glimpse of corrupt religion in a stronghold of religion—just as it existed in Holy Rome under the medieval popes—and of lack of morality that attends sophisticated society in every age.

Religion and Morals. Sharper and sharper became Isaiah's commentary. He once demanded attention for a message, probably in the temple, at an occasion where there was a great assembly. Leaders and people are likened to those of Sodom and Gomorrah, cities that were destroyed for their sinfulness (Gen. 19:24).

> Hear the word of the LORD,
>   you rulers of Sodom!
> Give ear to the teaching of our God,
>   you people of Gomorrah!
> "What to me is the multitude of your sacrifices?
>   says the LORD;
> I have had enough of burnt offerings of rams
>   and the fat of fed beasts;
> I do not delight in the blood of bulls,
>   or of lambs, or of he-goats.
>
> "When you come to appear before me,
>   who requires of you
>   this trampling of my courts?
> Bring no more vain offerings;

> incense is an abomination to me.
> New moon and sabbath and the calling of assemblies—
>   I cannot endure iniquity and solemn assembly.
> Your new moons and your appointed feasts
>   my soul hates;
> they have become a burden to me,
>   I am weary of bearing them.
> When you spread forth your hands,
>   I will hide my eyes from you;
> even though you make many prayers,
>   I will not listen;
>   your hands are full of blood.
> Wash yourselves; make yourselves clean;
>   remove the evil of your doings
>   from before my eyes;
> cease to do evil,
>   learn to do good;
> seek justice,
>   correct oppression;
> defend the fatherless,
>   plead for the widow." (1:10–17)

This great utterance reveals the prophet's rejection of reliance on sacrifice as a means of pacifying the deity. This was one of the basic props of all ancient religion, according to the famous principle, "I give that you may give." It still permeates religion on the lower levels today. But Isaiah, like Hosea and Amos, has the true prophetic outlook. Religiousness is not pleasing to God unless it strives with all its might for morality and is penitent because of constant failure to measure up to the ethical norms.

Equally discerning is the criticism on which Isaiah based his ironic prediction of the wonderful things the Lord would do with "this people."

> "Because this people draw near with their mouth
>   and honor me with their lips,
>   while their hearts are far from me,
> and their fear of me is a commandment of men learned by rote;
> therefore, behold, I will again
>   do marvelous things with this people,
>   wonderful and marvelous;
> and the wisdom of their wise men shall perish,
>   and the discernment of their discerning men shall be hid." (29:13–14)

Coming Calamities. Isaiah, like his predecessors, seeks to frighten the sinner and thus to induce repentance or change of ways. In a great poem he draws vivid pictures of the calamities the Lord will send (3:1–8). Social chaos and revolution are among them. When the economy gets upset, when defeat in war creates confusion, then anarchy can prevail:

> For, behold, the Lord, the LORD of hosts,
>   is taking away from Jerusalem and from Judah
> stay and staff . . .
> the mighty man and the soldier,
>   the judge and the prophet,
>   the diviner and the elder,
> the captain of fifty
>   and the man of rank,
> the counselor and the skilful magician
>   and the expert in charms.
> And I will make boys their princes,
>   and babes shall rule over them.
> And the people will oppress one another,
>   every man his fellow
>   and every man his neighbor;
> the youth will be insolent to the elder,
>   and the base fellow to the honorable. (3:1–5)

But the leading calamities are military in nature. He even presupposes the fall of the Davidic dynasty and that no one of the old aristocracy will be willing to take the responsibility of governing the heap of ruins that will be left. Projecting himself into that future situation he explains the reasons for the collapse:

> For Jerusalem has stumbled,
>   and Judah has fallen;
> because their speech and their deeds are against the LORD,
>   defying his glorious presence. (3:8)

It is clear that the ethical deficiencies are viewed as the undoing of state and capital.

But Isaiah advances to a more comprehensive idea of God's judgment. Perhaps the oracles of Amos had come to his attention. Tekoa was close enough to Jerusalem to make it seem certain that when Amos's sayings were assembled they were circulated among the partisans of prophetic views and strivings. It was Amos who, so far as we can see, had first enunciated the idea of a day of judgment on Israel and had expanded that to include a judgment on other peoples for their moral wrongdoings. Isaiah sees all the earth as full of God's glory, and hence under the sway of his power and accountable to him. But he adds an element not found in Amos: Human pride and vanity are intolerable to God. Isaiah's day of the Lord is one in which he will come with the terrors that are at his disposal to punish all pride in the world:

> For the LORD of hosts has a day
>   against all that is proud and lofty,
>   against all that is lifted up and high;
> against all the cedars of Lebanon,
>   lofty and lifted up;
>   and against all the oaks of Bashan;
> against all the high mountains,
>   and against all the lofty hills;
> against every high tower,
>   and against every fortified wall;
> against all the ships of Tarshish,
>   and against all the beautiful craft.
> And the haughtiness of man shall be humbled,
>   and the pride of men shall be brought low;
>   and the LORD alone will be exalted in that day.
> And the idols shall utterly pass away.
> And men shall enter the caves of the rocks
>   and the holes of the ground,
> from before the terror of the LORD,
>   and from the glory of his majesty,
>   when he rises to terrify the earth. (2:12–19)

The day of the Lord is thus described in figurative terms of a terrible tempest and earthquake which will lay low all that is proud—trees, mountains, and works of men—such as oceangoing ships and fortresses with walls and towers. It is a day that will humble all the pride of man. God will prove himself alone the powerful and exalted one.

Isaiah and Israel

But events in the outside world soon demanded Isaiah's attention. Above all it was the fate of the northern kingdom that concerned him. A lengthy poem, originally consisting of five stanzas, bears witness to this. It is a kind of philosophy of Israel's history and may have been inspired by a desire to emulate Amos (cf. Amos 4:6–12). The Lord, Isaiah says, has dealt this people repeated blows because of its pride and sinfulness. He now is ready to deliver another and final one. Each stanza except the last ends in a refrain:

> For all this his anger is not turned away
> and his hand is stretched out still.

According to a view generally accepted in modern times the fifth and last stanza, preceded by the refrain of a missing fourth stanza, was left behind in 5:25–27 in connection with editorial activity attending the insertion of a separate booklet, 6:1–9:7. We cannot dwell here on the details of this poem except to notice wherein Isaiah, at the time of this utterance, saw the coming final catastrophe planned by the Lord. If 5:26–27 is indeed the original fifth stanza he was obsessed, as Jeremiah later was, by a peril from the north.

> He will raise a signal for a nation afar off,
>   and whistle for it from the ends of the earth;
> and lo, swiftly, speedily it comes!
> None is weary, none stumbles,
>   none slumbers or sleeps,
> not a waistcloth is loose,
>   not a sandal-thong broken;
> their arrows are sharp,
>   all their bows bent,
> their horses' hoofs seem like flint,
>   and their wheels like the whirlwind.
> Their roaring is like a lion,
>   like young lions they roar;
> they growl and seize their prey,
>   they carry it off, and none can rescue. (5:26–29)

The nation meant is usually taken to be the Assyrians; but they were not "at the ends of the earth." The description would best fit the Cimmerians, who came down through the Caspian Gates and spread terror in the lands north of Assyria. But since their inroads began in 707, one would have to infer that this is not the original conclusion of a poem written before the fall of Samaria (721). One might, however, think of the Medes, an Iranian people, who preceded the Cimmerians and against whom the Assyrian king Tiglathpileser III had campaigned in 737.

In another remarkable poem Isaiah assails Samaria, which he compares to a proud crown on a hill above a rich valley. Unfortunately the beautiful city is in the hands of men bereft of judgment through alcoholism:

> The proud crown of the drunkards of Ephraim
> will be trodden under foot;
> and the fading flower of its glorious beauty,
> which is on the head of the rich valley,
> will be like a first-ripe fig before the summer:
> when a man sees it, he eats it up
> as soon as it is in his hand. (28:3-4)

Here, we think, Isaiah clearly realized that it would be the Assyrian who would eat the first-ripe, the juiciest, tenderest fig. The illustration indicates how quickly Samaria will be taken.

The Prophet Micah

About the time when Isaiah's attention was drawn to the northern kingdom the prophet Micah must have been similarly moved, for he too prophesied against Samaria (1:2-7). His home is given as Moresheth, or Moresheth-gath (1:14) in southwestern Judah, evidently near the Philistine city of Gath. He does not have the imagination and poetic ability of his great contemporary, but he is able to speak forcefully and directly. In a saying against the kind of prophets who mislead the people by predicting "peace" (i.e., weal, welfare) for pay (3:5-8) he asserts his own strong prophetic consciousness:

> But as for me, I am filled with power,
> with the Spirit of the LORD,
> and with justice and might,
> to declare to Jacob his transgression
> and to Israel his sin. (3:8)

Like Isaiah he criticizes the rich and the powerful. Several of his sayings are directed against the "heads of Jacob and rulers of the house of Israel" (3:1-4; 9-12), and, as the second passage shows, he means those of Judah. This suggests that at the time of these utterances Samaria had already fallen and that Judah had become heir to the names "Jacob" and "Israel"; for these names were previously claimed by and used for the northern kingdom (cf. Isa. 10:11).

Hear this, you heads of the house of Jacob
and rulers of the house of Israel,
who abhor justice
and pervert all equity,
who build Zion with blood
and Jerusalem with wrong.
Its heads give judgment for a bribe,
its priests teach for hire,
its prophets divine for money;
yet they lean upon the LORD and say,
"Is not the LORD in the midst of us?
No evil shall come upon us."
Therefore because of you
Zion shall be plowed as a field;
Jerusalem shall become a heap of ruins,
and the mountain of the house a wooded height. (3:9–12)

From the book of Jeremiah (26:16 ff.) we learn that Micah came to Jerusalem with this very message in the time of King Hezekiah. The prophet had been arrested, but had been released, thanks to influential men who may have been impressed by his consciousness of authority, as revealed in his words against the prophets. His visit to the capital may have occurred at a period when Isaiah had retired temporarily from the prophetic activity. There is no indication of contact between them. The prophets of old passed each other like ships in the night.

In one oracle (1:8–16) Micah warns the people of his own area of coming disaster, punning on the names of their towns. Some of the places he mentions are obscure or unknown. But Lachish (verse 13) was important, as we shall have occasion to see. It was a military outpost of Judah. In what sense, one must wonder, was that town "the beginning of sin to the daughter of Zion"? Had some cult Micah considered injurious been imported from there, or is the allusion political or military? There is no way of knowing. The excavations at the site of Lachish have yielded no answer.

Other Oracles of Micah? According to some scholars the authentic prophecies of Micah are restricted to chapters 1–3. Two further sections, chapters 4–5 and 6–7, are now appended to the book. In the latter section there are some materials which quite possibly were Micah's. Particularly valuable among these is the poem on God's controversy with Israel (6:1–8). Israel, convicted before the mountains by the

Lord, penitently asks its counselors, as a devotee does the priest, about the appropriate means of penance:

> "With what shall I come before the LORD,
>   and bow myself before God on high?
> Shall I come before him with burnt offerings,
>   with calves a year old?
> Will the LORD be pleased with thousands of rams,
>   with ten thousands of rivers of oil?
> Shall I give my first-born for my transgression,
>   the fruit of my body for the sin of my soul?" (6:6–7)

The prophet replies instead of the priest:

> He has showed you, O man, what is good;
>   and what does the LORD require of you
> but to do justice, and to love kindness,
>   and to walk humbly with your God? (6:8)

The utterance gives a classical definition of true religion.

The two pieces following the great passage, a second oracle against the people of Samaria (6:9–16) and a lament over moral decline in Judah (7:1–6), are likewise in the vein of Micah 1–3. But the psalm-like conclusion of the book (7:7–20) cannot very well be attributed to the prophet. Gunkel, the leading master of form-critical study, called it a "prophetic liturgy." The whole poem is a song of trust in God. Its dating depends on who is addressed in 7:8, "Rejoice not over me, O my enemy." The usual assumption is that Edom is meant, and that a postexilic Jewish vantage point is to be assumed. A recent theory holds that Assyria is the enemy and that the speaker is an Israelite and not the Judean Micah.

The preceding section, chapters 4–5, consists mainly of prophecies of hope. Leading off is 4:1–4, the great poem dealing with the temple of the future that is found also in Isaiah 2:1–4. It was evidently put here editorially to offset the prophecy of the destruction of the temple predicted by Micah in the final poem of chapter 3. The conclusion of the prophecy is better preserved in the Micah version than in Isaiah. There is little in the entire section (4–5) that could make one think of Micah's time. In 4:9–12 we find a description of a future siege of Jerusalem in a near-apocalyptic vein, followed by a seemingly parallel verse (5:1) in which it is said that during a siege, "they strike upon the

cheek the ruler of Israel." If this is an allusion to a historical situation
it cannot be identified. The passage is of interest since a Gospel author
must have had it in mind in his passion narrative (John 18:22). In the
case of 5:5–6 the mention of Assyria and the land of Nimrod (Gen.
10:9) might seem to indicate origin in the Assyrian era. But one can
find no realistic basis in the historical situation of that period for
an expectation of seven or eight rulers, who would rule Assyria with
a drawn sword and deliver Israel or Judah from Assyrian invasion.
Since "Assyria" was used in later times as a term for Mesopotamia and
Syria (a word abbreviated from Assyria), this peculiar passage could
have arisen in that period. The time of the wars of the Diadochi
(323–301) would seem particularly suitable, for a considerable number of rulers then were fighting Antigonus, the man who strove to hold
together the empire of Alexander the Great. Antigonus had for his
base of power a city not far from the later Syrian Antioch.

The star piece in this section of Micah's book, however, is the one
that precedes the passage just referred to. It is the prophecy about the
future Messiah (5:2–4). There is no discernible reason why it should
be attributed to Micah, standing as it does amid a whole collection of
later prophecies (5:5–6; 7–9; 10–15). It is questionable, too, whether
the man who had so little use for Jerusalem had much interest in the
house of David, and the town from which he had come. The
prophecy presupposes the fall of the northern tribes, and probably also
that of the Davidic monarchy.

The prophecy begins with hailing the small town from which David,
founder of Judah's kingship, had come:

> But you, O Bethlehem Ephrathah,
>   who are little to be among the clans of Judah,
> from you shall come forth for me
>   one who is to be ruler in Israel,
> whose origin is from of old,
>   from ancient days.
> Therefore he shall give them up until the time
>   when she who is in travail has brought forth;
> then the rest of his brethren shall return
>   to the people of Israel.
> And he shall stand and feed his flock in the strength of the LORD,
>   in the majesty of the name of the LORD his God.
> And they shall dwell secure, for now he shall be great
>   to the ends of the earth. (5:2–4)

This passage may have been produced by a native of Bethlehem, which of old was in the hands of a Calebite clan called "Ephrath," (cf. Ruth 1:2; 1 Sam. 17:12). The town thus could be described in archaizing manner as Beth-Ephrath "house of Ephrath" (or as "Ephrathah"). The combination Bethlehem-Ephrathah is late and artificial, but clarifies the fact that Bethlehem is meant. The town allegedly is an insignificant one in the author's time. But the Lord has a way of choosing what is weak in the world to shame the strong (1 Cor. 1:27). Bethlehem is the place of his choice for the birth of the Messiah who is to come. In mysterious style the author speaks of this ruler's ancient lineage (i.e. his descent from David), and of his mother as "she who is (or will be) in travail." There is no indication as to when this king will be born, but until the predestined time arrives the people are "given up" helplessly to foreign domination. For this author the Jews are now "Israel," to which he hopes "the rest of his brethren" (i.e. the northern tribes carried off by the Assyrians) will be joined. When the Messiah comes he shall be great through the power of God, and his people shall dwell securely.

In consequence of this passage the belief that the Son of David, or "Messiah" would come from Bethlehem became fixed in the Jewish mind in the late centuries. Of necessity then Jesus had to come from there.

The Prophet in Retrospect

Micah is not as distinctive a figure as Amos, Hosea, or Isaiah. He has no specific slant in his idea of God, as Amos has in stressing the God of righteousness or as Hosea has in proclaiming the God of love, or as Isaiah has in preaching the God of holiness and world government. But like his great predecessors he sees that a rift has come about between the Lord and the nation. The morality the Lord expects of his people has given way to immorality all along the line and must provoke the divine judgment. But he was able to dissociate himself from Jerusalem much more than was possible for Isaiah, and to foresee its utter, unqualified destruction. Furthermore he regards the poor and humble as God's people (to the exclusion of their oppressors), and thus paves the way for him who said, "Blessed are you poor, for yours is the kingdom of God" (Luke 6:20).

4 ISAIAH AND THE STRUGGLE OF NATIONS

In the Time of Tiglathpileser III

The Syro-Ephraimite War. It soon became Isaiah's task to serve as the Lord's prophet in troubled times. The new and vigorous Assyrian ruler Tiglathpileser III (745–727) had resumed the strong policy of imperial expansion. He had driven back the Urartaeans of Lake Van, who had pushed down into Syria, and he had taken and destroyed the Syrian city of Arpad (near modern Aleppo), which had been unfaithful in its allegiance to Assyria. The threat of Assyrian peril, reminiscent of that which had prevailed under the earlier kings Ashurnazirpal and Shalmaneser III, drove Syria, under its king Rezin of Damascus, to build an alliance. Pekah of Israel was Rezin's satellite, and had to participate. Since Tiglathpileser had again turned his attention to campaigns in northern countries in 736–735, there was time to exert pressure on recalcitrants. Judah's King Jotham (756–741) had apparently refused to join, and hostile actions had been undertaken against him (2 Kings 15:37). His death left his untried son Ahaz (c. 741–725) as successor, and apparently provided an opportunity for more decisive action by Rezin and Pekah. When news of a purpose of overthrowing Ahaz and appointing a puppet king over Judah reached Jerusalem, the city and the Davidic house were terrified (Isa. 7:1 ff.).

In that situation Isaiah was prompted to bear a message of the Lord to Ahaz, who at the moment was evidently concerned with preparations for a siege. The prophet was to take along his small child Shear-jashub and go to a water reservoir, where he would find the king.

The message Isaiah was to give the ruler was one of reassurance: The onslaught of the two kings will fail; each is only head of his kingdom and cannot be more than that, and both are like burned-out torchbutts. The prophet was to warn his sovereign:

> "If you will not believe,
> surely you shall not be established." (7:9)

We are not told how Isaiah carried out this instruction. This may be due to a loss or abridgment of text. But it clearly leaves a gap in the record.

The occasion at which Isaiah is said to have delivered the message has been called the hour in which "faith" was born. In any case it is an hour in which it was classically stressed. When God has spoken and promised something that seems difficult of realization there is an obligation to trust him. In this instance he had informed Ahaz that there was no need for fear. The assurance was absolute. Ahaz's disbelief could not change it, and so the warning words "you shall not be established" must look beyond this crisis to future developments.

In delivering his warning the prophet may have divined what was going on in the king's mind. He may have felt that Ahaz was thinking of how he might checkmate his two adversaries by worldly means. It seems unlikely that Isaiah had any direct knowledge of the king's secret diplomacy, but it would not have been difficult to guess that he would seek foreign aid. Such a thing had already been done by an earlier king of Judah (1 Kings 15:18). Isaiah's warning, one may suppose, was intended to deter Ahaz from such a step.

The directive to the prophet to take along Shear-jashub must also have had a meaning, and that meaning must lie in the son's name. "Shear-jashub" probably means "a remnant will return." The child must have been a mere toddler if it was born and named after Isaiah's call (c. 736). It would be most in line with the message Isaiah had received at that time (6:9–12) if the significance of the name were ominous: "(Only) a remnant will return." "Remnant" is really a military word, at home in the strategy of annihilation. "Return" thus could refer to the homecoming of escapees after military disaster. If that were the case the point of taking the child along could have been to warn against fighting any battle outside of the city. But the word "return" is often used with the religious nuance of "returning to the LORD," or repenting. The meaning would then rather be that of an affirmation of hope on the part of Isaiah himself, in spite of the dreadful prediction of disaster given him at his call (6:11–12). A passage that is probably of later origin (10:31) operates with the phrase "a remnant will return" in this religious sense. But it is difficult to see what a future repentant remnant could have meant to King Ahaz at this time. His concern was with the present preservation of his people and of his throne. True prophecy is timely and relevant to the situation. It thus seems likely that the name Shear-jashub was understood in an ominous sense by Isaiah, and that the presence of the child bearing it served to reinforce what was only hinted at in the warning "you shall not be established."

The Immanuel Prophecy. Into the gap made by loss or omission of the account of how Isaiah carried out his assignment has been placed a continuation of his interview with the king (7:10–17). It assumes that the king put no stock in the warning of Isaiah, and that the latter then pressed the matter further.

In this passage Isaiah offered a miraculous "sign" to Ahaz to persuade him to believe that he had spoken with divine authority. The king declined to put the Lord to the test (Exod. 17:2; Num. 14:22) by asking for a sign. He was evidently superstitious; such "testing," he might fear, could have dangerous side effects. Isaiah thereupon rebuked him for wearying him and his God, and added a prediction:

> "Therefore the Lord himself will give you a sign. Behold, a young woman shall conceive and bear a son, and shall call his name Immanuel. He shall eat curds and honey when he knows how to refuse the evil and choose the good. For before the child knows how to refuse the evil and choose the good, the land before whose two kings you are in dread will be deserted. The LORD will bring upon you and upon your people and upon your father's house such days as have not come since the day that Ephraim departed from Judah—the king of Assyria." (7:14–17)

This is one of the most controversial prophecies in all history. One thing is certain. Since the first century Christians have regarded it as a direct prophecy of Christ, and it is that fact which has lent it an abiding interest. But the new biblical scholarship that came up in the eighteenth century did away with older scholastic and antique principles of interpretation, and made it more difficult to maintain the historic position. The scriptural authors in all periods, we must now hold, were men of their time, and those of the New Testament read earlier Scripture with the eyes of their own time. We, however, must put ourselves back into the situation of the original writer or speaker when seeking to understand any utterance. If one does that here the Immanuel prophecy at best could be one of a Messiah within the scope of the time (if, indeed, the expectation of such a one existed that early), but not a direct prophecy of the birth of Jesus.

Such modern views should not disturb anyone. What words have come to mean for people is often more important than what they actually meant when they were first uttered. One cannot but recognize that age-long interpretation, rich in satisfaction and noble sentiment, has its place and its value. There is no reason why we should not follow the summons addressed to the people of God in a medieval hymn in the Advent season:

> "Rejoice! Rejoice! Emmanuel
> Shall come to thee, O Israel."

Immanuel, or Emmanuel (as the ancient Greek translation and the New Testament transcribe it) is a name that in substance means "God is on our side." When Gideon was greeted with the words, "The Lord is with you," he replied, "Pray, sir, if the Lord is with us (Heb. *immanu*), why then has all this befallen us?" (Judg. 6:12 ff.). He was referring to the recurring invasions and plunderings of the country by desert Arabs. This catastrophic situation raised doubt as to the Lord's ability or will to protect his people. One must expect that the same question disturbed Jerusalem, when the news came of an impending joint attack by Rezin of Damascus and Pekah of Israel. It allegedly brought Isaiah to the fore, as we have heard. The affirmation "God is with us," concluding a powerful utterance against attacking peoples (8:10), and the refrain "The Lord of hosts is with us" in a psalm of similar spirit (Ps. 46:7, 11), support the idea that the name implied, primarily, belief in divine help in a national crisis. It was probably an existing personal name, for the Elephantine papyri of the fifth century B.C. mention a Jew named *Immanuiah*, "The Lord is with us."

If one starts with the assumption that the sign promised Ahaz had to be pertinent to the situation and carry assurance of divine help, a prophecy of a Messiah would seem useless. Any aid at this juncture had to come from God himself. Only the existence and name of the child, and the time mentioned when what is implied in the name will be realized, can count. As to the former point, it seems probable that the birth of the child must be imminent to have any value for Ahaz. Hence many scholars render "Behold the young woman *is* with child." As to the time of fulfillment verse 16 is clear enough: Before the child is a few years old the land before whose two kings Ahaz is in dread will be forsaken. Verse 15 ("He shall eat curds" etc.) can either be eliminated, as standing unnaturally between the name and its explanation, or be put after verse 16, where it would provide a transition to verse 17("The LORD will bring upon you" etc.). In the latter case the eating of curds and honey would suggest hardship in Judah in the interim between the birth of the child and the time indicated in verse 16 (cf. below on v. 21). The young woman's act in naming her child "Immanuel" would then be one of a faith contrasting markedly with Ahaz's unbelief.

Is the author of the passage thinking of an individual child? Some go so far as to assert that he means it collectively: Any young woman may then call her son Immanuel. But that seems incredible in view of the time-lag between the naming of the child and the fulfillment of what the name implies. Some go further and, omitting verse 15, eliminate the words "before whose two kings you are in dread" from verse 16. When that is done the sense of the prophecy is changed to one of doom for Judah. This has the advantage of making verse 17, with its prediction of Assyrian invasion, and the appended short prophecies 7:18–25 follow naturally after verse 16. The Immanuel children then are viewed as suggestive of the holy remnant (cf. 6:13; 37:31).

But it seems unwarranted for the Lord to reverse his intention and send so much affliction on Judah just because Ahaz did not wish to put him to the test. The style of the saying, furthermore, is the one found in narratives of individual deliverers or heroes. The following comparison will make this plain.

Isa. 7:14	Gen. 16:11
"Behold, a young woman shall conceive and bear a son, and shall call his name Immanuel."	"Behold, you are with child, and shall bear a son; you shall call his name Ishmael."

Ishmael is so named because the Lord has given heed (Heb. *shama'*) to Hagar's affliction. Similarly one may say that the point of the name Immanuel lies in the prediction of the forsakenness of the lands of the enemy as stated in 8:16. For this will prove that God is with Judah. One may insist that to eliminate the words which specify the nature of the help is to miss the point of the whole situation as seen by the narrator.

But who is going to be the mother of an individual Immanuel? Will it be one of Ahaz's own wives who will give this name to her child? This idea has suggested a theory that the allusion is to the birth of Hezekiah, Ahaz's son, who, according to a later story, experienced such a wonderful deliverance (chapter 37). That view is already entertained in a Jewish midrash, and was perhaps suggested by 2 Chron. 32:8, where Hezekiah says of Sennacherib, "With him is an arm of flesh; but with us (immanu) is the LORD our God." Or is Isaiah prophesying about his own wife? That theory is currently exercising an appeal, and has suggested to some that Isaiah's wife soon bore a son whom she named Immanuel, as predicted.

But the messianic interpretation of the passage can still be defended on the basis of 7:15, "He shall eat curds and honey," when compared with verses 21–22.

> In that day a man will keep alive a young cow and two sheep; and because of the abundance of milk which they give, he will eat curds; for every one that is left in the land will eat curds and honey. (7:21)

Curds and honey can be regarded as a motif of the blessed times or regions as in the phrase "land flowing with milk and honey" (Exod. 3:8). In further support of this one can adduce the exclamation "O Immanuel" in 8:8. The Immanuel prophecy can then be grouped with the prophecies of Micah 5:3 and Isaiah 9:6, in which the Messiah's mother also remains cloaked in mystery. The scope for a messianic interpretation can be broadened by drawing on parallels from antiquity, such as the famous fourth eclogue of Virgil. On this basis, one can assert that Isaiah is now going a step further than in 7:17. In his anger over the refusal of Ahaz to ask for a sign he is predicting that the dynasty will fall and the country be overwhelmed by the Assyrians, and that a mysterious child, given the name "God is with us," will be born and grow up in these times and become the deliverer of the future.

It seems highly probable, however, that in 7:22 the words "and because of the abundance of milk which they give, he will eat curds" are an interpolation; for all the other short prophecies grouped together in

7:18–25 deal with future invasion and desolation of the land by the Assyrians. That then may also be the case with 7:15 and with the "O Immanuel" of 8:8. When the changes (if such they are) were made, people had already begun to seek deeper meaning in scripture and were looking for prophetic utterances that might be relevant to their own day. The name Immanuel certainly invited connection with the Messiah, and once it was regarded as a messianic title it would cease to be a commonly used personal name.

Such a messianic interpretation may already have been shared and carried further by the ancient translators in Hellenistic Egypt who rendered the book of Isaiah into Greek c. 200 B.C., for they substituted for the word "young woman" (in 7:14) the Greek word for "virgin." It is possible that they were influenced in this by the cry raised at Alexandria at the festival of the birth of the sun god, "The virgin (-goddess) has born a son." Since early gentile Christians used the Greek Bible translation as authoritative, its rendering led them to take the prediction of Isaiah 7:14 as prophecy of the virgin birth of Jesus, as is done in Matthew 1:23 and, without direct reference to Isaiah, in Luke 1:26 ff. The Septuagint thus paved the way for a tenet that was considered very important in the early Church, and which has had an enormous impact on Catholicism. If later Greek Bible translations, made by Jews in the Christian era, avoided using the word "virgin" in Isaiah 7:14 and rendered "young woman," this was no doubt due to Jewish dissatisfaction with the Christian use of the passage, as given in the Septuagint.

Political Action of Ahaz and the Reaction of Isaiah. Ahaz did not heed the warning to be unafraid of Rezin and Pekah. He could not see the shakiness of their thrones, of which the prophet spoke in his inspired message, and he followed the course from which the Lord had sought to deter him. This is clearly reported in a historical account:

> So Ahaz sent messengers to Tiglathpileser king of Assyria, saying, "I am your servant and your son. Come up, and rescue me from the hand of the king of Syria and from the hand of the king of Israel, who are attacking me." (2 Kings 16:7)

This act of Ahaz was to have far-reaching consequences. It created obligations for the future. According to Assyrian custom Ahaz had to accept a vassal treaty, though mention of this has been omitted from the biblical record. Economically the treaty meant heavy annual tribute. Religiously it meant a denial of the Lord's sovereignty, and it opened the gates to the worship of foreign gods. Politically it gave the foreign power the right to expect loyalty and obedience in return for protection. Transgression would invite terrible retribution. This was to befall Judah a generation later, as we shall hear.

An oracle of Isaiah gives his reaction to the act of Ahaz which evidently enjoyed full popular support. The prophet must have uttered the words immediately following public knowledge of Tiglathpileser's acceptance of the king's request:

> "Because this people have refused the waters of Shiloah that flow gently, and melt in fear before Rezin and the son of Remaliah; therefore, behold, the Lord is bringing up against them the waters of the River, mighty and many, the king of Assyria and all his glory; and it will rise over all its channels and go over all its banks; and it will sweep on into Judah, it will overflow and pass on, reaching even to the neck; and its outspread wings will fill the breadth of your land, O Immanuel." (8:6–8)

The extra lines about Rezin and Pekah and the king of Assyria are probably explanatory glosses. They were unnecessary for the contemporaries but helpful for later readers. As we have seen, it is possible that "O Immanuel" is also editorial in origin. It could have been added on the basis of the thought that the Immanuel child (or children, if collectively interpreted) would be alive when the prophesied Assyrian invasion of Judah became a reality. Or it could just have been supplied to effect a transition to 8:9–10, which ends with "God is with us" (Hebrew, *immanu 'el*). If the name was introduced later into 8:8 the piece may originally have ended with "its land" rather than "your land." However that may be, the poem is in accord with Isaiah's exhortation to rely on the Lord, and construes the bid for Assyrian aid made by Ahaz as rejection of the waters of Shiloah—the water channel coming from the Gihon spring, on which the city's life depended. These waters, then, are a figure for the divine help available to God's people. The River of many waters is the Euphrates.

Tiglathpileser's response to the appeal of Ahaz must have been his campaign to Philistia in 734. According to a newly published inscription, he first campaigned in Phoenicia, and from there passed through Israelite territory. It seems probable that Pekah's army was defeated

in resisting the Assyrian's passage (see page 63). But many years were
still to pass before the predicted Assyrian flood would overwhelm Judah.
The events in the north were to hold the stage for a decade to come.

The Son with the Ominous Name. According to a first person report
(8:1–4), hence going back to Isaiah himself, the prophet predicted
certain events that took place in 735–732 at a time when nobody believed them possible. The prediction is not dated but the time can
perhaps be inferred from the account. He was commanded by the Lord
to inscribe on a large tablet (perhaps of clay set in a wooden mold)
an inscription in "common characters" (better, "in human script").
This, we believe, is stressed because the words were the Lord's, though
not supernaturally inscribed in "the writing of God" like the ten commandments in the tables of stone (Exod. 32:16).

The words he was to incise were "Belonging to Maher-shalal-hash-
baz," a name meaning "spoil speeds, prey hastes." This was cryptic, like
a Delphic oracle, and perhaps not yet fully understood by Isaiah himself; but he knew the meaning would become clear later on. He provided
validation by procuring two reliable witnesses, one a priest and the other
evidently a prominent laymen—both men of standing—who may have
watched with a feeling of awe as he engraved the mysterious words.

Apparently Isaiah sought to beget a child on that same day. When
a son was born after ten lunar months he received another divine
communication:

> "Call his name Maher-shalal-hash-baz; for before the child knows how to
> cry 'My father' or 'My mother,' the wealth of Damascus and the spoil of
> Samaria will be carried away before the king of Assyria." (8:3b–4)

Now the meaning of the mysterious inscription was unveiled. The
spoiler and those to be despoiled were identified. The infant bearing
the prophecy for a name advertised it concretely, as Hosea's son Jezreel
had by his name forecast the end of King Jehu's dynasty. Isaiah, of
course, must have produced his tablet, and the witnesses who could
swear that he had written the words nearly a year ago, when there was
no discernible indication yet of catastrophic events. It must have been
clear by now that Tiglathpileser was bent on crippling the alliance that
was forming against him. But it was not clear whether he could take
Damascus and Samaria, or whether that was his real objective. The

campaign to Philistia in 734—if that had already taken place—could indicate that he was bent on threatening Egypt. But Isaiah's oracle said: Within a year Damascus and Samaria will fall. Assuming that he was right for Damascus, the oracle would have been spoken in 733, for in 732 Damascus was taken. In 733 the northern and eastern regions of the kingdom of Israel were attacked—events reported without a date in 2 Kings 15:29. Samaria did not have to be besieged, for Israel's King Pekah was assassinated, and his slayer, Hoshea, reigned in his stead (2 Kings 15:30). Since Tiglathpileser states that he appointed him, and received ten talents of gold and a quantity of talents of silver from him, the prophecy was fully vindicated. Besides this money the Assyrian king carried off to Assyria the captives and spoils of the Israelite cities that had fallen.

An Allusion to Israel's Grievous Losses.   A brief oracle, referring to the tragic events of 733, though in retrospect, may be mentioned here. It was originally independent of the messianic prophecy of 9:2 ff., but came to be taken in conjunction with the latter.

> In the former time he [i.e., the LORD] brought into contempt the land of Zebulun and the land of Naphtali, but in the latter time he will make glorious the way of the sea, the land beyond the Jordan, Galilee of the nations. (9:1)

This became significant to a Gospel author (Matt. 4:15 ff.) as a prediction of Christ's appearance in the tribal areas of Zebulun and Naphtali, which were crossed by "the way of the sea" (the road leading to the coast), as well as of his ministry in the land beyond the Jordan (the country of the Gadarenes, Matt. 8:28). The tribal areas mentioned belonged geographically to "the Galilee (i.e., the 'circle country,' *galil*) of the nations," perhaps so-named because it was ringed by heathen cities. Contrary to those who scoffed at the idea that the Messiah or even a prophet would come from Galilee (cf. John 7:41, 52) the evangelist found evidence in this prophecy that the light of the messianic deliverance would dawn there for the people sitting in darkness (9:2 ff.). Since the prediction in 9:1, though brief like those in 7:18 ff., can stand by itself (as we have assumed was originally the case), one can well regard it as fulfilled in Christ's ministry. However, the author, whether Isaiah or someone else, was thinking only of a

restoration to prosperity and therewith glory for a region that had fallen
into contempt through the ruin wrought by Tiglathpileser. The vicinity
of the Hellenistic cities not only gave Jesus the opportunity to have
contact with gentiles and to find them receptive for his person and
message, but prepared the way for the transition of Christianity to the
gentile sphere. Here again the principle that what words come to mean
may be more important than what they originally meant is applicable.

Isaiah's Retirement. Events were now taking their predicted tragic
course. The prophet was conscious of a restraint being imposed upon
him by the will of the Lord:

> For the LORD spoke thus to me with his strong hand upon me, and warned
> me not to walk in the way of this people, saying: "Do not call conspiracy
> all that this people call conspiracy, and do not fear what they fear, nor
> be in dread. But the LORD of hosts, him you shall regard as holy; let him
> be your fear, and let him be your dread. (8:11–13)

The words "call conspiracy" are probably to be emended to "call holy"
to correspond with "regard as holy" in verse 13. It is difficult to see
in any case what "conspiracy" has to do in this connection. It makes
excellent sense, however, if Isaiah is to separate himself from the popular
reliance on the holy place and all the holy objects and rites conducted
in it. He adds as his own parting shot the grim prediction that the
Lord will become a stumbling block to both houses of Israel, a trap
and snare particularly to the inhabitants of Jerusalem (vv. 14–15).

The command to cease his prophetic activity seems to have followed
directly after this revelation. Isaiah reports that he was told:

> Bind up the testimony, seal the teaching among my disciples. I will wait
> for the LORD, who is hiding his face from the house of Jacob, and I will
> hope in him. Behold, I and the children whom the LORD has given me
> are signs and portents in Israel from the LORD of hosts, who dwells on
> Mount Zion. (8:16–18)

Apparently then his "disciples" were to conserve his teachings, and this
may have implied writing them down. The only visible sign of what
Isaiah stood for was to be his person with his name which he may
have taken to mean "The LORD is help," and the children the Lord
has given him—Shear-jashub and Maher-shalal-hash-baz. Since the latter's name portended the fall of Damascus and Samaria the oracle may
antedate the fall of the former city.

In the Time of Tiglathpileser's Successors

The Oracle Against the Philistines.   With the fall of Damascus in 732 resistance was temporarily at an end in the Syro-Palestinian sphere. There seems to have been no concerted attempt to rebel at Tiglathpileser's death in 727. His successor, Shalmaneser V (726–722), was governor of a Syrian province when he succeeded to the throne of his father, and no doubt had things firmly in hand in the north. This is less certain in the case of the south. It is quite possible that the year of the death of Tiglathpileser was also that of the death of Ahaz, king of Judah, and that an oracle referring to Philistine messengers was given to Isaiah at that time. It marks a resumption of his activity, and may have been addressed to the ministers of the new king, Hezekiah.

> In the year that King Ahaz died came this oracle:
> "Rejoice not, O Philistia, all of you,
> > that the rod which smote you is broken,
> for from the serpent's root will come forth an adder,
> > and its fruit will be a flying serpent. . . .
> Wail, O gate; cry, O city;
> > melt in fear, O Philistia, all of you!
> For smoke comes out of the north,
> > and there is no straggler in his ranks."
> What will one answer the messengers of the nation?
> "The LORD has founded Zion,
> > and in her the afflicted of his people find refuge." (14:28–29, 31–32)

Tiglathpileser had smitten Philistia, and so could be compared to a rod. But in his role as bringer on of successors in office this figure was useless, and so the poet shifts to the figure of the serpent. The adder is probably Shalmaneser V, Tiglathpileser's son, and the flying serpent (described as the adder's "fruit") would then be Shalmaneser's son. Actually, however, a usurper named Sargon II succeeded Shalmaneser, but he was indeed more terrible than Shalmaneser. Philistia is then warned of an oncoming Assyrian army, burning cities as it advances. The prophet apparently suggests neutrality for Judah in reliance on the Lord.

King Hoshea and the Last Days of Samaria.   In 724 King Hoshea of Israel defaulted on his tribute to Assyria. Shalmaneser allegedly "found treachery" in him for sending messengers "to So, king of Egypt" (2

Kings 17:4). As has been recognized recently the words "to So, king of Egypt" should really be rendered with a very slight emendation "to Sais, to the king of Egypt." Though Egypt in general was under Ethiopian dominion at this time, the city of Sais (called Sa' in the Assyrian texts) was virtually independent. The king in question must have been Tefnakht (730–720).

Shalmaneser was able to seize the person of King Hoshea, but the leadership in Samaria, knowing well the fate in store for it, refused to surrender and so the city was placed under siege. The length of the siege is given as three years (2 Kings 17:5). It was probably a mere holding operation to permit the forces of self-destruction to take their course. Actually, Shalmaneser did not live to occupy Samaria. It fell like the ripe fig, to which Isaiah had compared it (28:4), into the hands of Sargon in 721 B.C.

The Mission from Ethiopia.   With the usurpation of Sargon II (721–705), the Assyrian realm was shaken. The vassal states could entertain new hope and started to form alliances to shake off the Assyrian yoke. It seems quite possible that it was at this time that a diplomatic mission from Ethiopia came to Judah to seek its participation in such an alliance (18:1 ff.). But Isaiah declared that the Lord would remain detached from the events, and predicted a battle in which the allies (?) would lose heavily. Since Sargon came to Philistia in 720 and since Ethiopians are pictured on a relief from his palace as participants in the battle of Raphia, in which he drove back the Egyptians and captured the Philistine leader Hanun of Gaza, it seems to us that the prophecy can be understood from this time.

The Illness of Hezekiah.   Isaiah's importance must have risen if his counsel of standing aloof was followed. We find him going in and out at Hezekiah's palace at the time of the king's illness (38:1 ff.). First he informed the king that he would soon die, but when Hezekiah prayed to be spared the prophet was sent back to grant him a fifteen-year lease on life. A sign to reassure the ruler was allegedly given at this occasion—"the sun turned back on the dial the ten steps by which it had declined" (38:8). Thanks to the Isaiah scroll from Qumran it has now been realized that there was no real "sun dial," but that the allusion is to the steps of an outside staircase leading up to the palace roof. The "sign" is clearly legendary and a more original element (left out here but preserved in the 2 Kings text) reveals that Isaiah cured the king with a fig plaster (2 Kings 20:7). The receding of the sun was so incredible that the storyteller in 2 Chronicles did not relate it but contented himself with saying that the Lord gave Hezekiah a sign (2 Chron. 32:24). Unquestionably, however, the illness of Hezekiah and his living thereafter for another fifteen years are facts. Unfortunately, the chronology of Hezekiah's reign is uncertain at both ends. If one accepts the view that he died in 700 then the illness would have occurred in 715.

The Embassy of Merodach-baladan. Tied together with Isaiah's role in connection with the illness of Hezekiah is the report of his reaction to the visit of ambassadors from distant Babylonia (39:1–8). They were sent by Merodach-baladan (*Marduk-apal-iddina*), formerly a ruler of a principality in the marshes at the Persian Gulf, who had gained sovereignty over Babylon in 721. He was driven out by Sargon in 710, but after the latter's death in 705 and Sennacherib's accession he became king of Babylon a second time. If one accepts a date of 700 for the death of Hezekiah and 715 or 714 for his illness, then the visit of the ambassadors must have taken place during the first period of Merodach-baladan's kingship at Babylon. Courtesy embassies were well known in the ancient Orient, but the suspicion that their purpose was one of espionage was bound to arise (cf. 2 Sam. 10:1–5). In this case geographical distance made such an objective unlikely to Hezekiah, but not to the prophet Isaiah. One must, however, suppose that the embassy had another purpose than the one stated or the one suspected by Isaiah —to line up Judah (and no doubt other western states by similar embassies) for an alliance against Assyria. Hezekiah felt flattered and showed the visitors his treasures. For this he was reproved by Isaiah. The prophet allegedly predicted that the day would come when Hezekiah's treasures and those of his father would be carried off to Babylon, and that some of his descendants would become eunuchs in the palace of the king of Babylon. This is too definite and, from the vantage point of the contemporary situation, too improbable to be a genuine prediction—it is a prediction reformulated in the light of known happenings (hence in the Babylonian exile). The storyteller goes on to stress Hezekiah's indifference to the fate of his descendants. This implies a serious criticism of him. We have no doubt that the report of the incident came from the entourage of King Jehoiachin (2 Kings 24:15; 25:27 ff.). It blamed Hezekiah for having aroused the lust of the Babylonians for the treasure of the kings of Judah and therewith having brought on Nebuchadnezzar's taking of Jerusalem. It illustrated, on the level of the Judean royal house, the complaint of the exiles that the sins of the ancestors were being visited on the descendants (Ezek. 18:2 ff.).

The Sign Against Egypt and Ethiopia. A slightly later situation is reflected in chapter 20—a third-person report about what Isaiah did in 713–711 B.C. He was commanded by the Lord to take off the sackcloth (evidently his habitual attire at this time) and sandals. This meant that he was to go about naked and barefoot. His action, of course, was to be a prophetic "sign," or "omen." No reason was given; it would be disclosed later (as in 8:1–4). Such conduct raised the questions: What is the prophet driving at? When will he tell us what it means? He may have been directed to take the step about the time that the king of the Philistine city of Ashdod, with encouragement from Egypt and Ethiopia, sought to lead a conspiracy against Assyria. What Isaiah was forecasting did not come to pass as swiftly as he may have thought, for the Assyrians appointed another king at Ashdod, and a usurper had to seize power before the real rebellion broke out there in 711. Isaiah thus had to wait more than two years before being released from his miserable state of exposure to cold in the rainy season and to the sun in the hot season. When the news arrived that an Assyrian force was on the way to besiege Ashdod, the explanatory oracle came:

> "As my servant Isaiah has walked naked and barefoot for three years as a sign and a portent against Egypt and Ethiopia, so shall the king of Assyria lead away the Egyptians captives and the Ethiopians exiles, both the young and the old, naked and barefoot, with buttocks uncovered, to the shame of Egypt." (20:3–4)

Male prisoners are shown on Assyrian monuments being led away completely naked, with a yoke at the neck.

Isaiah's sign was not just touching a matter of general interest. It had been from the beginning a warning not to get involved in the war that would result from Ashdod's rebellion. We know from Assyrian sources that Hezekiah had involved himself to some extent, in spite of the prophet. Sargon lists Judah, Moab, and Edom among the allies of Ashdod. But when Isaiah gave his clear-cut oracle, at the time of the Assyrian campaign, there was still an opportunity to withdraw. To urge this was Isaiah's purpose. In predicting what "the inhabitants of this coast land" would say, Isaiah is evidently voicing what would be the feeling of Ashdod's allies after the city's fall; it is noteworthy that Sargon, too, assumes such a maritime point of view when he speaks of "Judah, Edom, and Moab who dwell by the sea."

Thrown into confusion by the speed of the Assyrian advance, the allies left Ashdod to its fate. Egypt and Ethiopia, to their shame, failed in their promised support. Not only Ashdod but its seaport as well as Gath were besieged, destroyed, and resettled with colonists from the East. The Ethiopian king even handed over to Sargon the fugitive leader of Ashdod's rebellion. It was an ignominious debacle, and we may be sure that Judah had to pay increased tribute or indemnity. Isaiah's reputation for prophetic insight and foresight must have been vastly enhanced by these events.

In the Time of Sennacherib

Renewed Preparations for Revolt. The real test for Isaiah as prophet, however, was still to come. Unquestionably life in Judah had been made more burdensome by Sargon. What had been tolerable, though costly, under Ahaz became a "yoke" under Hezekiah. Such conditions inevitably bred hope of deliverance and efforts to bring it about. Other peoples that had suffered under invasion were likewise ready to risk rebellion. In the background were greater powers lending encouragement. Merodach-baladan, who had regained the kingship of Babylon at the time of Sargon's death (705), was no doubt among them. But greater hope could be placed in Egypt, now headed by the Ethiopian Shabaka (c. 716–701). Egypt was again actively interested in what went on in Asia.

An oracle of Isaiah on "the beasts of the Negeb" reflects the passing of the desert sheiks and their south-Arabian caravan trade into Egyptian control:

> Through a land of trouble and anguish,
>   from where come the lioness and the lion,
>   the viper and the flying serpent, .

> they carry their riches on the backs of asses,
> and their treasures on the humps of camels,
> to a people that cannot profit them.
> For Egypt's help is worthless and empty,
> therefore I have called her
> "Rahab who sits still." (30:6–7)

Egypt here is compared to Rahab, a name of the mythical primeval monster and adversary of the creator-god (cf. 51:9; Ps. 87:4), classically represented by Tiamat in the Creation Epic of Babylon. The words "who sits still," if a correct rendering, characterize Egypt as a "do nothing" power.

To the years just before 701 one may also attribute some oracles reflecting Isaiah's concern with Judah's preparations for war and trust in Egyptian support. Evidently Hezekiah did not consult the prophet, who would have said things he did not want to hear. The lesson of the events of 720 and 711 was evidently forgotten by leaders and people:

> "Woe to the rebellious children," says the LORD,
> "who carry out a plan, but not mine;
> and who make a league, but not of my spirit,
> that they may add sin to sin;
> who set out to go down to Egypt,
> without asking for my counsel,
> to take refuge in the protection of Pharaoh,
> and to seek shelter in the shadow of Egypt!
> Therefore shall the protection of Pharaoh turn to your shame,
> and the shelter in the shadow of Egypt to your humiliation.
> For though his officials are at Zoan
> and his envoys reach Hanes,
> every one comes to shame
> through a people that cannot profit them,
> that brings neither help nor profit, but shame and disgrace." (30:1–5)

That the Pharaoh's officials were in Zoan (Tanis) and his envoys in Hanes (Heracleopolis parva) indicates that the Ethiopian Shabaka was now getting control of the delta region, though local rulers still existed at the two cities named.

Importation of war materials from Egypt, such as horses and chariots, soon began in earnest. Isaiah heaped bitter scorn on this rearmament, and on the Egyptians themselves, who had agreed to furnish troops and leadership for the struggle.

> Woe to those who go down to Egypt for help
>   and rely on horses,
> who trust in chariots because they are many
>   and in horsemen because they are very strong,
> but do not look to the Holy One of Israel
>   or consult the LORD!
> And yet he is wise and brings disaster,
>   he does not call back his words,
> but will arise against the house of the evildoers,
>   and against the helpers of those who work iniquity.
> The Egyptians are men, and not God;
>   and their horses are flesh, and not spirit.
> When the LORD stretches out his hand,
>   the helper will stumble, and he who is helped will fall,
> and they will all perish together. (31:1-3)

The remark that the Egyptians are men, and not God, and their horses "flesh" and not "spirit," shows how deeply the leaders of Judah were impressed with the Egyptian military potential. But however mighty the soldiers and horses may be, Isaiah insists that there is nothing supernatural in their makeup. The Lord, who is "spirit" in essence, is on the opposing side, and there can be no question that "spirit" will prevail in a conflict with "flesh." The Lord need only extend his hand to strike, and the allies will all perish together.

In a remarkable oracle that seems to have lost its introduction (30:8-14), Isaiah is told to write something down before the people on a tablet or in a "book." The latter word should not be taken literally, for it can apply to an inscription (as is documented by a Phoenician one from a north Syrian city). What was to be inscribed on the tablet was necessarily short (cf. 8:1), but there is no direct indication of what it was. Some would find the inscription in the last words of the preceding oracle ("Rahab who sits still"), but that ironic remark would not seem important enough to warrant the solemnity of the saying. What is at issue in this oracle is trust in the Lord. The saying to be engraved on the tablet must have been of such a nature. Perhaps it is the one about "returning and rest" at the beginning of the next piece (30:15-17). The latter then would be the direct continuation of verses 8-14:

> And now, go, write it before them on a tablet,
>   and inscribe it in a book,
> that it may be for the time to come

as a witness for ever.
For they are a rebellious people,
   lying sons,
sons who will not hear
   the instruction of the LORD;
who say to the seers, "See not";
   and to the prophets, "Prophesy not to us what is right;
speak to us smooth things,
   prophesy illusions,
leave the way, turn aside from the path,
   let us hear no more of the Holy One of Israel."
Therefore thus says the Holy One of Israel,
"Because you despise this word,
   and trust in oppression and perverseness,
   and rely on them;
therefore this iniquity shall be to you
   like a break in a high wall, bulging out, and about to collapse,
   whose crash comes suddenly, in an instant;
and its breaking is like that of a potter's vessel
   which is smashed so ruthlessly
that among its fragments not a sherd is found
   with which to take fire from the hearth,
   or to dip up water out of the cistern."

But it was all in vain. They despised "this word" of what was right and trusted in their own ways of oppression and perverseness.

Full of the consciousness of the impending crisis, Isaiah pointed to the only right course for his people and then painted the picture of what he foresaw as the result of the new militarism:

For thus said the Lord GOD, the Holy One of Israel,
   "In returning and rest you shall be saved;
   in quietness and in trust shall be your strength."
And you would not, but you said,
"No! We will speed upon horses,"
   therefore you shall speed away;
and "We will ride upon swift steeds,"
   therefore your pursuers shall be swift.
A thousand shall flee at the threat of one,
   at the threat of five you shall flee,
till you are left
   like a flagstaff on the top of a mountain,
   like a signal on a hill. (30:15–17)

The restatement of the Lord's words concerning the proper course is

followed by the prophet's mournful "And you would not." Again one
must recall Jesus and his lament over Jerusalem, "How often would
I have gathered your children together...and you would not" (Matt.
23:37). The prophecy of flight and of being left like a flagstaff was to
be wholly vindicated, as we shall see.

Rising Peril. Ominous news came from northern theaters of war. The
Assyrian king Sennacherib took Babylon in 703 and therewith Merodach-
baladan's second reign at that city was ended. Thus one of the most
powerful of the allies was eliminated. In 702 Sennacherib campaigned
in the far north, and there too subdued rebels. By now qualms of
anxiety must have come to the leaders in Jerusalem. Isaiah's warnings,
however, were scoffed at. Like Hosea (13:14) he may have prophesied
that "death and Sheol" would overwhelm them. In reply, his adversaries
boasted that they had made "a covenant with death and Sheol" and
so had nothing to fear. By their own reckoning they would be safe in
their mountain stronghold. The floodwaters of an Assyrian campaign
(cf. 8:7-8) would sweep through the coastal plain only, as in the days
of Tiglathpileser and Sargon. They bragged, too, of their clever diplomatic deals, which Isaiah aptly calls "lies" and "falsehoods." After
setting up a glimpse of the future intended by the Lord (in vv. 16–17a,
of which we will speak later) Isaiah strikes back at the scoffers. The
reckoning of the Lord must come first:

> "Hail will sweep away the refuge of lies,
>   and waters will overwhelm the shelter."
> Then your covenant with death will be annulled,
>   and your agreement with Sheol will not stand;
> when the overwhelming scourge passes through
>   you will be beaten down by it.
> As often as it passes through it will take you;
>   for morning by morning it will pass through,
>   by day and by night;
> and it will be sheer terror to understand the message.
> For the bed is too short to stretch oneself on it,
>   and the covering too narrow to wrap oneself in it.
> For the LORD will rise up as on Mount Perazim,
>   he will be wroth as in the valley of Gibeon;
> to do his deed—strange is his deed!
>   and to work his work—alien is his work!
> Now therefore do not scoff,

lest your bonds be made strong;
for I have heard a decree of destruction
from the Lord GOD of hosts upon the whole land. (28:17b–22)

The fury of the Lord will be turned against Judah, as it once was turned against his people's foes at Mount Perazim (2 Sam. 5:17 ff.) and at Gibeon (Josh. 10:10 ff.). The prophet warns against their increasing the amount of sin already stacked up by continuing their scoffing. His dictum is: Destruction upon the whole land is decreed. This is in line with the prediction of the Lord in giving him his commission (6:12).

In another situation, apparently at a banquet at which even priests and prophets were drunk, some taunted Isaiah, saying:

"Whom will he teach knowledge,
  and to whom will he explain the message?
Those who are weaned from the milk,
  those taken from the breast?" (28:9)

His utterances were mocked with words that perhaps were intended to be gibberish (28:10), or magical language. To this he replied:

Nay, but by men of strange lips
  and with an alien tongue
the LORD will speak to this people
  to whom he has said,
"This is rest;
  give rest to the weary;
and this is repose";
  yet they would not hear. (28:11–12)

Therefore, he concludes, the word of the Lord will be meaningless to them:

that they may go, and fall backward,
  and be broken, and snared, and taken. (28:13b)

In another oracle (29:1–8) the prophet, in bitter grief, addresses Jerusalem, giving it the surname "Ariel." He fondly thinks of Jerusalem as "the city where David encamped." He thus idealizes the beginning of its history (cf. 1:21–26). But he predicts that the Lord will encamp round about the city (with hostile intent) and it shall become like an *ariel* ("an altar-hearth," cf. Ezek. 43:15). A gruesome picture of voices coming out of the city's rubble seems to conclude this passage.

Sennacherib's Campaign of 701 B.C. In spite of Isaiah's grim warnings, Hezekiah and his ministers involved themselves deeply in the intrigues against Assyrian rule. A whole league of nations from Phoenicia to Edom came into being. Egypt and Ethiopia lent promises of support. From the Assyrian sources we learn that King Padi of the Philistine city of Ekron, who was opposed to the rebellion, was handed over by the citizenry into the custody of Hezekiah. How jubilant the people of Jerusalem must have been, when a captive king was brought in! If Isaiah uttered any oracle at this time it has not been preserved.

Sennacherib came down "like a wolf on the fold." He first subjected the Phoenician rebels led by Sidon. The kings of Ashdod, of Moab, and of Edom prudently submitted when the Phoenician cities surrendered. Judah, therefore, was left—along with the Philistine kingdoms of Ashkelon and Ekron and the Egyptians—to face the oncoming storm. Arriving at the coastal plain, Sennacherib subdued Ashkelon and cities under its sway. On moving south and approaching Ekron, the real center of the rebellion, he found a powerful Egyptian army barring his way. The "kings" of Egypt (i.e., rulers of the delta cities with their troop contingents) and the archers, chariots, and horses of their overlord, the king of Ethiopia, formed in battle array near Eltekeh (a town mentioned as once Danite in Josh. 19:44). Sennacherib defeated them, and then besieged and took Eltekeh and Timnah. The way to Ekron now lay open. The city evidently surrendered, but Sennacherib held a fearful judgment over the guilty. He reappointed Padi (held captive in Jerusalem) as king over Ekron.

Judah now stood alone. If Sennacherib's inscription relates the events chronologically he first proceeded to subject the outlying forty-six walled cities of Hezekiah's kingdom. This process must have taken much time. It seems quite likely, however, that right after the battle of Eltekeh he sent a force to invest Jerusalem. Hezekiah, who had withdrawn all his best soldiers from the border fortresses for the defense of his capital, was now locked in "like a bird in a cage."

When the grim process of the reduction of all outlying Judean cities had been completed and only Lachish and Libnah remained, the separate task forces of Sennacherib could concentrate in the direction of Jerusalem. Terror seized Hezekiah and his soldiery. Many of them fled, presumably in the same direction as their successors were to do in 587 (cf. 2 Kings 25:4). Now was fulfilled what Isaiah had foretold of the flight of the military (30:15–17; see page 106). Surrender was the only possible course. Hezekiah's surrender made it unnecessary for Sennacherib to prosecute the siege of Jerusalem to the end. In regulating affairs he not only increased the annual tribute but gave all of Judah, except an enclave around Jerusalem, to Ashdod, Ekron, and Gaza. The Assyrian relates that Hezekiah sent after him to Nineveh "thirty talents of gold, 800 talents of silver, precious stones" (here follow other valuable objects), "as well as his daughters, palace women, and male and female musicians. To present his tribute and to pay homage he sent his ambassador."

Hebrew Versions of What Happened. A brief Hebrew historical account of what had taken place is given in 2 Kings 18:13–16. It confirms the essentials of Sennacherib's account. It not only admits that Sennacherib took all the fortified cities of Judah, but that Hezekiah surrendered abjectly and agreed to bear whatever was demanded, if only the Assyrian would withdraw from him (i.e., without prosecuting the siege of Jerusalem). For the indemnity imposed, the 2 Kings account gives exactly the same number of talents of gold as the Assyrian report, but a lesser quantity of talents of silver (300 instead of 800). The individual who wrote the Hebrew account was evidently a scribe in the temple. He was especially pained by the stripping of the gold covering from the temple gates. He does not mention other humiliating conditions that Hezekiah was forced to accept, such as the yielding up of his daughters, palace women (i.e., his harem), and musicians, and so perhaps no longer knew about them. But he gives the information that the surrender offer was sent to the Assyrian king when he was besieging Lachish. Sennacherib had this siege portrayed on reliefs in his palace at Nineveh; perhaps because it marked his final triumph in this war.

Nations do not like to recall their humiliations. Later history may not even record them, as is the case with the Assyrian rule over Egypt, which Egypt's own historians buried in silence. Or, later history may twist matters, so that a great defeat is turned into a victory. It would be strange if Hebrew historical writings did not provide examples of such procedures too. A case of the second type, we hold, is found in a further story about Sennacherib's campaign in 2 Kings 18:17–19:37. It is given again in Isaiah 36:2 ff., where it is not preceded by the whole short account of 2 Kings 18:13–16, but only by the first verse of it (2 Kings 18:13; Isaiah 36:1), which is needed as introduction. Elimination of the other verses was very much in the interest of the credibility of this second account, in which the author of the new and dramatic story dwells especially on the surrender demand that Sennacherib sent to Jerusalem from Lachish. It attributes to Isaiah the patriotic role of urging rejection of the demand. But actually Hezekiah submitted, as the short report of 2 Kings 18:13–16, in agreement with Sennacherib's annals, states.

There has naturally been a great reluctance to concede that the second story is in error. It is argued on the basis of the connection in 2 Kings that the Assyrian king, after receiving Hezekiah's tribute, treacherously went back on his word and demanded the surrender of Jerusalem. But that runs contrary to the fact reported by Sennacherib that the tribute was sent to Nineveh later in the charge of Hezekiah's ambassador. Hezekiah had only accepted the terms at Lachish.

Evidently the author of the surrender-refusal story did not know the "short report." He gathered his lore from popular tradition, and notably from quarters exalting the person of Isaiah. Fading of historical memory, rather than willful deception, can account for his picture of the events. He must have written many years after the time of the happenings. He thinks of Sennacherib as being led back home to his death (which is thought of as taking place shortly after this campaign), whereas in reality that sovereign's reign lasted for another twenty years; and he holds Tirhakah to have been ruler of Ethiopia in 701, whereas he did not attain that status until thirteen years later. If the mention of Tirhakah is taken by some scholars to prove that there was a later campaign of Sennacherib which ended in the manner described, this is unconvincing.

In accounting for the origin of the surrender-refusal tale one must think too of changing political realities. Assyrian power had declined late in the reign of Ashurbanipal (c. 630). Assyria's hold on the Syro-Palestinian provinces had weakened. A new nationalism has asserted

itself among the conquered peoples, including Jews. It was a fact that
Jerusalem had not been taken and destroyed. It was also a fact that a
prophet named Isaiah had been the leading prophet of that time. People
began to believe that Sennacherib had been prevented by the Lord
from taking Jerusalem, and that it was Isaiah who had advised him to
refuse the surrender demand. "Anti-Assyrian" or nationalistic oracles
were now attributed to Isaiah. The story includes a sample (37:23–29)
and others are found in 8:9–10; 10:5–19, 24–26; 14:24–27. Some genuine
oracles of Isaiah, too, may have been revised in the process (29:5–8;
17:12–14; 18:1–7). A picture of Sennacherib as boasting and vaunting
himself against the God of Israel was created, thus providing a strong
reason for an intervention by the Lord. If the author had the Lord
predict that he would cause Sennacherib to retreat on hearing a rumor,
a later editor found this too tame, and satisfied his desire for the
miraculous by having the angel of the Lord slay 185,000 besiegers
in one night (37:36; cf. Exod. 12:29). Thus in the final form of the
story the Assyrian took an immense beating. No urge in moral man
is deeper than the desire of seeing an evildoer get his due. Having
painted Sennacherib black and Hezekiah white, the storyteller had
produced a tale that was eminently satisfactory to Jewish readers.

We see no possibility of a nationalistic interlude in the ministry of
Isaiah and do not think that he believed in the inviolability of Zion
any more than did his contemporary Micah. The presuppositions for
depending on the Lord's help that Isaiah actually had set up (as in
30:15; 7:4, 9b; 28:16) were violated by Hezekiah's political schem-
ing, of which Sennacherib's account gives clear indication. Furthermore, breach of allegiance to the sovereign power, which had required
loyalty sworn to with solemn oaths in the name of one's own God,
cannot have been taken lightly by Isaiah. When we see how Jeremiah
remained true to his position in the face of the Chaldean investment
of Jerusalem, and how Ezekiel regarded Jerusalem's rebellion against
Nebuchadnezzar (Ezek. 17:15), one must become skeptical of any
aberration of Isaiah from the path that he had trod so long. Since,
furthermore, Isaiah's attitude after the departure of Sennacherib was
the same as it was before his coming, a nationalistic interlude becomes
difficult to comprehend psychologically. That is not to say, however,
that Isaiah may not have foreseen that Jerusalem would be spared

temporarily; but he certainly would have attributed this to the mercy
of God, not to a victory over the enemy of God.

In the Wake of the Disaster. After Sennacherib's acceptance of the
surrender of Hezekiah, the siege of Jerusalem by the forces engaged in
the holding operation was lifted. The city populace, recently so penitent,
exulted over the relief from its imprisonment and short rations. Isaiah
could not understand this jubilation, which showed how unregenerate
the hearts were, and in the "Oracle concerning the valley of vision,"
expressed his grief.

> What do you mean that you have gone up,
>   all of you, to the housetops,
> you who are full of shoutings,
>   tumultuous city, exultant town?
> Your slain are not slain with the sword
>   or dead in battle.
> All your rulers have fled together,
>   without the bow they were captured.
> All of you who were found were captured,
>   though they had fled far away.
> Therefore I said:
> "Look away from me,
>   let me weep bitter tears;
> do not labor to comfort me
>   for the destruction of the daughter of my people." (22:1–4)

He thus alludes to the flight and capture of the leaders (without mention of the troops, to whom Sennacherib refers), to demonstrations
made by the besiegers who consisted of auxiliaries from Elam and
Kir and to his call to repentance and mourning.

> In that day the Lord GOD of hosts
>   called to weeping and mourning,
>   to baldness and girding with sackcloth;
> and behold, joy and gladness,
>   slaying oxen and killing sheep,
>   eating flesh and drinking wine.
> "Let us eat and drink,
>   for tomorrow we die."
> The LORD of hosts has revealed himself in my ears:
> "Surely this iniquity will not be forgiven you

> till you die,"
> says the Lord GOD of hosts. (22:12–14)

The sin of callous indifference to the fate of all the cities of Judah,
this gluttony which thinks only of the belly and sees nothing in life but
the pleasures of the senses, as expressed in the worldly dictum "Let
us eat and drink, for tomorrow we die" (22:13), is to Isaiah a sin
that they will have to atone for by death.

Life in Jerusalem must have settled down to a very dreary existence.
Starvation must have reigned, since there was no harvest until the
third year (37:30). With a large part of Judah in the hands of the
Philistines, with Moabites and Edomites, who had gotten away unscathed, posing a constant threat that was curbed only by Assyrian
recognition and support of Hezekiah's small city-state, life was one
of increasing insecurity and poverty. Yet the punishments inflicted had
not sobered or bettered the people. The same evils that had gone on
before went on now. It seemed as though a base and wicked population
was bent on inviting more retribution on its own head. And so Isaiah
uttered the great oracle which reveals the magnitude of what had
happened and gives the true picture of Sennacherib's dreadful work.

> Ah, sinful nation,
>   a people laden with iniquity,
> offspring of evildoers,
>   sons who deal corruptly!
> They have foresaken the LORD,
>   they have despised the Holy One of Israel,
>   they are utterly estranged.
> Why will you still be smitten,
>   that you continue to rebel?
> The whole head is sick,
>   and the whole heart faint.
> From the sole of the foot even to the head,
>   there is no soundness in it,
> but bruises and sores
>   and bleeding wounds;
> they are not pressed out, or bound up,
>   or softened with oil.
> Your country lies desolate,
>   your cities are burned with fire;
> in your very presence
>   aliens devour your land;

> it is desolate, as overthrown by aliens.
> And the daughter of Zion is left
>   like a booth in a vineyard,
>   like a lodge in a cucumber field,
>   like a besieged city. (1:4–9)

Jerusalem—a mere booth in a vineyard, a lodge in a cucumber field—
apt illustrations, in view of the reduction of territory that Sennacherib
relates and about which the Book of Kings preserves silence. With the
different imagery of "flagstaff" and "signal," Isaiah had predicted
this outcome (30:17).

Isaiah's Hope

Did Isaiah entertain a hope for his city and people? There would
certainly be little advantage in a hope to those to whom he prophesied
that the sin of their materialistic philosophy would not be forgiven them.
But he had carried with him from the outset the hope that a remnant,
at least, would turn about and take the right road to moral and religious
conduct and would enjoy the Lord's favor. In his invective against
the scoffers he had proclaimed that the Lord would lay a cornerstone
for the foundation of a new and better Zion (evidently implying that
the old one would be destroyed):

> therefore thus says the Lord GOD,
> "Behold, I am laying in Zion for a foundation
>   a stone, a tested stone,
> a precious cornerstone, of a sure foundation:
>   'He who believes will not be in haste.'
> And I will make justice the line,
>   and righteousness the plummet;
> and hail will sweep away the refuge of lies,
>   and waters will overwhelm the shelter." (28:16–17)

The foundation thus would consist of implicit trust in the Lord alone,
and justice and righteousness would serve as line and plummet in
the erection of the well-built structure of the new city and state. The
current immoral order of statecraft would be done away with.

We may think of the aged Isaiah as dreaming more and more of
the future change. In the great lament over the once faithful city

he closes with a ray of hope. After the Lord had smelted the dross
out of it he foresees:

> And I will restore your judges as at the first,
>   and your counselors as at the beginning.
> Afterward you shall be called the city of righteousness,
>   the faithful city." (1:26)

He does not mention the kingship here. Hezekiah's policy had brought
his people into the dust. Yet, as is apparent from Isaiah's idealizing
allusions to Jerusalem's beginnings and his fond mention of David,
the prophet was not one who would abolish the house of David. Just
as he entertained the hope of new leaders and counselors comparable
to those at the beginning, so he may also have entertained the hope
of a new and superior ruler for David's house.

A prophecy of this nature, which could fit the mood of a man who
believed in the ultimate revival of the kingship and of the kingdom,
is that of chapter 9. In it the author hails the birth of a babe of
destiny of Davidic descent that when grown to manhood would
break the foreign yoke as in Gideon's time (Judg. 7:22 ff.) and
establish peace. Just as the Egyptian pharaohs had names describing
their supposedly divine qualities or their superior attributes, so this
babe of the future, after his achievements in young manhood, will have
royal titles:

> The people who walked in darkness
>   have seen a great light;
> those who dwelt in a land of deep darkness,
>   on them has light shined.
> Thou hast multiplied the nation,
>   thou hast increased its joy;
> they rejoice before thee
>   as with joy at the harvest,
>   as men rejoice when they divide the spoil.
> For the yoke of his burden,
>   and the staff for his shoulder,
>   the rod of his oppressor,
>   thou hast broken as on the day of Midian.
> For every boot of the tramping warrior in battle tumult
>   and every garment rolled in blood
>   will be burned as fuel for the fire.
> For to us a child is born,

> to us a son is given;
> and the government will be upon his shoulder,
>   and his name will be called
> "Wonderful Counselor, Mighty God,
>   Everlasting Father, Prince of Peace."
> Of the increase of his government and of peace
>   there will be no end,
> upon the throne of David, and over his kingdom,
>   to establish it, and to uphold it
> with justice and with righteousness
>   from this time forth and for evermore.
> The zeal of the Lord of hosts will do this. (9:2–7)

Some of Isaiah's characteristic ideas appear here. The kingdom of the future will be upheld in justice and righteousness. The faith element is present in the speaker's own certainty that this would be brought about by the zeal of the Lord of hosts (cf. 37:32). The mystical view of the ideal kingship of the future is one element that surprises—such a title as wonderful counselor is closely parallel to what Isaiah says of God (28:29). The oracle remains dynastic, national, and regional. It is still quite far removed from any such transcendent thought of the Messiah as was entertained at the threshold of the New Testament.

Two other great passages concerned with the future are found in the first part of the book of Isaiah—the messianic prophecy about the shoot from the stump of Jesse (11:1–9) and the prophecy of universal peace (2:2–4). Their authenticity is uncertain, but it matters little whether they are by Isaiah or by some unknown prophet. They have their weight and worth in themselves. The first is monarchically oriented; the second is wholly theocratic:

> There shall come forth a shoot from the stump of Jesse,
>   and a branch shall grow out of his roots.
> And the Spirit of the Lord shall rest upon him,
>   the spirit of wisdom and understanding,
>   the spirit of counsel and might,
>   the spirit of knowledge and the fear of the Lord.
> And his delight shall be in the fear of the Lord.
>
> He shall not judge by what his eyes see,
>   or decide by what his ears hear;
> but with righteousness he shall judge the poor,
>   and decide with equity for the meek of the earth;

and he shall smite the earth with the rod of his mouth,
and with the breath of his lips he shall slay the wicked.
Righteousness shall be the girdle of his waist,
and faithfulness the girdle of his loins.

The wolf shall dwell with the lamb,
and the leopard shall lie down with the kid,
and the calf and the lion and the fatling together,
and a little child shall lead them.
The cow and the bear shall feed;
their young shall lie down together;
and the lion shall eat straw like the ox.
The sucking child shall play over the hole of the asp,
and the weaned child shall put his hand on the adder's den.
They shall not hurt or destroy
in all my holy mountain;
for the earth shall be full of the knowledge of the Lord
as the waters cover the sea. (11:1-9)

The prophecy seemingly presupposes that the Davidic dynasty has fallen. It allows for the possibility that from the roots of the stump of Jesse a branch shall grow out. That of course is figurative for the king of the future. Taken literally, the words indicate that the author expects the Messiah to come from the family of Jesse, the father of David, and perhaps from descendants of David's brothers. He stresses the coming ruler's possession of the Spirit of the Lord, his piety and morality, his concern for the poor, his ability to deal in terrifying sternness with the wicked. Into the picture of his reign the author draws that of the restored golden age, when even the savage beasts are harmless. Particularly safe will be all the Lord's holy mountain. Knowledge of God will overspread the earth. It is a fine prophecy, but somewhat limited in usefulness by its royalistic presuppositions.

The allusion to the holy mountain, on which the peace of God prevails, shows kinship in thought with the other great passage (2:2-4). The latter seems to be expressly attributed to Isaiah in the title: "The words which Isaiah the son of Amoz saw concerning Judah and Jerusalem." However, this title was not formulated to apply to this piece alone, but rather to a whole collection of Isaiah's oracles. One must assume that there was a gap in the manuscript, and that this prophecy was written into it. As was already noted, it appears also in Micah 4:1-4, where it is likewise not original, but where the concluding verse is preserved:

> It shall come to pass in the latter days
>> that the mountain of the house of the LORD
> shall be established as the highest of the mountains,
>> and shall be raised above the hills;
> and all the nations shall flow to it,
>> and many peoples shall come, and say:
> "Come, let us go up to the mountain of the LORD,
>> to the house of the God of Jacob;
> that he may teach us his ways
>> and that we may walk in his paths."
> For out of Zion shall go forth the law,
>> and the word of the LORD from Jerusalem.
> He shall judge between the nations,
>> and shall decide for many peoples;
> and they shall beat their swords into plowshares,
>> and their spears into pruning hooks;
> nation shall not lift up sword against nation,
>> neither shall they learn war any more; (2:2–4)
> but they shall sit every man under his vine and
>> under his fig tree,
> and none shall make them afraid;
> for the mouth of the LORD of hosts has spoken.
>> (Micah 4:4)

In both Isaiah and Micah a liturgical comment is appended after the passage, but different in each case. The editors thus drew on different sources for the prophecy.

The author of this prophecy predicted the elevation of the temple mount, so that it would be visible from all quarters, and, like a beacon, draw all peoples to itself. He is thus dependent on Ezekiel's vision of the new lofty Jerusalem (40:2) and on Deutero-Isaiah's and Trito-Isaiah's conceptions of the attraction of gentiles to the holy city. But noteworthy is the absence of the idea of a return or bringing back of exiles. From this we may infer that Jerusalem was again well populated in the author's time. Impressed with the indoctrination he has received, the author of this piece feels that the Mosaic law has something to offer the world. He sees the possibility of world peace and disarmament under the arbitrament of the Lord. What he has heard about the influence of western temple-states and oracle-centers in achieving settlements of disputes probably sparked this great idea. The peoples, by their own decision, will come to the Jerusalem temple to learn the ways of the Lord.

Such thoughts could well have arisen in the period after the death

of Alexander the Great in 323. The constant warfare among his successors must have created a war-weariness among the peoples and the
desire for a just settlement of disputes. While these wars were fought
mainly by mercenaries, they brought much hardship to the populations
of the districts where they happened to be fought. Crops were ruined,
animals were requisitioned, and people were abused or intimidated
by the military. Small wonder, then, that this author's ideal was that
everyone should be able to sit unafraid under his vine or fig tree.
Through the Christian scriptures the passage has had a potent influence on the minds of men, but the organizations that have sprung
up for peacekeeping purposes are not yet imbued with the law of the
God of Jacob.

Isaiah in Retrospect

Isaiah stands before the mind of the ages as the prophet of faith.
Faith was not a common concept in religion before him. He helped
give it currency, and moreover he carried faith out of the purely
personal sphere into the larger one of public life. Trust in the Lord was
his counsel; do not trust in arms or in alliances. Through a tradition begun by him we have "In God we trust" on our nation's coinage and
in our national anthem the climactic words "And this be our motto: 'In
God is our trust.'" But one cannot trust in God and expect his help
when one is under his displeasure. The narrative in 36–37 about Isaiah's
role in 701 overlooks this. It obscures the fact that Sennacherib's campaign was a terrible judgment of the Lord over Judah. The real Isaiah
in numerous oracles had forecast just such a judgment.

Isaiah was by nature an extrovert and man of action. He spoke fear-
lessly what the Lord instructed him to say. Naturally he provoked opposition. His sayings show him to have been mocked and reviled. The
policies he recommended were not followed; his advice was not sought
when the policies leading to disaster were formulated. He had the feeling that the purpose of his ministry was to increase opposition to God's
will and ways and thus hasten the inevitable judgment. He saw more
clearly than any other prophet that the Lord was a "holy" and hence
unapproachable God, and that one could stand in his presence only
after one's sins had been forgiven. Like his predecessor Amos he placed

no value at all on cult or ceremonies, when carried on by those who disregard God's law in everyday life.

Judgment of God was Isaiah's first word, but not his last. He believed that after still another judgment, more definitive than under Hezekiah, there would be a renewed beginning for his people. It was impossible for him to give them up entirely. A remnant would turn to God and become the founding fathers of a new and better nation. He must have thought of a divinely caused regeneration, for his experience with men's perversity must have left him without illusions as to human nature. He foresaw the building of a new city of God or temple of God, in place of a destroyed one, with faith as the firm foundation of religion. It would be a city with righteous leadership, as of old, and perhaps even with a descendant of David as its first king.

It was of world historical importance that Isaiah set such a goal before the minds of men. The goal was limited by the fact that he could as yet think only in terms of a national religion. He could not yet think in terms of a God who was the father of all men. The glorified future which he awaited was a restoration of an idealized past age, or purified counterpart of the present world. But the edifice of the future which he foresaw was capable of becoming more than a renewed Davidic Jerusalem. And the remnant that would form the constituency of this transcendent Zion was already taking shape as a kind of church of believers within a still unbelieving nation. Those in whose hearts Isaiah's words lived on, his disciples or followers, comprised that church which was to be the hope of mankind, but which would attain to worldwide influence and importance only through Jesus of Nazareth and his greatest interpreter, Paul.

5 THE REVIVAL OF PROPHECY: ZEPHANIAH AND THE YOUNG JEREMIAH

Historical Transition

FOR HALF A CENTURY or more after the passing of Isaiah the voice of prophecy was hushed. King Hezekiah was succeeded by his son Manasseh, who had a very long reign (c. 696–642 B.C.). He proved himself a loyal supporter of his Assyrian masters. He seems to have been rewarded by getting back most of the territory that Sennacherib had cut off from Judah. He was even allowed to have a small army, for we learn from the Assyrian inscriptions that Manasseh with his troops participated in Ashurbanipal's expedition to Egypt in 663. But under Manasseh evil times befell the religion of the Lord. He carried on a reign of terror against all opposition. "Moreover Manasseh shed very much innocent blood, till he had filled Jerusalem from one end to another," says a historian (2 Kings 21:16). Prophets who dared criticize his heathenish actions must have been among his main victims (Jer. 2:30). If the idea of a Jerusalem "killing the prophets" became established in the minds of later generations (Matt. 23:37; Luke 13:34) this was due to him more than to any other ruler.

Manasseh's policies were continued by his son Amon during his brief reign. Amon's successor, Josiah (639–609), was only eight years old at his accession. During his early years there must have been a regency until he was old enough to assert his own will. Naturally then, the policy that had been shaped by Manasseh and continued by Amon prevailed for many years. But it may well be that eventually persecution of prophets fighting for the worship of the Lord was relaxed.

The Prophet Zephaniah

An indication of this relaxation is to be seen in the fact that Jerusalem soon had a prophet who spoke out critically and apparently with impunity. This was Zephaniah, whose appearance may have taken place about 630 or a few years later. He attacked the corruption of religion that had developed under Manasseh, and thus prepared the way for Jeremiah's more powerful assault. He therefore deserves our interest as the latter's forerunner.

Zephaniah has the longest pedigree of any of the prophets; it is carried back to the fourth ancestor, who was a Hezekiah. It seems very likely that this means King Hezekiah, for such a genealogy would not have been traced except for the purpose of getting back to a big name. The time differences would fit, too, and no other Hezekiah is reported for the preexilic period. Given the polygamy of the kings of Judah, the city on Zion hill, below the royal palace, must have been full of royal descendants.

Zephaniah's prophecy has not come down without some revision and additions. It has been made more satisfying to Jewish readers of a later period by being broadened with predictions of a world judgment (1:2–3, 18b). The real Zephaniah was interested only in what was going to be done to Judah and Jerusalem in the course of imminent military events:

> "I will stretch out my hand against Judah,
>   and against all the inhabitants of Jerusalem;
> and I will cut off from this place the remnant of Baal
>   and the name of the idolatrous priests;
> those who bow down on the roofs
>   to the host of the heavens;
> those who bow down and swear to the LORD
>   and yet swear by Milcom;
> those who have turned back from following the LORD,
>   who do not seek the LORD or inquire of him." (1:4–6)

Zephaniah has harsh words for the leadership:

> "I will punish the officials and the king's sons
>   and all who array themselves in foreign attire.
> On that day I will punish
>   every one who leaps over the threshold,

> and those who fill their master's house
> with violence and fraud." (1:8b–9)

Assyrian style of dress must have been imitated by the aristocracy in this period. The Philistine superstitious custom of leaping over the threshold (1 Sam. 5:5) was evidently in vogue with the court servants, who were filling the royal coffers with gold gotten by violence and treacherous means.

But the prophet is not just concerned with the acropolis city. There had evidently been an expansion of Jerusalem to the northern part of the western ridge, and here, too, he held, the judgment would strike (1:10–13). He hears wails going up from the Fish Gate in the north (Neh. 3:3); from the Second Quarter in the west (2 Kings 22:14); and from the "mortar"—perhaps the head of the valley between the two ridges where the Phoenician traders (literally, "Canaanites") and the money changers had their shops. Scattered through the city, however, is a class of skeptics who, figuratively speaking, are "thickening upon their lees" (like wine left to thicken after the fermentation process is completed) and hence of sluggish nature; they asserted that "The LORD will not do good, nor will he do ill." The Lord will search Jerusalem with lamps, says the prophet, to ferret them out and punish them

The climax of Zephaniah's prophesying is his classic prediction of the coming "day of the LORD" (1:14 ff.). Thus the ideas of Amos and Isaiah, who had spoken of such a day, were still being perpetuated:

> The great day of the LORD is near,
>   near and hastening fast;
> the sound of the day of the LORD is bitter,
>   the mighty man cries aloud there.
> A day of wrath is that day,
>   a day of distress and anguish,
> a day of ruin and devastation,
>   a day of darkness and gloom,
> a day of clouds and thick darkness,
>   a day of trumpet blast and battle cry
> against the fortified cities
>   and against the lofty battlements.
> I will bring distress on men,
>   so that they shall walk like the blind,
>   because they have sinned against the Lord;

> their blood shall be poured out like dust,
> and their flesh like dung. (1:14–17)

He urges holding an assembly of repentance in the face of this coming outpouring of God's wrath, and he has a particular hope for a humble, godfearing minority:

> Seek the LORD, all you humble of the land,
> who do his commands;
> seek righteousness, seek humility;
> perhaps you may be hidden
> on the day of the wrath of the LORD. (2:3)

Like Amos, Zephaniah sees the Lord's judgment as also striking some other peoples—the Philistine cities, the "Cherethites" (people of Cretan origin) of the southern seacoast and the Ethiopians (2:4–7, 12). He apparently anticipated Nahum in predicting the fall of Nineveh (2:13–15). Less certain is the authenticity of the oracle against Moab and Ammon (2:8–11). When Zephaniah passed from the scene the time was ripe for the Lord to send his greater servant, Jeremiah.

The Young Jeremiah

Jeremiah may have been born about 645. He saw the light of day in a small town called Anathoth. The name lingers to this day at 'Anāta, a village three miles north of Jerusalem. But the town of Anathoth, as archaeological exploration has shown, lay on a height half a mile to the southwest of the modern village.

Jeremiah's Background. Jeremiah is described in the editorial title of his book as "the son of Hilkiah, of the priests who were in Anathoth in the land of Benjamin." It was to his estate at Anathoth that King David's chief priest Abiathar had retired when ousted from office by Solomon (1 Kings 2:26). It seems likely that the town was still mainly inhabited by his descendants and supporters. But that Hilkiah was of the "priests" need not be taken to mean active priests. Certainly Jeremiah shows little concern with priestly viewpoints. It is unlikely that the Zadokite priesthood showed any favor to the deposed line. If Hilkiah acted as priest it would have been at the small sanctuary of Anathoth itself. The emphasis on "the land of Benjamin" suggests that a distinctive Benjaminite—and that is to say north-Israelite—emphasis was maintained at Anathoth. It must be recalled that the father of Abiathar had been the priest of Nob—a nearby small town which was destroyed by Saul because the priests had aided David (1 Sam. 22:19). Abiathar's ancestral connections, furthermore, had been with the priesthood of Shiloh, in the hill country of Ephraim. Jeremiah's allusions to Shiloh (cf. 7:12–14) suggest knowledge of the fact.

From the height of ancient Anathoth the boy Jeremiah had a wide view. To the east he could overlook the upper end of the Dead Sea, the Jordan valley, and the mountains of Gilead. Since an old road coming from Jericho and heading for the coastal plain passed north of Jerusalem, he may have seen many a caravan coming from the East and carrying among the export products the famous "balm of Gilead." That was a resin much in demand in Egypt for embalming, but also for beauty care and medicinal use.

In antiquity a youth from such a town and of such a family had little chance to become prominent. The desire to become a prophet and thus to attempt to play the only public role open to him may well have stirred within him. External pressures of relatives, however, must have been steering him toward conformity. He should labor in garden, orchard, or vineyard. We may imagine him as standing at the parting of the ways in brooding and dejection.

Jeremiah's Call. Then (about 626) something happened. He heard a voice speaking to him, and knew it to be that of the Lord. His inner ear heard it, but there was no accompanying vision of God such as had been accorded Isaiah. He thus did not have the full endowment of his predecessor—any more than Elisha had the full measure of Elijah's spirit (2 Kings 2:9). Nor did Jeremiah have Isaiah's appreciation of his own sinfulness and unworthiness, and of God's awesome holiness. He relates in a matter-of-fact manner how the Lord spoke to him without his being shriven. But the God in whom he believes is one who determines men's destinies even before they are born, and so his idea of him is intellectualized:

> "Before I formed you in the womb I knew you,
> and before you were born I consecrated you;
> I appointed you a prophet to the nations." (1:5)

The experience was not recorded until thirty-five years later (36:32) and so it may be that consciousness of all the messages he had received in the interim about foreign peoples made him view his office in a broader light than in the actual hour of his calling. It seems likely that he at first was told only that he was to be a prophet to "my people." In retrospect he knew that he was more—that he had a ministry to the whole world.

Characteristically the young man quailed at the assignment of being prophet to his nation, for he was sensitive by nature. Like Moses (Exod. 4:10 ff.) he made an excuse. "Ah, Lord GOD! Behold, I do not know how to speak, for I am only a youth." He was aware that only after a man had earned the respect of his neighbors could he arise in the gatherings of men and speak with self-assurance. The notice of his election to the prophetic office thus seemed to him to be premature. But in the background of his hesitancy was another reason— fear. He was afraid of having to suffer torture or even death, like many prophets before him (2:30).

But the Lord rejects Jeremiah's excuse:

> "Do not say, 'I am only a youth';
> for to all to whom I send you you shall go,
> and whatever I command you you shall speak." (1:7)

He was just to be the Lord's messenger. He did not, like other men, have to choose to whom he should speak or what he should say. The mustering of courage need not trouble him. No uncertainty need inhibit him. He could be fearless of consequences in the consciousness that he was under divine protection and would be delivered from the martyr's fate.

On receiving these words Jeremiah had the sensation that his mouth was being touched by an invisible hand. This experience was accompanied by the words:

> "Behold, I have put my words in your mouth.
> See, I have set you this day over nations and over kingdoms,
> to pluck up and to break down,
> to destroy and to overthrow,
> to build and to plant." (1:9b–10)

Here again retrospective appreciation of the significance of his prophetic ministry may have shaped the installation formula. It would have been sufficient for the moment that Jeremiah received assurance that he had been appointed God's messenger to his people, and that the word he bore was potent to exercise both a negative and a positive effect.

A visionary experience seems to have followed either directly or very soon upon this peculiar ordination. He saw a rod which he recognized as the "watch-shrub" or almond (Hebrew, shaqed). It must have been in the season when the shrub bore neither leaf nor flower. The heavenly voice approved of his discernment and interpreted the vision. The watch-shrub was to remind him that the Lord was "watching" over his word to fulfill it. He thus was not to lose faith in the efficacy of the Word, when there was a seeming lag in fulfillment. God's time is not our time. Of this he may be sure—God's word does not come back empty (Isa. 55:11).

All this was still only preparatory. No actual message had as yet been given. A first revelation of what he was to say was, however, accorded to him in another vision. He saw a pot—presumably one of huge size and under which the fire has been blown to high heat—facing away from the north. It therefore was about ready to boil over and spill its contents toward the south. This was interpreted by the divine voice as signifying:

> "Out of the north evil shall break forth
> upon all the inhabitants of the land." (1:14)

One must suspect that the further explanation predicting a siege of Jerusalem is again an elaboration formulated on the basis of later insight. The threat of evil brewing from the north was sufficient. Integral in the situation, however, are the interpretation of that evil as divine judgment for apostasy (v. 16) and the charge to deliver this message:

> "But you, gird up your loins; arise, and say to
> them everything that I command you. Do not be
> dismayed by them, lest I dismay you before
> them." (1:17)

This is supplemented by further reassurance, which, however, may have been drawn into the text here from a later occasion (15:20; see page 144). The editors of the book of Jeremiah may have desired to include at the beginning of the book everything about Jeremiah's commission, and to indicate his full stature at the outset.

Jeremiah's Beginnings. It is possible that Jeremiah began to have his seizures of inspiration in his home town. However, the command to go to Jerusalem and proclaim the Lord's message in its hearing now stands at the beginning of his prophecies of chapters 2–6. Even though this may be due to mere editorial arrangement, either by Jeremiah or later editors, it creates an uncertainty about assuming a period of activity before coming to the capital.

If anything was first formulated at Anathoth it may have been some of the prophecies about the northern peril that are scattered through chapters 4–6, for they are in line with the early vision of the boiling pot (1:13 ff.). These six (or seven?) pieces may not now be quite in the exact form or sequence in which they were first uttered. Twenty or more years lay between the time of his call and his dictation of his prophecies to Baruch (36:32). Some retouching may have been done by Jeremiah at that occasion in the light of unfolding historical events. His idea of who the northern foe was may have shifted several times. But these productions have the excited quality of visions, and they differ from the more measured discourses among which they are interspersed.

We may imagine the young man seized by the divine impulse as he was surrounded by a group of bystanders, some moved with fear, some with annoyance, and some with skepticism or even scoffing. The prophetic inspiration was close to insanity in its physical symptoms, and the question always was: Is the man really a prophet or is he mad? Even the insane person was viewed with a certain amount of awe, as is still the case in the Near East.

Particularly characteristic is the sixth of these poems:

> "Behold, a people is coming from the north country,
>   a great nation is stirring from the farthest parts of the earth.
> They lay hold on bow and spear,
>   they are cruel and have no mercy,
>   the sound of them is like the roaring sea;
> they ride upon horses,
>   set in array as a man for battle,
>   against you, O daughter of Zion!"

We have heard the report of it,
  our hands fall helpless;
anguish has taken hold of us,
  pain as of a woman in travail.
Go not forth into the field,
  nor walk on the road;
for the enemy has a sword,
  terror is on every side.
O daughter of my people, gird on sackcloth,
  and roll in ashes;
make mourning as for an only son,
  most bitter lamentation;
for suddenly the destroyer
  will come upon us. (6:22–26)

When Jeremiah spoke these words he was thinking of a people more distant than those with whom Judah had had contact in the past. The "farthest parts of the earth" in his time were not sought as close by as the Euphrates-Tigris regions. The usual view is that Jeremiah was thinking of the Scythians. The report of a Scythian dominion over the Medes and an incursion by them from Palestine up to the very border of Egypt (Herodotus, 1, 103 ff.), is largely responsible for this view. But the report of Herodotus arouses skepticism. The Scythians were allied with the Assyrians, and with their aid they kept the Medes in check. It seems unlikely that they would have overrun Assyria itself and penetrated into Syria before the death of Ashurbanipal (626), and still less is this possible after the Medes had thrown off the Scythian yoke c. 626–625. The Medes, too, were still more or less nomadic, though now establishing a capital city at Ecbatana under their king Kyaxares.

In the fourth of these poems (5:15–17) the nation from afar is called "an enduring nation," "an ancient nation." This sounds as though the Babylonians would be the invaders, for they certainly were a nation with a long history. If the next lines read "a nation whose language you do not know, nor can you understand what they say," this would suit the Indo-European speech of the Medes better, and thus may belong to the original wording, while the allusion to the antiquity of the people may represent revision.

A historical moment seems reflected in the first of these songs (4:5–8), which has a special introductory formula:

> Declare in Judah, and proclaim in Jerusalem, and say,
> "Blow the trumpet through the land;
> cry aloud and say,
> 'Assemble, and let us go
> into the fortified cities!'
> Raise a standard toward Zion,
> flee for safety, stay not,
> for I bring evil from the north,
> and great destruction.
> A lion has gone up from his thicket,
> a destroyer of nations has set out;
> he has gone forth from his place
> to make your land a waste;
> your cities will be ruins
> without inhabitant.
> For this gird you with sackcloth,
> lament and wail;
> for the fierce anger of the Lord
> has not turned back from us."

The "lion [that] has gone up from his thicket," who is at the same time called "a destroyer of nations," would seem best to fit a great individual leader like Kyaxares or Nabopolassar. The former's overthrow of the Scythians had just occurred, and he thus was a rising figure on the horizon, as Cyrus was when Deutero-Isaiah began to prophesy in the next century.

In the second song (4:11–18) Jeremiah hears voices, first from Dan in the extreme north and then from Mount Ephraim, announce the coming of the besiegers. In the fifth song (6:1–8) he bids the Benjaminite community in Jerusalem to flee and forecasts a siege of the city. In the third song (4:29–31) he sees the inhabitants of the cities taking flight and seeking refuge in thickets and among rocks. He addresses Jerusalem with vivid words:

> And you, O desolate one,
> what do you mean that you dress in scarlet,
> that you deck yourself with ornaments of gold,
> that you enlarge your eyes with paint?
> In vain you beautify yourself.
> Your lovers despise you;
> they seek your life.
> For I heard a cry as of a woman in travail,
> anguish as of one bringing forth her first child,

the cry of the daughter of Zion gasping for breath,
   stretching out her hands,   .
"Woe is me! I am fainting before murderers." (4:30–31)

Indeed, this is a powerful and terrible description of the agony of a
city doomed to fall. It is no wonder that the young Jeremiah suffered
physically from the torture of such messages. We hear him cry out:

My anguish, my anguish! I writhe in pain!
   Oh, the walls of my heart!
My heart is beating wildly;
   I cannot keep silent;
for I hear the sound of the trumpet,
   the alarm of war. (4:19)

Then he rises to an appreciation of God's pity for those who will have
to suffer all this coming misery:

"For my people are foolish,
   they know me not; .
they are stupid children,
   they have no understanding.
They are skilled in doing evil,
   but how to do good they know not." (4:22)

The Loner. Relatives, friends, and neighbors may have thought the
cure for the young prophet, who was sending forth such seemingly unnecessary alarms, was matrimony. Family responsibility would absorb
his energies, and family happiness would mellow his nature. But they
were rebuffed. Jeremiah announced that he had received a revelation
from the Lord, which forbade his marrying; for marriage would mean
involving a new family in the horrors he saw impending (16:1 ff.). He
was also prohibited from entering a house of mourning, or a house of
feasting, because, in view of the Lord's disfavor, there would be no
consolation and no occasions of rejoicing:

"For thus says the LORD of hosts, the God of Israel: Behold, I will make
to cease from this place, before your eyes and in your days, the voice of
mirth and the voice of gladness, the voice of the bridegroom and the voice
of the bride." (16:9)

His personal life was thus to be a prophecy of disaster, a sign to all the
people.

Jeremiah in Jerusalem. Behind the dread northern peril was the anger of the Lord, without whom nothing at all happens on the stage of history. That anger had to have a cause. Jeremiah had to go to Jerusalem to see at firsthand the reasons for God's anger and to deliver his message where it counted most. Anathoth, inhabited by priests of the old order of Abiathar, was no doubt steeped in the ancient piety, for Jeremiah did not have to break with an aberrant type of religion. It does not seem likely that his departure from Anathoth implied an immediate transfer to residence in the city. The latter was, after all, only a short distance from home. But now he was able to observe for himself what was going on. Soon he must have begun to utter prophetic criticism there, coupled with threats of divine retribution.

What were the charges Jeremiah had to present as moral basis for the threat of doom?

The basic one was that of apostasy, for which he could think of no parallel in either the west or the east:

> "Therefore I still contend with you,
>   says the LORD,
> and with your children's children I
>   will contend.
> For cross to the coasts of Cyprus and see,
>   or send to Kedar and examine with care;
>   see if there has been such a thing.
> Has a nation changed its gods,
>   even though they are no gods?
> But my people have changed their glory (i.e., their God)
>   for that which does not profit.
> Be appalled, O heavens, at this,
>   be shocked, be utterly desolate,
>   says the LORD,
> for my people have committed two evils:
>   they have forsaken me,
> the fountain of living waters,
>   and hewed out cisterns for themselves,
> broken cisterns,
>   that can hold no water. (2:9–13)

This powerful appeal to the heavens reminds one of the great opening utterance of the book of Isaiah. The contrast of the perennial fountain and the leaky cisterns must have been especially vivid to a Palestinian because of the porous nature of the rock into which cisterns were cut.

What was the nature of this apostasy? The narrative of 2 Kings 21 accuses King Manasseh of having done things more wicked than all that the Amorites had done of old. He had restored the high places, erected altars of Baal, made an Asherah, as Ahab had done, and worshiped all the hosts of heaven and served them. The altars for the hosts of heaven he set up in the two courts of the temple. The graven image of Asherah he set up in the house of the Lord. He burned his son as an offering, practiced soothsaying and augury and dealt with mediums and wizards. Religious syncretism prevailed. It was basically a revival of Canaanite worship, such as was also carried on in Phoenicia, but with inclusion of elements of the astral religion of the Assyrians. The story of the reforms in 2 Kings 23:4–16 supplements the picture.

Jeremiah himself does not go into much detail about all this paganism. He follows in the footsteps of Hosea by referring to it as "harlotry" which is practiced "upon every high hill and under every green tree" (2:20):

> Lift up your eyes to the bare heights, and see!
> Where have you not been lain with?
> By the waysides you have sat awaiting lovers
> like an Arab in the wilderness.
> You have polluted the land
> with your vile harlotry. (3:2)

Sometimes the allusion to harlotry, however, seems to be more than a figure for idolatry:

> When I fed them to the full,
> they committed adultery
> and trooped to the houses of harlots.
> They were well-fed lusty stallions,
> each neighing for his neighbor's wife.
> Shall I not punish them for these things?
>   says the LORD;
> and shall I not avenge myself
> on a nation such as this? (5:7b–9)

Apparently the orgies at the high places provided opportunities for actual adultery without peril of penalty, as in the Israel of Hosea.

Jeremiah refers, too, to "abominations" that were set up in the Lord's presence (4:1, cf. 7:30) and to the people's having made gods for themselves (2:28). In rejecting the city's claim, "I am not defiled, I have not gone after the Baals," Jeremiah answers:

> "Look at your way in the valley;
> know what you have done—"(2:23b)

This is an allusion to the high place of Topheth in the valley of the son of Hinnom (7:31 ff.). In the latter connection we also hear of the worship of "the queen of heaven" and of drink offerings poured out to other gods (7:17–18).

One allusion to idolatrous practice poses a perplexity:

> "As a thief is shamed when caught,
> so the house of Israel shall be shamed:
> they, their kings, their princes,
> their priests, and their prophets,
> who say to a tree, 'You are my father,'
> and to a stone, 'You gave me birth.' " (2:26)

The "tree" can hardly be the sacred post called Asherah, since that seems to have been a symbol of the goddess of that name, nor can the stone be the "pillar," which is often a phallic emblem and suggested a male divinity. Since "tree" is masculine in Hebrew and "stone" feminine, the gender of the words may have influenced Jeremiah's connecting them with the sex of the divinities.

While Jeremiah puts the religious apostasy first, he is not blind to the social sins which so greatly disturbed Amos and Isaiah. Indeed, he immediately connects an accusation of this kind with his people's cultic errancy of seeking lovers (the Baals):

> Also on your skirts is found
> the lifeblood of guiltless poor;
> you did not find them breaking in.
> Yet in spite of all these things
> you say, 'I am innocent;
> surely his anger has turned from me.'
> Behold, I will bring you to judgment
> for saying, 'I have not sinned.' (2:34–35)

Elsewhere he singles out men who are prospering by means of oppression:

Like a basket full of birds,
   their houses are full of treachery;
therefore they have become great and rich,
   they have grown fat and sleek.
They know no bounds in deeds of wickedness;
   they judge not with justice
the cause of the fatherless, to make it prosper,
   and they do not defend the rights of the needy.
Shall I not punish them for these things?
                           says the LORD,
  and shall I not avenge myself
  on a nation such as this?" (5:27–29)

In passing he even broadens his accusation as to the quest for wealth:

"For from the least to the greatest of them,
   every one is greedy for unjust gain." (6:13a)

He probes more deeply into social life, too, when he warns:

Let every one beware of his neighbor,
   and put no trust in any brother;
for every brother is a supplanter,
   and every neighbor goes about as a slanderer.
Every one deceives his neighbor,
   and no one speaks the truth;
they have taught their tongue to speak lies;
   they commit iniquity and are too weary to repent.
Heaping oppression upon oppression, and deceit upon deceit,
   they refuse to know me, says the LORD.

Their tongue is a deadly arrow;
   it speaks deceitfully;
with his mouth each speaks peaceably to his neighbor,
   but in his heart he plans an ambush for him. (9:4–6, 8)

What impresses Jeremiah particularly about the sins of his people is the willful and conscious persistence in them. The people have no desire to change their evil ways (2:25). They take no correction (2:30). Such an attitude, he holds, is sheer rebellion. Furthermore it is base ingratitude toward the Lord, when seen against all that he has done for his people.

But Jeremiah not only castigates his people—he urges repentance; he calls for a return to the Lord:

> "If you return, O Israel,
> > > says the LORD,
> > to me you should return.
> If you remove your abominations from my presence,
> > and do not waver,
> and if you swear, 'As the LORD lives,'
> > in truth, in justice, and in uprightness,
> then nations shall bless themselves in him,
> > and in him shall they glory."

For thus says the LORD to the men of Judah and to the inhabitants of Jerusalem:

> > "Break up your fallow ground,
> > and sow not among thorns.
> > Circumcise yourselves to the LORD,
> > > remove the foreskin of your hearts,
> > > O men of Judah and inhabitants of Jerusalem;
> > lest my wrath go forth like fire,
> > > and burn with none to quench it,
> > > because of the evil of your doings." (4:1–4)

Later Judaism was to stress circumcision as distinctive of the chosen people, but Jeremiah knows that it was not peculiar to Israel (9:25). It here is turned into a mere figure for something else, viz. removal of uncleanness from the heart, instead of ritualistic uncleanness from the body. This saying must have influenced Paul's attitude on circumcision, and thus have had a profound effect in bringing about the emancipation of Christianity from Judaism.

As was the case with Hosea, Jeremiah indulges again and again in nostalgic reflection on the relation of God and people in the nation's beginnings. The oracle placed at the very head of his Jerusalem utterances starts off with this as keynote:

> "Go and proclaim in the hearing of Jerusalem, Thus says the LORD,
> > I remember the devotion of your youth,
> > > your love as a bride,
> > how you followed me in the wilderness,
> > > in a land not sown." (2:2)

As those who eat of the forbidden first fruits which were to be given to the Lord (Lev. 22:10), so those who "ate of" Israel (such as the Amalekites, and the Canaanites? Num. 14:43 ff.) became guilty and were swiftly punished by the Lord. How different, Jeremiah implies, is the recent state of affairs, where others have "eaten" of Israel with impunity. He thinks of the occupation of Palestine in an idealistic way. But swiftly the Hebrews "defiled the land." Priests, political leaders, and prophets are blamed. In another passage he contrasts God's purpose with the result achieved:

> " 'I thought
>> how I would set you among my sons,
> and give you a pleasant land,
>> a heritage most beauteous of all nations.
> And I thought you would call me, My Father,
>> and would not turn from following me.
> Surely, as a faithless wife leaves her husband,
>> so have you been faithless to me,
>>> O house of Israel,
>>>> says the LORD.' " (3:19–20)

This is anthropomorphic thinking about God, since the deity is held to be unable to foresee the outcome; but it is highly effective nonetheless.

The Hegira of Jeremiah.   Far from finding any response to his charges and threats delivered in the name of the Lord, Jeremiah found himself the object of ridicule and abuse. Complaints about his activities must have reached Anathoth. Relatives were ashamed. In the second of his so-called Confessions (12:1–6)—really his discourses with God— it is revealed to him that worse things lie ahead than the pain he had complained of as he saw the wicked prosper:

> "If you have raced with men on foot, and they have wearied you,
>> how will you compete with horses?
> And if in a safe land you fall down,
>> how will you do in the jungle of the Jordan?" (12:5)

He then is told by the Lord that he cannot trust his own family:

> "For even your brothers and the house of your father,
>> even they have dealt treacherously with you;
>> they are in full cry after you;
> believe them not,
>> though they speak fair words to you." (12:6)

This is an early near-parallel to the experience Jesus was to have with "his own," who sought to restrain him from carrying on his prophetic ministry (Mark 3:21).

It seems certain that Jeremiah left Anathoth after these experiences, just as Jesus left Nazareth, or Mohammed left Mecca. But reports of what Jeremiah was saying and doing in Jerusalem naturally came back. People were incensed that the young prophet was bringing discredit on his town. There was even a plot to murder him. In the first Confession (11:18–23), he alludes to a warning he had received from the Lord concerning this danger. Prior to receiving it he had been "like a gentle lamb led to the slaughter":

> I did not know it was against me
>   they devised schemes, saying,
> "Let us destroy the tree with its fruit,
>   let us cut him off from the land of the living,
>   that his name be remembered no more." (11:19)

A prose report about an oracle he uttered against the men of Anathoth represents the matter somewhat differently. It says that the citizens had threatened him openly, "Do not prophesy in the name of the LORD, or you will die by our hand" (11:21). Jeremiah thereupon allegedly predicted their extermination:

> therefore thus says the LORD of hosts: "Behold, I will punish them; the young men shall die by the sword; their sons and their daughters shall die by famine; and none of them shall be left. For I will bring evil upon the men of Anathoth, the year of their punishment." (11:22–23)

It seems probable that the wording of this prose report mirrors the actual fate of the people of Anathoth at the time of the fall of Jerusalem. The more dependable utterance is that of 11:18–19.

The Intensified Ministry. Separated from his family and townsmen, Jeremiah faced a hostile Jerusalem. We may imagine that he threw himself even more energetically into his prophetic activity. The latter now took on a new turn. Of this a command given him affords us a momentary glimpse:

> Run to and fro through the streets of Jerusalem,
>   look and take note!
> Search her squares to see
>   if you can find a man,

> one who does justice
>   and seeks truth;
> that I may pardon her. (5:1)

Abraham of old had asked the Lord whether he would refrain from
destroying Sodom if there were a certain number of righteous men in
it; he had haggled with the Lord over the number, but had not dared
to carry his inquiry to the point of asking whether he would spare the
city if there was just one righteous man in it (Gen. 18:22 ff.). But
here the Lord, with a compassion and mercy that passes understanding,
consents not to destroy Jerusalem for the sake of one doer of justice
if Jeremiah can find him. Like the Cynic Diogenes, who went to the
market of Athens with a lantern at noontime seeking human beings,
Jeremiah went through the streets of Jerusalem seeking a man con-
forming to the Hebrew ideal. He searched first among the ordinary
citizenry, perhaps expecting to find among it greater respect for the
ancient ways. But no repentant man was to be found among them:

> Then I said, "These are only the poor,
>   they have no sense;
> for they do not know the way of the LORD,
>   the law of their God. (5:4)

But in the upper stratum to which he then turned, and which included
priests, prophets, and other intellectuals, he found a similar breaking
loose from all the restraints of religion and morals. The conclusion
was plain. Pardon for the city was impossible.

The Lord compares Jeremiah's new role of evaluating the moral
worth of numerous individuals to that of an assayer, who determines
the purity of monetary metal:

> "I have made you an assayer and tester among my people,
>   that you may know and assay their ways.
> They are all stubbornly rebellious,
>   going about with slanders;
> they are bronze and iron,
>   all of them act corruptly.
> The bellows blow fiercely,
>   the lead is consumed by the fire;
> in vain the refining goes on,
>   for the wicked are not removed.
> Refuse silver they are called,
>   for the LORD has rejected them." (6:27–30)

This then has been the result of his investigation: This population is absolutely worthless.

The discovery must have been a great shock to Jeremiah. It was hard to believe that the people of Judah were so faithless, and it was even harder to believe that the Lord would discard them. Repeated messages of this kind were needed to persuade him of the seriousness of the divine intention.

The Sign of the Waistcloth. Among these messages must be reckoned the very peculiar one that involved a symbolical act with a "waistcloth," or girdle (13:1–11). This was the ordinary linen undergarment worn by a man. It is often pictured in Egyptian art, and slaves are nearly always shown wearing only this cloth. The waistcloths of the Egyptian aristocracy were, of course, ornate. A finely made waistcloth was a source of pride to an ancient man.

The incident is related in the first person, and thus goes back to Jeremiah himself. He is told by the Lord to buy the waistcloth and wear it, but not wash it. Later he is commanded to take it to the Euphrates and hide it there in a cleft in the rock. "After many days" he is instructed to go and retrieve it. He found the waistcloth spoiled; "it was good for nothing." The lesson to be drawn was that God will "spoil the pride of Judah and the great pride of Jerusalem."

It seems strange that Jeremiah should have to make two journeys to the Euphrates (presumably from Jerusalem to Aleppo and thence to Carchemish) and back for so trivial a purpose as providing an illustration of the rot of a buried waistcloth. If the place were significant, if the meaning were that the rot was caused by contact with the soil of pagan gods, or that the land of the Euphrates would be the ruin of Judah, then one could accept the journey as meaningful. Since no such meaning is given, it is questionable whether one should supply it. As the text stands, the emphasis is on spoilage of the things Jerusalem and Judah are proud of, as a man is proud of his waistcloth. This can mean only destruction of the beautiful country and the beautiful acropolis of Zion because of the people's refusal to repent and their sin in stubbornly following other gods. But spoilage of a waistcloth could be shown sufficiently by burying it near at hand. The question then is whether a textual error or misunderstanding is not involved. It should be noticed that there is no word "river" preceding the name (as e.g. in 2 Kings 23:29; 24:7) to prove that the Euphrates was actually meant. Some scholars think that the word rendered "Euphrates" (Hebrew, *Perath*) really referred to Parah (which in the spelling of Jeremiah's time would have been Parath), a town of Benjamin (Josh. 18:23), where a watercourse (still called Wadi *Fāra*) starts descending to the Jordan. Even easier would be the supposition that Perath is shortened from Ephrath, the place near Ramah where the ancestral mother of Benjamin, Rachel, was buried (Gen. 35:19). We know that Jeremiah had an interest in that locality (31:15). But there are other interpretations—e.g., that the story is just an allegory—or that Jeremiah played a kind of game as Ezekiel once did (Ezek. 4:1 ff.). Though no certainty can be reached on where Jeremiah went (if indeed, he went anywhere), the actual point of the whole incident is clear enough—the Lord will spoil the pride of Judah and Jerusalem.

Unacceptable Repentance. There were occasions when there was a seeming return to the Lord. At one of these times Jeremiah made it plain that renewed acceptance was not to be taken for granted.

> "If a man divorces his wife
>   and she goes from him
> and becomes another man's wife,
>   will he return to her?
> Would not that land be greatly polluted?
> You have played the harlot with many lovers;
>   and would you return to me?
>   says the LORD." (3:1)

To take back a divorced wife after she has married someone else was socially impossible in Jeremiah's world—a thing we have already mentioned in discussing Hosea's marriage. How then can a people defiled by following pagan gods expect renewed acceptance by the Lord?

Such an occasion of seeming repentance developed in connection with a drought (14:1–10). What such a disaster was like in Palestine is made clear in the opening description, by such vivid touches as the doe abandoning her newborn fawn and the wild asses standing on the bare heights panting for air. A piteous prayer of the people which then is quoted is rejected by the Lord.

In an appended prose passage of conversation between the Lord and Jeremiah (14:11–16), the latter is told not to pray for his people since the Lord has decreed their destruction by three scourges—sword, famine, and pestilence. But this material does not appear to belong to the drought situation, since Jeremiah refers to reassuring predictions of the false prophets that none of the things mentioned will occur. A supplementary oracle, partly in prose, says:

> "Though Moses and Samuel stood before me, yet my heart would not turn toward this people. Send them out of my sight, and let them go! And when they ask you, 'Where shall we go?' you shall say to them, 'Thus says the LORD:
> "Those who are for pestilence, to pestilence,
> and those who are for the sword, to the sword;
> those who are for famine, to famine,
> and those who are for captivity, to captivity." ' (15:1-2)

For Jeremiah the Benjaminite, Moses and Samuel loom large as intercessors for their people (Exod. 32:30 ff.; 1 Sam. 7:5 ff.). But even their intercession would not avail.

A Spiritual Crisis

We may well believe that after seeing the hopelessness of his ministry Jeremiah fell into a deep melancholy. Thus his third Confession (15:10-21) begins with the lament:

> Woe is me, my mother, that you bore me, a man of strife and contention to the whole land! I have not lent, nor have I borrowed, yet all of them curse me. (15:10)

God's words had been his joy in life. He had otherwise had a sad existence because God's hand was upon him. In dissatisfaction he cries:

> Why is my pain unceasing,
> my wound incurable,
> refusing to be healed?
> Wilt thou be to me like a deceitful brook,
> like waters that fail? (15:18)

Apparently this discontent with God's ways led him to the realization that he had overstepped the bounds. For in his response the Lord says:

> Therefore thus says the LORD:
> "If you return, I will restore you,
> and you shall stand before me.
> If you utter what is precious, and not what is worthless,
> you shall be as my mouth.

> They shall turn to you,
>> but you shall not turn to them. (15:19)

Jeremiah's continuance in the prophetic office rested on his "return" or, as we would say, "repentance." But to fit him for the task that now confronts him, the Lord confers on him a new hardness and gives fresh reassurance of aid:

> And I will make you to this people
>> a fortified wall of bronze;
> they will fight against you,
>> but they shall not prevail over you,
> for I am with you
>> to save you and deliver you,
>>> says the LORD. (15:20)

The full significance of this occasion has been somewhat dimmed by editorial borrowing of these words to enrich the report of his original installation (1:18 ff.). In reality the words are original here only. The passage marks a new stage in the prophet's development.

The early ministry of Jeremiah thus gives us his message in powerful, emotionally laden utterance. There is as yet no direct concern with special historical crises in Judah, as was to be the case later. He is not involved in ethical perplexities as to his own actions. But, at the point where he now stands he has seemingly arrived at the end of useful service. It now remains for the Lord himself to act and vindicate his prophet's warnings.

Out of this first phase of the prophet's activity emerges the picture of an individual who felt himself elected and sent by the Lord as messenger to his people to inform them of the judgment that would soon befall them because of their religious and moral corruption, and their stubborn refusal to heed the Lord's call to repent. It was a hard task for a man to stand alone, bereft of normal support by family or clan, facing the scorn, the ridicule, the hatred and even the treachery of men. It would seem to require a heroic nature to endure it. Jeremiah did not have that nature constitutionally. He was a sensitive person. But he felt equipped by the Lord with the power needed for the vocation and thus became equal to the entrusted task. And so he too must belong to the grand army of those whom the author of the Letter to the Hebrews had in mind, who through faith "won strength out of weakness" and "of whom the world was not worthy."

Jeremiah and the Political Scene. The world situation underwent rapid change. The dramatic developments brought the prophet out of the sphere of anticipation of things to come to the realities of the hour. There is no indication as yet that he had any contact with the king and high officials or knew more than the average man of government policies. But by merely loitering in the City Gate, where men gathered in those days, he could have seen ambassadors and messengers going forth on errands to other countries and draw some inferences. Assyria was declining under Ashurbanipal's son and successor (Ashur-etil-ilani, 625–621). Babylonia, where the Chaldean Nabopolassar had begun a revolution against Assyrian rule in 626, was the scene of continuous fighting. This did not affect Judah directly but it resulted in bringing the Egyptian Pharaoh Psamtik I into southern Palestine. A twenty-nine year "siege" of Ashdod, the capital of Assyria's Philistine provinces, is reported by Herodotus. This may mean no more than that Psamtik left Assyrian officials holding the city, but occupied the rest of the country.

Judah could not be indifferent to this altered situation. Pro-Egyptian sentiment arose, and loyalty to the Assyrian overlord weakened. Observing this trend, Jeremiah charged the people of Judah:

> How lightly you gad about,
>   changing your way!
> You shall be put to shame by Egypt
>   as you were put to shame by Assyria.
> From it too you will come away
>   with your hands upon your head,
> For the LORD has rejected those in whom you trust,
>   and you will not prosper by them. (2:36–37)

The prediction was evidently fulfilled very soon. Psamtik presumably sought to collect tribute from Judah and was resisted. There must have been a disastrous warlike clash between Josiah's forces and the Egyptians and then a vacillation in Judah between pro-Assyrian and pro-Egyptian sentiment, for Jeremiah can say:

> Moreover, the men of Memphis and Tahpanhes
>   have broken the crown of your head. . . .
> And now what do you gain by going to Egypt,
>   to drink the waters of the Nile?
> Or what do you gain by going to Assyria,
>   to drink the waters of the Euphrates? (2:16, 18)

Unfortunately the story of Josiah's relations with Egypt at this time has been omitted from the biblical record, just as was the case with that of Ahab's relations with Assyria, of which the Assyrian inscriptions alone have given us a glimpse.

The Reformation of Josiah. In 621, the year of the death of the king of Assyria (Ashur-etil-ilani) and of the accession of his successor (Sin-shar-ishkun, 620–612), Jeremiah saw an astonishing event take place in Judah. The religious apostasy against which he had fought was suddenly swept away by an act of King Josiah. This act was based on a book found in the temple (2 Kings 22:8). Modern biblical scholarship holds that this book of the law is incorporated in the book of Deuteronomy (chapters 12–26), for the religious reforms reported in 2 Kings 23 agree with the regulations given there.

There must have been a political reason for such an act. It was clear in 621 that Nabopolassar of Babylon had succeeded in breaking the Assyrian domination of his land. He was apparently determined to go further and to subject Assyria itself. Josiah and his council must have decided that a new power constellation was evolving and that Judah must pull itself up by the bootstraps to be ready for a role in it. North of Judah began Assyrian provincial lands, carved out of what had once been part of the Hebrew people's heritage. It was natural for Josiah to aspire to restore the realm of his forefathers and the dominant position of the city of Jerusalem. The first thing to do was to animate the people of Judah with a new religious zeal for the Lord, who, according to tradition, had done such mighty deeds in days of old for his people.

The most startling element in the program was the centralization of worship at Jerusalem. The local temples and shrines were thereby declared illegal, and what had gone on there had to be terminated. Only at Jerusalem could one satisfy one's religious needs. Clever planners had thought this out. The religious life would be unified. Jerusalem would be dominant, its economy would be helped by pilgrimage. A strong bid was made for the support of the poor by laws giving them relief.

Jeremiah and the Reformation. One must wonder why Jeremiah's name is not mentioned in the narrative about the reformation. Before Josiah acted he sent trusted advisers to inquire of the Lord; they went to a prophetess named Huldah in the "Second Quarter" of the city (2 Kings 22:14). Why not to the man who had so powerfully assailed the prevailing apostasy? This of course is a question about which one can only speculate. For one thing Jeremiah was an outsider—a Benjaminite. Furthermore, since Huldah was the wife of a high official it could be taken for granted that this inquiry would remain less noticed and be held confidential. Action in promulgating the reforms had to be sudden and dramatic, before opposition could crystalize. Given the powerful hold of heathenism on the people, revolution could easily have thwarted reform. In any case, no inference as to Jeremiah's whereabouts at the time of the reform can be drawn from the fact that he is not mentioned in the report of 2 Kings about the reformation.

If Jeremiah was present at the great gathering in the temple at which the king read the lawbook to those assembled and where the covenant was made to obey it, he left no record of his thoughts or feelings. After his inability to discover a single righteous man in all Jerusalem he cannot have been convinced that there was sincere change of heart on the part of the people. But he may have felt that God, in his sovereign power, had decided to give them a reprieve and had chosen means other than words spoken by prophets to bring about a change, if that were possible. The thing that would have pleased him most was the action against idolatry (2 Kings 23:10–14). But he must have known very well that idolatry would only be driven underground and might come to the surface again at any favorable moment.

There are several allusions in sayings of Jeremiah which are commonly

construed as revealing his dissatisfaction with the Deuteronomic law
code. His assertion, "my people know not the ordinance of the LORD"
(8:7) led to the reply, "We are wise, and the law of the LORD is with
us" (8:8a). That this response refers to possession of the new legal
code seems certain. Jeremiah's rejoinder was:

> But, behold, the false pen of the scribes
> has made it into a lie. (8:8b)

Is Jeremiah here accusing the scribes of having committed a forgery by
putting forth a code which they themselves had prepared, claiming that
it was the law given by Moses? It seems more likely that Jeremiah saw
in this law evidence of man-made perversion of God's requirements. If
it prescribed sacrifice and other cultic activities he must have regarded all this as not true of the Mosaic era; for like his great predecessors he denies that God desired sacrifices or that such were brought
in the Mosaic era (cf. 7:21 ff.; 6:20). It is a question, too, whether
Jeremiah approved of the centralization of worship at Jerusalem and
consequent abolition of all local temples. This worked hardship on those
living at a distance, especially on women. It impoverished the priests of
the towns, since the Jerusalem priests, in disregard of the Deuteronomic
ordinance (Deut. 18:6-8), balked at letting the town priests officiate
at their temple (cf. 2 Kings 23:9). Furthermore if the restraints on
prophetic activity (Deut. 18:20-22) stood in Josiah's code, Jeremiah
may not have felt too happy about these regulations either.

Another passage that sometimes is taken to refer to the code of
Josiah is that in which Jeremiah proclaims, "Cursed be the man who
does not heed the words of this covenant" (11:1 ff.). But this is
prose material, like the temple sermon (see page 160), and at best a
reproduction of a poetic oracle which the traditioner was unable to
give verbatim. Since the curse is immediately followed by allusion
to the covenant made in the Exodus period it is very doubtful
whether Jeremiah was thinking of the Deuteronomic law. If the text
intended to convey such an impression it would have to be regarded
as in a class with the section on the sabbath day (17:19-27), which
is clearly out of line with Jeremiah's thinking, and is thus to be
taken as a later addition.

Actually, whether Jeremiah realized it or not, the Deuteronomic
law was a first tolling of the bell for the end of prophecy. Not only

did the restraints which this law imposed upon prophets make it perilous to prophesy; its introduction marked the birth of an entirely new religious principle. Authority henceforth was to reside in a document in the hands of priestly interpreters. Religion was to become a religion of the book. Though the influence of the prophetic ethic on the book was considerable, it still remained a matter of the letter rather than of the spirit. While this law was to remain in force for a few short years only, it was to be revived and become triumphant two centuries later as part of an authoritative Pentateuch, and then prophecy would become officially extinct. Indeed, the lawbook of Josiah was destined to be the nucleus around which the other sacred writings would crystallize.

So we have a book religion to this day, and derive most of our religious thought from wellsprings that flowed ages ago.

The Hope for the Northern Tribes. What Jeremiah said or did in the twelve years between the reformation in 621 and the death of Josiah in 609 is not preserved. In view of his later remark (25:3) that he had spoken for twenty-three years, from the thirteenth year of Josiah (626) to "this day" (i.e., 605), he must have said many things. Tremendous military events in Babylonia and Mesopotamia were shaking the world. The prophet must have become increasingly certain that his early predictions about the northern peril were on the way to realization. He must have been deeply concerned, too, about the Israelites who had been deported to Mesopotamia and Media. They were right in the path of the Median army that in 614–612 was taking advantage of Assyria's struggle with the Babylonians to push down into Assyria itself. At some time during these years he could perhaps have spoken or written some of the materials contained in a special booklet now forming chapters 30 and 31 of the book bearing his name. In it the return of the tribes is not merely called for as at an earlier occasion (3:6–13), but anticipated. Jeremiah hears the weeping of the ancestral mother of his own Benjaminite tribe:

> "A voice is heard in Ramah,
>   lamentation and bitter weeping.
> Rachel is weeping for her children;
>   she refuses to be comforted for her children,
>   because they are not."

Thus says the LORD:
"Keep your voice from weeping,
    and your eyes from tears;
for your work shall be rewarded,
                    says the LORD,
    and they shall come back from the land of the enemy.
There is hope for your future,
                    says the LORD,
    and your children shall come back to their own country." (31:15–17)

He hears Ephraim confessing its sins and praying for return, and then the Lord saying to himself:

Is Ephraim my dear son?
    Is he my darling child?
For as often as I speak against him,
    I do remember him still.
Therefore my heart yearns for him;
    I will surely have mercy on him,
                    says the LORD. (31:20)

The prophet then urges that preparations be made for the migrating host, and he chides the hesitant ones who are reluctant to leave their foreign homes. The closing couplet is uncertain as to meaning. As taken by the Revised Standard Version, it pictures how wonderfully safe the journey will be made by the Lord:

"Set up waymarks for yourself,
    make yourself guideposts;
consider well the highway,
    the road by which you went.
Return, O virgin Israel,
    return to these your cities.
How long will you waver,
    O faithless daughter?
For the LORD has created a new thing on the earth:
    a woman protects a man." (31:21–22)

The New Covenant. Whether Jeremiah uttered the famous prophecy of the New Covenant (31:31–34), the jewel of this booklet, is a moot point. Its placement amid a series of obviously later additions and its single allusion to Judah (which would presuppose Judah's exile) stand in the way. Since the section is in prose, it could be a later paraphrase of what Jeremiah had given in poetic form. In that case the allusion to Judah, which is not repeated in verse 33, may be a gloss. The epochal words are:

> "Behold, the days are coming, says the LORD, when I will make a new covenant with the house of Israel and the house of Judah, not like the covenant which I made with their fathers when I took them by the hand to bring them out of the land of Egypt, my covenant which they broke, though I was their husband, says the LORD. But this is the covenant which I will make with the house of Israel after those days, says the LORD: I will put my law within them, and I will write it upon their hearts; and I will be their God, and they shall be my people. And no longer shall each man teach his neighbor and each his brother, saying, 'Know the LORD,' for they shall all know me, from the least of them to the greatest, says the LORD; for I will forgive their iniquity, and I will remember their sin no more." (31:31–34)

Just as the past history of Israel was inaugurated by a covenant at the time of the Exodus from Egypt, so the new cycle beginning with a return will be marked by a covenant. But this new covenant will be different. It will not be imposed outwardly in a relationship that can be broken. This had, indeed, been done by Israel, as described with the marriage symbolism so prominently used by Hosea. Rather it will involve a creative transformation of men. The law of this new covenant will be written in the heart (or "conscience," a term the Hebrew language did not have). There thus will be no future discord between the Lord and his people. Teaching knowledge of God to people will become unnecessary, for all will know him. All the sins of the past will have been forgiven and forgotten by the Lord.

It was a lovely dream, like the one referred to in the concluding remark of a previous oracle (31:26). It could only be entertained by virtue of faith in the power of the creator. God alone can do something about it by going to the heart of the matter.

It was with this thought, lifted out of the purely national context to a universally human one, that early Christianity came to regard itself as a new order—the new covenant foretold by Jeremiah. Experience soon showed, however, that what seemed within human grasp was beyond attainment, since God had not changed the heart. What he had done was to make more powerful agents of inner purification available through the person of Jesus and the Spirit sent by him. Through the

Christian take-over of the Old Testament this prediction is set before
men of all time like a shining beacon, drawing them out of the realm
of darkness toward that of light.

The World Situation. Not only is Jeremiah silent about the world
situation after 621, but there is also a gap for the years 622–617 in
the invaluable Babylonian Chronicle texts. Where they reopen, in
the summer of 616, we find Nabopolassar of Babylon reducing As-
syrian-controlled principalities in the Middle Euphrates region, but with
Assyrian and Egyptian forces pursuing Nabopolassar's men for a distance as they returned to Babylon. This mention of Egyptian cooperation with the Assyrians came as a great surprise when the text was first
published in 1923. It had not been realized from 2 Kings 23:29 that
the Pharaohs sought to aid Assyria (see page 157). Pharaoh Psamtik,
though eager to take over Assyrian provinces in Palestine and Syria,
evidently became concerned about losing Assyria as a bulwark against
the growing strength of the peoples of the north and east. In 615 that
which he must have most feared, happened. The Medes under their
king Kyaxares moved against Assyria, taking possession of a northern
province. In the following year they attacked the early Assyrian capital
of Ashur. Nabopolassar, who had previously attempted a siege of the
city, came too late to share in the spoils. The Medes, as the Chronicle
text notes, murdered the greater part of the population. Nabopolassar
and Kyaxares met and formed an alliance, and then each returned
home. Two years later they jointly attacked Nineveh, the capital of
Assyria.

Assuredly Jeremiah must have predicted the fall of Nineveh. The
man called "to pluck up and to break down, to destroy and to overthrow" (1:10), must have had a hand in this matter by announcing it
in advance, thereby—as he believed—helping to bring it about. But
whatever he may have said about it has perished.

The Prophet Nahum and the Fall of Nineveh

We are recompensed, however, for Jeremiah's seeming silence about
one of ancient history's greatest events by some utterances of a contemporary prophet named Nahum.

Who Nahum was and where he lived is hard to say. He is called the

"Elkoshite," i.e., a man from a town named Elkosh. But no such town is mentioned anywhere else in the Old Testament. Tradition of the first century A.D. sought it in Micah's region, on the Philistine border. Since the Assyrian armies had passed back and forth over this area again and again for over a century one could well understand the emotion that lies behind Nahum's words if he was, indeed, from that part of the country. So vividly does Nahum describe the destruction of Nineveh that some scholars hold the book to have been a kind of liturgy celebrating the fall of the famous city. But others believe the prophet is predicting what was going to come to pass. Perhaps the siege was already in progress.

The city is described as still confident of being able to repel its foes. Nahum taunts her with the example of another metropolis:

> Are you better than Thebes
>   that sat by the Nile,
> with water around her,
>   her rampart a sea,
>   and water her wall?
> Ethiopia was her strength,
>   Egypt too, and that without limit;
>   Put and the Libyans were her helpers. (3:8–9)

Thebes (or No-Amon) was taken by Ashurbanipal's army in 663, and since troops from Judah had participated as auxiliaries, authentic knowledge of this destruction must have been widely available.

According to the Babylonian Chronicle texts the siege and fall of Nineveh took place in 612 (not in 606 as formerly believed). The Assyrian king Sin-shar-ishkun apparently perished, but part of the defenders escaped and set up a new capital at Haran under Ashur-uballit as ruler.

A closing requiem may have been added to Nahum's book after the event of the fall of Nineveh became known:

> Your shepherds are asleep,
>   O king of Assyria;
>   your nobles slumber.
> Your people are scattered on the mountains
>   with none to gather them.
> There is no assuaging your hurt,
>   your wound is grievous.

> All who hear the news of you
>   clap their hands over you.
> For upon whom has not come
>   your unceasing evil? (3:18–19)

If the address to the king is original and not to be deleted on metrical grounds, it would seem to reflect knowledge of the fact that an Assyrian ruler was still in existence.

Nineveh's fall caused deep satisfaction in all the countries that had suffered from Assyrian ruthlessness. So terrible was the destruction of the city that its very location was forgotten. Xenophon passed in sight of its vast ruin mounds two hundred years later without knowing that "Ninos" had lain there, and Diodorus even places it on the Euphrates instead of on the Tigris. It was not until the nineteenth century that Austin Henry Layard, taking up Botta's abandoned effort to probe the great mounds opposite Mosul, penetrated into the palace of Sennacherib and could tell the world that Nineveh was found.

PART 2

PROPHETS OF THE CHALDEAN ERA

7 AT THE BEGINNING OF THE NEW AGE: JEREMIAH AND HABAKKUK

The Historical Scene. In the spring of 609 we find a new Pharaoh, Necho II (or Neco) marching from the coastal plain to the plain of Esdraelon en route to Syria and the Euphrates. The way led past the Assyrian provincial center at Megiddo. A brief biblical report relates:

> In his (i.e., Josiah's) days Pharaoh Neco king of Egypt went up to the king of Assyria to the river Euphrates. King Josiah went to meet him; and Pharaoh Neco slew him at Megiddo, when he saw him. (2 Kings 23:29)

The second Book of Chronicles reports in more detail, but perhaps not as dependably (2 Chronicles 35:20 ff.). But the haste of Necho mentioned there, we now can see, was certainly in keeping with the Pharaoh's need of getting to the Euphrates with reinforcements to aid the Assyrian ruler. The latter had abandoned Haran and retreated to Syria, but was planning to stage a comeback.

The Babylonian Chronicle text relates what happened when Necho got to the Euphrates. In July 609 Ashur-uballit "with a great Egyptian army crossed the river and marched against the city of Haran to conquer it." It must thus have been a powerful force that Pharaoh Necho had brought with him. The Egyptian ruler probably stayed in Syria. The campaign failed, for Ashur-uballit found it wiser to abandon the siege of Haran, when Nabopolassar and his Babylonian army approached in September, and retreated to Syria.

According to the Chronicles story (2 Chron. 35:25–26), all Judah and Jerusalem mourned for Josiah, and Jeremiah also uttered a lament for him. No such lament, however, is found in the book of Jeremiah.

It probably stood in a repertory of laments used by "the singing men and women." That collection is not preserved, so there is no way of knowing whether it was authentic or just attributed to him. That he thought well of Josiah is shown by a passing remark about him (22:15–16).

In this situation where the leaders of Judah must have been awaiting a signal from Pharaoh Necho before acting on the succession, the "people of the land" asserted themselves. They installed Josiah's fourth son Shallum (1 Chron. 3:15), who took the name of Jehoahaz (2 Kings 23:30). The Deuteronomic stricture about this king's "doing evil" suggests that he did not maintain the centralization of cult, but allowed the local sanctuaries to be revived, therewith opening the door to a renewal of corrupt worship. This would fit with his debt to his supporters, the people from outside of the capital city. As a younger son he may have resided in the country himself.

Pharaoh Necho, however, from his post in Syria now asserted the right to appoint a successor to Josiah. He summoned Jehoahaz to appear before him. There was nothing the new king could do but go. His departure took place while the mourning for Josiah was still in progress —hence probably within a forty-day mourning period. It led Jeremiah to clairvoyant utterance:

> Weep not for him who is dead,
>   nor bemoan him;
> but weep bitterly for him who goes away,
>   for he shall return no more
>   to see his native land. (22:10)

Jehoahaz was, indeed, taken to Egypt in bonds and died there (2 Kings 23:31–34).

Necho now appointed Josiah's second son, Eliakim (2 Kings 23:34), whose name he changed to Jehoiakim, in place of his brother. That Jehoiakim formally acknowledged Egyptian overlordship before being recognized is self-evident. Furthermore, he had to agree to pay a tribute of a hundred talents of silver and one talent of gold (2 Kings 23:33).

Jehoiakim, according to the later verdict, "did what was evil in the sight of the LORD, according to all that his fathers had done" (2 Kings 23:37). This general statement receives confirmation and detailed illustration from the words and the story of Jeremiah. For the prophet was to carry on his activity in Jerusalem for eleven years under this ruler.

All the heathenism suppressed by Josiah's reform was permitted to return—with some Egyptian innovations added. The prophet could thus resume the ministry of assailing apostasy that he had carried on before the reformation.

The Temple Sermon. In the accession year of Jehoiakim (hence still in 609 or the first months of 608) Jeremiah delivered an important message of the Lord in the temple. A narrative account in chapter 26 tells briefly of the discourse and of the happenings that followed it, while a longer version of the discourse is found in chapter 7. The latter is more specific about what led Jeremiah to speak. It was the oft repeated cry, "This is the temple of the Lord, the temple of the Lord, the temple of the Lord." It must have been a scene of religious fanaticism. What caused the emphasis on this assertion is not stated, but Jeremiah's words make it probable that it was a case of clinging desperately to the dogma of the inviolability of Zion, which had been developed by successors and admirers of Isaiah and had received new emphasis through the centralization of worship. The insecurity was great after the hopes for restoration of the Hebrew borders from Dan to Beersheba were frustrated and the good king Josiah was slain. Instead of being rid of foreign control Judah had only exchanged an Assyrian master for an Egyptian one. There may have been a strong patriotic desire to throw off this new yoke. Why hesitate? No foe could take Jerusalem, the fanatics cried. It was the place where the Lord had caused his name to dwell. In this way, perhaps, we can reconstruct the mood of the day.

Jeremiah was directed by the Lord to stand in the court of the temple and proclaim his message. The short version of it in chapter 26 simply threatens this temple with the same fate as befell the earlier one at Shiloh unless the people walked in the law the Lord had set before them and listened to his prophets. In the threat here made a bit of forgotten history emerges, for there is no other report of the destruction of Shiloh. However, the Danish excavations at the site of this temple have revealed that it must indeed have been destroyed at the time of the loss of the ark of the covenant related in 1 Samuel 4. The Israelite defeat at Aphek was thus followed by an inland thrust of the Philistines.

That part of the sermon of chapter 7 which parallels the summary of chapter 26 elaborates more specifically on the moral requirements: amending one's ways and doings, executing justice one with another, avoiding oppression of the unprotected, shedding of innocent blood, and going after other gods. The prophet also launches into other charges, and gives the threat in more detail:

"Behold, you trust in deceptive words to no avail. Will you steal, murder, commit adultery, swear falsely, burn incense to Baal, and go after other gods that you have not known, and then come and stand before me in this house, which is called by my name, and say, 'We are delivered!'—only to go on doing all these abominations? Has this house, which is called by my name, become a den of robbers in your eyes? Behold, I myself have seen it, says the LORD. Go now to my place that was in Shiloh, where I made my name dwell at first, and see what I did to it for the wickedness of my people Israel. And now, because you have done all these things, says the LORD, and when I spoke to you persistently you did not listen, and when I called you, you did not answer, therefore I will do to the house which is called by my name, and in which you trust, and to the place which I gave to you and to your fathers, as I did to Shiloh. And I will cast you out of my sight, as I cast out all your kinsmen, all the offspring of Ephraim." (7:8–15)

As the message relative to the actual occasion is suitably concluded with the threat against the temple, it seems likely that the further utterances in 7:16–34 were put here editorially to make this sermon representative of Jeremiah's total message. A similar procedure was followed in the case of the Sermon on the Mount (Matt. 5–7), which has been enriched with sayings of Jesus found in other connections in the older tradition. In this supplementary material Jeremiah is told first not to pray for this people (cf. 11:14 and 14:11). The Lord then speaks of the cult of the queen of heaven, in which parents and children cooperate, by baking cakes in her honor (cf. 44:17 ff.). In another more permanently valuable piece, the Lord ironically bids the people to add burnt offerings to regular sacrifice (i.e., eat both and hence have more profit, for the burnt offerings were normally burnt up entirely), and then declares he did not require sacrifice of their ancestors at the time of the Exodus. What he had demanded was obedience: "Walk in all the way that I command you" (7:23). But they did not listen, in spite of all the prophets sent to them, and they will not listen now to Jeremiah. He is to single them out as the nation that did not obey its god, and did not accept discipline. Truth (i.e., faithfulness) has perished in their case. A snatch of the original poetic wording was evidently remembered and included by the traditioner—an invitation to mourn over the rejection of this generation by the Lord (7:29).

The concluding part of the temple sermon (7:30 ff.) deals with the horrible custom of infant sacrifice at the Topheth ("place of burning") in the valley of the son (or sons) of Hinnom on the south side of Jerusalem. The worst of it was that this sacrifice was brought to the Lord—not to Baal or the queen of heaven. The requirement to give the first born to the Lord (cf. Exod. 24:19) was sharpened under Canaanite influence to disallow redemption of human beings (Exod. 22:29b–30). In the coming disaster, the prophet says, Topheth is to lose its name and become a burial ground, and Hinnom is to be renamed "valley of Slaughter."

Jeremiah in Peril

Uriah's Fate. When Jeremiah uttered the threat that this temple would become like the one at Shiloh, he had said enough for that occasion, as already indicated. One can imagine the rage into which such words threw the priests and supporting cult-prophets and their followers. The tumult must have been like that which more than 600 years later broke out against Paul of Tarsus in this same area. Jeremiah was mobbed. "You shall die!" was the cry. How could he speak such blasphemous words? It seems prophetic that the charge of having spoken against the temple was also the one brought against Jesus (Mark 14:57 ff.).

The noise and uproar in the temple brought high officials from the palace to the scene. They seated themselves in the "new gate" that led into the temple area from the south. This was the signal to bring a person accused of having committed a misdemeanor before them to be judged. Priests and prophets charged Jeremiah with blasphemy against the temple of the Lord. But some important men from other cities or districts of Judah called attention to the fact that in Hezekiah's time the prophet Micah had made a similar prediction. Since they were able to quote it they apparently were from Micah's own area. Micah's charges, they said, had led to self-examination and repentance. Their considered opinion was, "We are about to bring great evil on ourselves" (i.e., inviting retribution for such an unjust act as killing a prophet). The account assumes, though it does not say so, that the case against Jeremiah was dismissed. He must, however, have been in great jeopardy, for it is recorded that only the powerful protection of Ahikam saved him. This individual's father, Shaphan, was one of the ministers of Josiah at the time of the reformation (2 Kings 22:12). Presumably, however, Jeremiah was forbidden to enter the temple court and had to hold his peace for some time thereafter.

The narrator of chapter 26 makes it clear that Jeremiah's protection was due to special providence by telling of another prophet who was not protected. He was Uriah of Kiriath-jearim. Apparently this man felt compelled to imitate Jeremiah's example and raise his voice in the temple. His appearance, however, must have been a hit-and-run affair. Before he could be arrested he escaped and fled to Egypt. But Jehoiakim sent an ambassador to Egypt to secure his extradition. The man was Elnathan, whose father is mentioned as a colleague of Ahikam under Josiah (2 Kings 22:12). We will hear of Elnathan again at a later juncture (36:12 ff.). The prophet Uriah was executed.

Jeremiah Attacks the King.   Jehoiakim was not a king after the heart of Jeremiah. In the time when "the people of the land" were being taxed to pay the indemnity imposed by Necho of Egypt, Jehoiakim decided to build himself a new, more modern palace. He was particular about getting cedar wood from Lebanon for its interior, hence he must have arranged for this at the very start of his reign with Necho, who held control of Syria. Such logs were rafted by the Phoenicians to the point on the coast from which they could best be transported inland to Jerusalem. While this building was going on Jeremiah uttered a woe upon Jehoiakim contrasting him with his pious father Josiah:

> "Woe to him who builds his house by unrighteousness,
>   and his upper rooms by injustice;
> who makes his neighbor serve him for nothing,
>   and does not give him his wages;
> who says, 'I will build myself a great house
>   with spacious upper rooms,'
> and cuts out windows for it,
>   paneling it with cedar,
>   and painting it with vermilion.
> Do you think you are a king
>   because you compete in cedar?
> Did not your father eat and drink
>   and do justice and righteousness?

> Then it was well with him.
> He judged the cause of the poor and needy;
>   then it was well.
> Is not this to know me?
>   says the LORD.
> But you have eyes and heart
>   only for your dishonest gain,
> for shedding innocent blood,
>   and for practicing oppression and violence." (22:13–17)

The charge that the king did not pay his workmen suggests that he drafted and exploited many of "the people of the land" who had favored his brother Jehoahaz. The accusation of his shedding innocent blood relates to proscriptions and confiscations, as were so common in the ancient world—even in Rome. The charge of Jeremiah is followed by a prediction concerning Jehoiakim's fate:

> Therefore thus says the LORD concerning Jehoiakim the son of Josiah, king of Judah:
> "They shall not lament for him, saying,
>   'Ah my brother!' or 'Ah sister!'
> They shall not lament for him, saying,
>   'Ah lord!' or 'Ah his majesty!'
> With the burial of an ass he shall be buried,
>   dragged and cast forth beyond the gates of Jerusalem." (22:18–19)

We will have occasion later to inquire whether this prediction was fulfilled.

Jeremiah and the Potter. It may have been around this time that Jeremiah made his divinely commanded visit to "the potter's house" (18:1–12). Pottery-making was a very essential craft in the world of his day, and a potter would naturally have his workshop near clayey ground where his needed material was conveniently at hand. At Jerusalem this would have been in the south, where the valley between the two ridges emerges, near the vale of Hinnom. Jeremiah watched how the potter did his work. What struck him particularly were the failures. If a pot did not get formed satisfactorily the potter broke down the material and started over again and reshaped it into another vessel. From this Jeremiah was to learn something about the ways of God. The house of Israel (here apparently meaning Judah), he was told, was like such a pot, and like the potter the Lord would have no hesitation in discarding it and shaping a new vessel that would be well made. A different application is introduced in verse 11 in the thought that the Lord was shaping evil against the people of Judah. But this idea is not followed out. The original revelation was only concerned with the rejection of the people which the Lord had been trying to mold as a potter molds a pot. The broadened interpretation, which would make the potter's act symbolical of the Lord's way with all nations (18:7-8), while valuable, may be regarded as revision in the light of Jeremiah's later enlarged perspective (1:15; see page 129).

According to the concluding instruction, which reverts to the beginning (18:5), the Lord was contemplating doing something else with this clay, the people of Judah. Repentance could save them, but they declare that they will persist in their willful, stubborn course (18:11-12). The divine purpose thus is being frustrated.

Jeremiah and his Enemies.   Jeremiah's utterances at this time aroused bitter enmity against him. A definite plan was reportedly hatched by those who believed the "regular" channels of revelation through priests and temple prophets to be adequate:

> Then they said, "Come, let us make plots against Jeremiah, for the law shall not perish from the priest, nor counsel from the wise, nor the word from the prophet. Come, let us smite him with the tongue, and let us not heed any of his words." (18:18)

The plan bears great similarity to the one later said to have been formed against Jesus (Mark 12:13). If they could entrap Jeremiah in some utterance that would permit accusing him before a court there might be no one to extend protection. On divining what they were up to, Jeremiah broke out into a prayer calling down retribution upon them (18:19-23). But perhaps Jeremiah's words are not to be taken as based wholly on wrong done him personally; he may be wishing that the punishments long announced by him would strike his enemies, rather than others not his enemies. And for this he could hardly be condemned. If some writers compare him—to his disadvantage—with Jesus and his teachings, this is wholly unjust. Jeremiah was neither a teacher nor a saint. His prophetic commission called for him to utter judgment against the wickedness of men.

The Act with the Flask. Presumably it was to the same potter whom he had visited earlier that Jeremiah went to buy an earthen flask (19:1–13). Showing it to some of the elders and priests, he invited them to come with him. Their willingness to go suggests that they knew a symbolical act was in prospect. It also indicates that they stood in some awe or fear of the man who did such things, and spoke messages from the Lord. Jeremiah led them to the outer entrance of the gate then called the Potsherd Gate. The name implies that it led out to the town rubbish dump, in or near the vale of Hinnom in the south. The account has been expanded with sermonic material suggested by what went on in the vale of Hinnom and its high place Topheth (cf. 7:30 ff.). Originally, however, anything said was secondary to the symbolical act. Jeremiah hurled the flask to the ground and broke it into pieces. Then he declared that just as one smashes a potter's vessel so that it cannot be mended, so the Lord is going to smash this people and this city (19:1 ff.).

It should be noted that this was a private ceremonial act. It is analagous to the ancient Egyptian magical custom of smashing vessels that had been inscribed with the names of foreign rulers and imprecations upon them (the so-called "execration texts"). Jeremiah's spectators must have shuddered, for in the superstitious view of the ancients the prophet was thought to be drawing the curse down upon his own people.

The story has a sequel (19:14–20:6). Jeremiah (apparently unaccompanied) next goes to the outer court of the temple and there warns the assembled persons:

> "Thus says the LORD of hosts, the God of Israel, Behold, I am bringing upon this city and upon all its towns all the evil that I have pronounced against it, because they have stiffened their neck, refusing to hear my words." (19:15)

It is noteworthy that he does not allude to the ceremony with the flask; this had been only for the invited persons. The chief overseer of the temple, Pashhur, a priest and apparently also a prophet, was incensed at Jeremiah's declaration. Had not King Jehoiakim forbidden that sort of disturbance? He had Jeremiah beaten and put in the stocks (20:1–2).

When Pashhur came in the morning to release Jeremiah the latter gave him a grim oracle (20:2–6). In it Jeremiah for the first time comes out flatly with the prediction that Judah would be given into the hands of the king of Babylon. We will revert again later to his personal prediction for the overseer (see page 178).

The Approaching World Crisis. What was the world situation confronting Jeremiah since Necho appointed Jehoiakim? In the light of the Babylonian Chronicle texts the historical events took the following course. The Egyptian forces, after the retreat of Ashur-uballit from Haran, continued to support the Assyrians. The latter must have been too weak to take the initiative again, for the Babylonian king Nabopolassar devoted the fall of 608 and the following spring (607) to a campaign in the northern mountains. Indeed, the Assyrians are not even mentioned again in the Chronicle text; henceforth it is only the Egyptian army that is referred to. In fall, 607, the adversaries began testing each other's strength in the front on the Euphrates, but Nabopolassar avoided a major clash. In the fall of 606, gravely ill, he left his army and returned to Babylon. The army retreated when the Egyptians came down against it.

In the following year (605), with the king of Babylon too ill to go forth, the crown prince Nebuchadnezzar took command of the Babylonian army and led it up the Euphrates, bent on striking a decisive blow.

Jeremiah's Forecast of the Battle. We can imagine in what anxiety the peoples awaited a decision in the long struggle of the great powers. In Judah Jehoiakim and his partisans were sure that Necho's forces would defeat the Babylonians. No doubt fresh Egyptian troops in great numbers had been observed streaming northward up the coastal plain to reinforce the army on the Euphrates. These included some of the most formidable fighting men known—Libyans, Carians, and Ethiopians. But Jeremiah uttered an oracle, forecasting defeat for the Egyptians. It is a classic of its kind. The poem describes in a few brush strokes the Egyptian army's preparations for battle, its dismay, the headlong flight:

> "Prepare buckler and shield,
>   and advance for battle!
> Harness the horses;
>   mount, O horsemen!
> Take your stations with your helmets,

>   polish your spears,
>   put on your coats of mail!
>   Why have I seen it?
>   They are dismayed
>   and have turned backward.
>   Their warriors are beaten down,
>   and have fled in haste;
>   they look not back—
>   terror on every side!
>   says the LORD.
>   The swift cannot flee away,
>   nor the warrior escape;
>   in the north by the river Euphrates
>   they have stumbled and fallen. (46:3–6)

After reverting to a prior situation—that of the Egyptian imperialistic expansion of the preceding years—the prophet returns again to the impending crucial battle and explains its significance in the light of the Lord's purpose:

>   That day is the day of the Lord GOD of hosts,
>   a day of vengeance,
>   to avenge himself on his foes.
>   The sword shall devour and be sated,
>   and drink its fill of their blood.
>   For the Lord GOD of hosts holds a sacrifice
>   in the north country by the river Euphrates. (46:10)

This is the Lord's judgment over his foes, the Egyptians. Without going into detail about the battle, which was sufficiently covered in the opening lines, Jeremiah taunts wounded Egypt:

>   "Go up to Gilead, and take balm,
>   O virgin daughter of Egypt!
>   In vain you have used many medicines;
>   there is no healing for you.
>   The nations have heard of your shame,
>   and the earth is full of your cry;
>   for warrior has stumbled against warrior;
>   they have both fallen together." (46:11–12)

Jeremiah's prediction proved accurate. The remark prefixed to the poem takes note of that fact:

> Concerning the army of Pharaoh Neco, king of Egypt, which was by the river Euphrates at Carchemish and which Nebuchadrezzar king of Babylon defeated in the fourth year of Jehoiakim the son of Josiah, king of Judah." (46:2)

Those words were the chief information about this battle of Carchemish prior to the publication in 1956 of a new Babylonian Chronicle text. The latter gives a fuller picture. It states that Nebuchadnezzar marched up the Euphrates and crossed it opposite Carchemish to go against the Egyptian army which lay there. It then says, in Wiseman's rendering:

> "He accomplished their defeat and to nonexistence beat them. As for the rest of the Egyptian army which had escaped from the defeat so quickly that no weapon had reached them, in the district of Hamath the Babylonian troops overtook and defeated them, so that not a single man escaped to his own country. At that time Nebuchadnezzar conquered the whole area of the Hatti country" (i.e., Syria).

It was indeed a great victory and at once established Nebuchadnezzar as a son worthy of his father.

After the battle of Carchemish and the takeover of much of Syria in 605, Nebuchadnezzar had to return to Babylon in September to succeed his father Nabopolassar. He then went to Syria once more and marched unopposed through it until February, taking heavy tribute back to Babylon with him. In April he celebrated the New Year's festival there and began his official first year. In June he mustered his army and marched about unopposed in the Hatti territory until Chislev (which month began November 24 in 604). "All the kings of Hatti-land came before him and he received their heavy tribute," says the Chronicle text.

Report of Another Temple Address. It may have been in the fall of that same year (604) that Jeremiah addressed "all the people of Judah and all the inhabitants of Jerusalem" in the only likely place where such a gathering is conceivable—in the temple (25:1–14). He recalled that for twenty-three years he had warned against provoking the Lord with idolatry. Since they did not heed him the Lord was going to send for all the tribes of the north and for Nebuchadnezzar his "servant" and bring them against this land and its inhabitants, as well as against the nations round about, and would utterly destroy them.

While this prose report of what the prophet said in poetic form was written down long afterward, it is interesting in that it reveals a harmonization between the prophecy of the northern peril and the actual historical peril that now threatened from the Babylonian quarter. Nebuchadnezzar, so Jeremiah now states, will have northern peoples among his auxiliary troops. Furthermore, Nebuchadnezzar is not viewed as a mere rod of God's anger, but rather positively appreciated as the Lord's "servant." Isaiah had never gone as far as that in thinking about the Assyrian kings. Jeremiah resigns himself to the thought that his people is too small and insignificant to produce a Nebuchadnezzar or Necho, but sees the God of Israel as giving dominion to whom he wills among the monarchs of the earth.

Jeremiah and the Philistine Campaign. It must have been about this time that Jeremiah clairvoyantly foresaw that Nebuchadnezzar would come down from the Syrian headquarters to Philistia. The Philistine coastal cities carried on commerce with Phoenician cities, notably Tyre and Sidon. These had not submitted to Nebuchadnezzar, and they evidently influenced the Philistines, under the lead of Ashkelon, to resist too.

In a vivid oracle (47:1–7) Jeremiah portrays the coming invasion of Philistia from the north. An erroneous caption—probably the survival of a different oracle that was lost or removed—has hindered scholars from recognizing that the Babylonians and not the Egyptians are meant. Jeremiah first describes terror befalling the people, and then states the reason for it in the following words:

> "because of the day that is coming to destroy
>   all the Philistines,
> to cut off from Tyre and Sidon
>   every helper that remains.
> For the Lord is destroying the Philistines,
>   the remnant of the coastland of Caphtor." (47:4)

He appeals to the sword of the Lord to return to the scabbard, but then asks,

> "How can it be quiet,
>   when the Lord has given it a charge?
> Against Ashkelon and against the seashore
>   he has appointed it." (47:7)

As Jeremiah foresaw, so it happened. Nebuchadnezzar swooped down from Syria through Israelite territory to Philistia in December of 604. Still within the month of December he took Ashkelon, captured the king, and turned the city into a ruin-mound.

Habakkuk, the Watchman

At about the same time another prophet, who did not view things as did Jeremiah, raised his voice in Jerusalem. Habakkuk's name does not sound Hebrew at all. Actually it is an Assyro-Babylonian one, though not of the most common type, for it is derived from a plant name. In response to his complaint about violence and lawlessness in the city, the Lord bids him contemplate the unbelievable work he is doing in the world at large through the Babylonians:

> Look among the nations, and see;
>   wonder and be astounded.
> For I am doing a work in your days
>   that you would not believe if told.
> For lo, I am rousing the Chaldeans,
>   that bitter and hasty nation,
> who march through the breadth of the earth,
>   to seize habitations not their own.
> Dread and terrible are they;
>   their justice and dignity proceed from themselves.
> Their horses are swifter than leopards,
>   more fierce than the evening wolves;
>   their horsemen press proudly on.
> Yea, their horsemen come from afar;
>   they fly like an eagle swift to devour.
> They all come for violence;
>   terror of them goes before them.
>   They gather captives like sand.
> At kings they scoff,
>   and of rulers they make sport.
> They laugh at every fortress,
>   for they heap up earth and take it.
> Then they sweep by like the wind and go on,
>   guilty men, whose own might is their god! (1:5–11)

This fits well with statements made in the new Chronicle text about Nebuchadnezzar's marching about unopposed in Hattiland, and taking cities like Ashkelon.

In another complaint (1:12–17) Habakkuk recognizes that the Lord has sent the Babylonians for a chastisement, but at the same time he reminds the Lord that he cannot be blind to this godlike exercise of sheer power by wicked men. Nebuchadnezzar is here compared to a fisherman who drags up all men as one drags up the fish of the sea with one's hook or net. Both comparisons take on vividness from ancient Oriental art. Thus subjected kings are sometimes shown on Assyrian sculptures as held by a line and hook, and as far back as Sumerian times a Babylonian stela portrays a god holding his dead enemies in a net. In dismay Habakkuk cries out:

> Is he then to keep on emptying his net,
> and mercilessly slaying nations for ever? (1:17)

The prophet then determines to stand up a tower (of Jerusalem's walls?)—perhaps by night (2:1, cf. Isa. 21:6 ff.). At this station he is to await a reply from the Lord. He is told to write "the vision" (i.e., the message of God that he would receive in a vision) on a tablet (in large letters) so that a running man may read it. The message can have consisted of only a few words (cf. Isa. 8:1). Furthermore, it must have been in accord with the woes against Nebuchadnezzar in 2:6–17. There are three possibilities—(1) the message may not yet have been given, but may only be awaited; (2) the message may have been lost from the text and replaced by chapter 3; (3) the message may be contained in the words:

> Behold, he whose soul is not upright in him shall fail,
> but the righteous shall live by his faith. (2:4)

The first line would apply to Nebuchadnezzar better if one renders it "Behold, puffed up, not upright is his soul in him." But it cannot be said that it furnishes the kind of message one would expect. The second line emphasizes the importance of faith (better, "faithfulness," Hebrew, emunah), i.e., steadfast adherence to the Lord and his word, as the road to survival and to a happy future (cf. Deut. 8:1; 30:16). This likewise is not what one would expect for the tablet inscription. But it is a very fine saying, worth lingering over. When Paul, in quoting this passage, deepened "faithfulness" to "faith" in the sense of complete trust in God (Rom. 1:17), he carried it to heights of importance it did not originally have. But the stimulus provided Paul by the words, and through him to the despairing monk Martin Luther, gave them a world-wide historical impact. *Sola fide*—through faith alone shall man be saved.

A psalm attributed to Habakkuk evidently survived in a poetic collection and was later appended to the prophecies. It describes the theophany of the Lord, as he comes to battle his foes. This is done in true Oriental manner, as a comparison with Marduk's theophany in the Babylonian Creation Epic makes plain. It provides a fitting conclusion to the little book.

Jeremiah's Scroll. In the year 605—perhaps after the battle of Carchemish—Jeremiah had received a command from the Lord to prepare a scroll containing all his prophecies from 626 to date. The prediction of the northern peril had become fully substantiated, and it was timely to prepare a record of all the warnings given in advance. Jeremiah sought the aid of a professional scribe, Baruch, in order to obtain a well-written manuscript, fit to set before important personages. The prophet no doubt dictated his oracles to him from memory.

The instruction to use the manuscript, however, did not come until the following year, December of 604, when a fast was held. Such fasts certainly required some advance notice to the towns of Judah, and this one may have been arranged before Nebuchadnezzar made his unexpected trip to Philistia. The Jerusalem assembly may have been convoked to pray for rain, for if the "early rains" did not arrive by the first day of Chislev (December) a fast was felt to be necessary (if we can rely on the antiquity of later Jewish custom in this matter). Since Nebuchadnezzar's campaign to Ashkelon was in progress by the time the people assembled, this must have lent ominous overtones to the occasion.

But there was an obstacle to be overcome to Jeremiah's reading of his oracles. For some unknown reason he was "debarred" from entering the temple, where the ceremonies of the fast naturally were held. He therefore sent Baruch to act on his behalf. The scribe spoke to a small gathering in the chamber of Gemariah son of Shaphan (hence a brother of Ahikam, who had protected Jeremiah). In the audience that heard

Baruch read the prophecies was a son of Gemariah, who reported the matter to the officials in the chancellery. These summoned Baruch and asked him to read them some of the contents of his scroll. On hearing them they were alarmed and decided to report to the king what they had heard. But first they advised Baruch to go into hiding along with Jeremiah. It is evident from this counsel that they expected an angry reaction to their report.

The king, who was in the winter palace, commanded the scroll to be brought and read before him. Over the protest of his ministers he destroyed it piecemeal in the brazier. He then commanded three of his courtiers to arrest Jeremiah and Baruch. The charge against them was put in question form: "Why have you written in the scroll that the king of Babylon will certainly come and destroy this land and cut off from it man and beast?" It seems unlikely that Jehoiakim would have asked this question had he already accepted Babylonian suzerainty. We may safely infer that his officials favored submission to Babylon, but that the king chose to rely on the protection of Necho of Egypt, whose vassal he was.

Jeremiah and Baruch must have been well hidden, for the search for them was fruitless.

The Second Scroll and the Oracle to Baruch. The prophet now received another message from the Lord. He was to record once more all the words that had stood on the destroyed scroll. It is noted especially that Jeremiah added more oracles of the same nature to this second scroll. The prophet, dictating his scroll by the feeble light of a lamp in the den or cavern where he was hiding, is an Old Testament counterpart to John writing the Revelation in exile on Patmos.

It may have been at this rewrite that Baruch felt great weariness of soul (36:27–28, 32). Things had turned out differently than he had anticipated. He had expected that Jeremiah's oracles would be heeded, and that he, as his representative, would win laurels. Instead he was in hiding somewhere, bereft of his usual activity of preparing contracts and letters for people, and had the drudgery of writing down the same baleful oracles and laments a second time. But the prophet had a divine message for him:

"Thus says the LORD, the God of Israel, to you, O Baruch: You said, 'Woe is me! for the LORD has added sorrow to my pain; I am weary with my groaning, and I find no rest.' Thus shall you say to him, Thus says the LORD: Behold, what I have built I am breaking down, and what I have planted I am plucking up—that is, the whole land. And do you seek great things for yourself? Seek them not; for, behold, I am bringing evil upon all flesh, says the LORD; but I will give you your life as a prize of war in all places to which you may go." (45:2–5)

The admonition given was not to seek great things for himself at a time when catastrophe for his country was imminent. But Baruch was at least assured of a charmed life, as the prophet had been at the time of his call, and should be grateful for that special grace, when so many would perish.

Jeremiah and the Campaign of 601. Further Babylonian campaigns in the west were carried on in 603 and in 602, but the Chronicle text is damaged here. Perhaps when Nebuchadnezzar carried home great tribute in 602, as it then reports, he was able to take along that of Jehoiakim of Judah. Though history fails to report the exact year of the latter's submission to the Babylonian ruler, it does state that he did submit, remaining loyal for three years, but then rebelled (2 Kings 24:1).

In the year 601 Nebuchadnezzar launched a campaign against Egypt. Just before this campaign Jeremiah uttered an oracle against Egypt (46:13–24, with an appended prose version in vv. 25–26) predicting its conquest. However, this first Babylonian attempt to subject that country was unsuccessful. The Babylonian Chronicle text states that the king of Egypt mustered his troops, and that in the battle that ensued both sides suffered heavy losses. Nebuchadnezzar and his army thereupon turned back and went to Babylon. There he remained the following year (600), gathering horses and chariots in great numbers. But no new campaign against Egypt followed.

In December 599 Nebuchadnezzar went to Syria and from there sent out raiding parties against the Arab tribes on the Syrian and Transjordanian frontier. At this time Jeremiah must have uttered his oracle against the Kedar (49:28–33, cf. Isa. 21:16–17), apparently the most important Arab tribe of the day. They still existed in Pliny's time (first century A.D.) as neighbors of the Nabataeans, who then were the dominant people. A biblical report mentions the Lord's sending bands of Chaldeans, Syrians, Moabites, and Ammonites against Judah (2 Kings 24:1 ff.). No doubt these acted on orders from Nebuchadnezzar to create serious trouble for Jehoiakim until the Babylonian was ready to deal with his rebellion. These harassment tactics could well have been employed during Nebuchadnezzar's campaign of 599 against the desert Arabs.

Jeremiah and the Rechabites. Among those who took refuge at Jerusalem, probably in this time of chaotic conditions (or according to others in 587) was the peculiar "house" (or clan) of the Rechabites. They were ultimately of Kenite extraction (1 Chron. 2:55). Since they were nomadic, they may have been camping outside the walls of the city. Jeremiah was commanded by the Lord to visit them and conduct them to a chamber in the temple (chapter 35). When he did so and offered them wine, as he had been told to do, they refused to touch it (as he knew they would), because of the ordinance of their ancestor Jehonadab, son of Rechab (2 Kings 10:15). They affirmed that they faithfully followed the manner of life Jehonadab had prescribed. Jeremiah thereupon gave them an oracle predicting that Jehonadab would never lack a descendant who would stand before the Lord. While this oracle may not have been fulfilled in the literal sense for the Rechabite clan, the persistence of its principles is noteworthy. The Arab world, out of which Kenites and Rechabites came and which stands before the one God of the Jews, follows the principle of alcoholic abstinence to this day. Christendom too, has always had adherents who have abstained from alcohol.

The loyalty of the Rechabites to their ancestors' directives served Jeremiah as an illustration in an address. What a contrast there was between their obedience to an ancestor's rules and the disobedience of the people of Judah to the Lord's own demands! Jeremiah then voiced the threat that the Lord was now going to bring upon Judah all the evil he had pronounced against them.

The First Fall of Jerusalem. Our sources give us no specific information as to what led Jehoiakim to rebel. But we may assume that Pharaoh Necho's success in halting the Babylonian invasion attempt of 601 had stirred hopes in other quarters. As Necho's protégé Jehoiakim must have been under heavy pressure to join an alliance with Egypt against Nebuchadnezzar. It must have seemed a formidable combination, or Jehoiakim would not have taken the risk.

Nebuchadnezzar showed himself the great ruler he actually was by striking swiftly, before the enemy's plans could be put into operation, and by recognizing the pivotal importance of Jerusalem for the command of the approaches to the south and east. The Babylonian Chronicle text states that in Chislev (December) of 598 he marched to the west and besieged "the city of Judah" (i.e., Jerusalem).

According to the biblical narrative (2 Kings 24) Jehoiakim died before the siege began, leaving his eighteen-year-old son and successor Jehoiachin to weather the storm. An oracle of Jeremiah may have been spoken soon after the new king was crowned and when Babylonian operations, which no doubt were carried out from a base in Philistia, were beginning:

> Say to the king and the queen mother:
> "Take a lowly seat,
> for your beautiful crown
>   has come down from your head."
> The cities of the Negeb are shut up,
>   with none to open them;
> All Judah is taken into exile,
>   wholly taken into exile. (13:18–19)

It seems likely that the shut-up cities were abandoned by flight of their inhabitants. The exile referred to is still in the future.

Another oracle, perhaps given after Jerusalem's siege began, and only preserved in prose reporting, offered Jehoiachin (whom Jeremiah calls "Coniah") a grim prognosis.

> "As I live, says the LORD, though Coniah the son of Jehoiakim, king of Judah, were the signet ring on my right hand, yet I would tear you off and give you into the hand of those who seek your life, into the hand of those of whom you are afraid, even into the hand of Nebuchadrezzar king of Babylon and into the hand of the Chaldeans. I will hurl you and the mother who bore you into another country, where you were not born, and there you shall die. But to the land to which they will long to return, there they shall not return." (22:24–27)

The king's mother mentioned in the two oracles was a daughter of Elnathan (2 Kings 24:8), the man who had arrested the prophet Uriah in Egypt (Jer. 26:22). She evidently played an important role, and perhaps gave the sensible advice of surrender.

According to the Babylonian Chronicle text Nebuchadnezzar on the second day of Adar (March 16, 597) "seized the city and captured the king." We learn from the biblical account that he carried off the royal family, ministers, soldiers, craftsmen, and smiths, leaving only the poor people in the land (2 Kings 24:12 ff.).

Punishment of the Guilty. Since Jerusalem was taken in early March Nebuchadnezzar had to return to his capital as soon as possible for the Babylonian New Year's festival in April. At this occasion the king had to "seize the hands" of Marduk, the god of Babylon. Nebuchadnezzar, therefore, left punishment of those Jews guilty of rebellious activity until the deportees arrived in Babylonia. Stern retribution was no doubt meted out. There is allusion to it in Jeremiah's angry words to Pashhur (see page 165), when the latter released him from the stocks. As this is a later account of what the prophet said it seems certain that knowledge of what actually had happened has shaped the formulation:

> "The LORD does not call your name Pashhur, but Terror on every side. For thus says the LORD: Behold, I will make you a terror to yourself and to all your friends. They shall fall by the sword of their enemies while you look on. And I will give all Judah into the hand of the king of Babylon; he shall carry them captive to Babylon, and shall slay them with the sword."
>
> (20:3b-4)

Executions must thus have been held. Pashhur himself may have been the last of a group to be executed, after watching all those who were his friends die. The phrase "terror (i.e., secret danger) on every side," which Jeremiah employed occasionally (6:25; 46:5; 49:29), seemed so appropriate that it could be used as a nickname for the man in speaking about him and his fate. If Pashhur was executed he must have been one of those held particularly culpable for the rebellion of Jehoiakim. That he was carried off seems certain, since a different man has his office later (29:26).

At this point we may ask: What of the prophecy that Jeremiah had uttered about Jehoiakim's fate (22:19; see page 163)? We are told Jehoiakim "slept with his fathers" (i.e., was buried in the royal tombs, 2 Kings 24:6). Some hold that this passage shows that Jeremiah had been mistaken in his prediction. But it seems very probable that Nebuchadnezzar, being thwarted in punishing a captive Jehoiakim, took vengeance on his corpse, and had it taken out of his tomb and thrown on the ground, thus giving it the "burial of an ass," as Jeremiah had foretold. We hear of similar acts by other ancient rulers—e.g., Ashurbanipal wreaking his revenge on the body of a king of the Sea Land, who had fled to Elam—and do not believe that Nebuchadnezzar was any less vindictive. It was a further punishment for the dead man that his son Jehoiachin was not recognized as successor, but was carried off three months later. The Chronicle text merely states, "He (Nebuchadnezzar) appointed there a king of his own choice." Of Jerusalem it only says: "He received its heavy tribute and sent it to Babylon." It does not mention the deportations, since they were not "news" to the ancients.

Jeremiah had a parting shot for Jehoiachin, as he went into exile. Some human sympathy seems to pervade it:

> Is this man Coniah a despised, broken pot,
>   a vessel no one cares for?
> Why are he and his children hurled and cast
>   into a land which they do not know?
> O land, land, land,
>   hear the word of the LORD!
> Thus says the LORD:
> "Write this man down as childless,
>   a man who shall not succeed in his days;
> for none of his offspring shall succeed
>   in sitting on the throne of David,
>   and ruling again in Judah." (22:28–30)

The prophecy of Jeremiah was fully vindicated some seventy-five years later, when Zerubbabel, the only descendant of Jehoiachin to receive an opportunity for political leadership, lost his post as governor of the restored community.

Nebuchadnezzar chose Jehoiakim's brother Mattaniah to be king, and changed his name to Zedekiah (2 Kings 24:17). As in the change of name by Necho (2 Kings 23:34) the act of change rather than the name itself was of significance, as showing the complete dependence of the vassal. In both cases the name may have been suggested by the appointee himself.

9 THE FINAL TRAGEDY AND JEREMIAH'S LAST DAYS

AT JERUSALEM Zedekiah sought to establish a new regime within the shattered land. Perhaps the earliest utterance of Jeremiah from this period is an oracle against the land of Elam, north of the Persian Gulf (49:34–39). The oracle is dated "in the beginning of the reign of Zedekiah king of Judah." If "beginning of the reign" is understood in the technical Babylonian manner it means: from the time of Zedekiah's appointment in March 597 until the Babylonian New Year's festival, which in that year took place at the end of April. Jeremiah predicts that the Lord will break Elam's bow, "the mainstay of their might," a phrase from which one may infer that the Elamite archers were especially famous (cf. Isa. 22:6). The Lord, he said, will set his throne in Elam and destroy their kings and princes. Elam thus had no unified kingdom at this time, any more than was the case in the time of Ashurbanipal. "The throne of the LORD" over a united Elam will be occupied by the man to whom he has given world dominion—Nebuchadnezzar (27:8). One may infer that in the spring of 597 rumors of an impending Elamite campaign against Babylon reached Jerusalem, and that those now going into exile were pinning great hopes on such a development. The rumors may have been premature, but in the following year, according to the Babylonian Chronicle text, the leading king of Elam made an invasion attempt, only to withdraw again before Nebuchadnezzar's powerful forces.

Warnings to Zedekiah

An oracle of Jeremiah addressed to "the house of the king" is critical of Zedekiah and his clan. It seems likely that it was uttered early in the new ruler's reign.

"Hear the word of the LORD, O house of David! Thus says the LORD:
> " 'Execute justice in the morning,
>> and deliver from the hand of the oppressor
>> him who has been robbed,
> lest my wrath go forth like fire,
>> and burn with none to quench it,
>> because of your evil doings.' " (21:11b–12)

Evidently the king and certain members of his family did not keep the usual early hours in handling appeals cases and were not zealous about procuring justice for those who had been robbed.

With this oracle is joined another addressing the inhabitants of the citadel—basically the king's clan and friends who felt safe on their height and boasted:

> "Who shall come down against us,
>> or who shall enter our habitations?" (21:13d)

Apparently the city had capitulated in 597 without experiencing capture of the citadel, and those dwelling there now were nursing the illusion that it was impregnable, or at any rate that there was no great peril in sight. Jeremiah threatened them as follows:

> "I will punish you according to the fruit of your doings, says the LORD;
> I will kindle a fire in her forest,
> and it shall devour all that is round about her." (21:14)

The "forest" referred to is figurative for the cedar wood used for beams and paneling in the royal palaces. From there the fire will start and spread.

Jeremiah and the Other Prophets. In the course of a few years hopes of a downfall of the realm of Nebuchadnezzar arose among the tributary nations. The people of Judah, too, urged on by nationalistic prophets, came to share them. Jeremiah was shocked by the influence these men

were able to exercise. He accused them of immorality—manifest proof
of their unfitness to be the Lord's servants—and considered them worse
than those prophets who had misled Israel in the days of Ahab:

> "In the prophets of Samaria
>   I saw an unsavory thing:
> they prophesied by Baal
>   and led my people Israel astray.
> But in the prophets of Jerusalem
>   I have seen a horrible thing:
> they commit adultery and walk in lies;
>   they strengthen the hands of evildoers,
>   so that no one turns from his wickedness;
> all of them have become like Sodom to me,
>   and its inhabitants like Gomorrah." (23:13–14)

He declared that they were filling people with vain hopes and were
speaking visions of their own minds, contrary to the authentic word
of the Lord as given by himself (23:16–17). The Lord disavows these
men:

> "I did not send the prophets,
>   yet they ran;
> I did not speak to them,
>   yet they prophesied.
> But if they had stood in my council,
>   then they would have proclaimed my words to my people,
> and they would have turned them from their evil way,
>   and from the evil of their doings." (23:21–22)

Clash with Hananiah. After a few years a situation arose in which
the temptation to rebel became very great. It was in 594, and nationalistic prophets were urging such a step (chapter 27). Messengers from
the kings of Edom, Moab, Ammon, Tyre, and Sidon had come to
Jerusalem to induce Zedekiah to join them. We may suppose that they
were in league with a movement in Babylonia itself to overthrow
Nebuchadnezzar. For from the new Babylonian Chronicle texts we
learn that a revolution broke out in Babylonia in December 595 and
lasted into January 594. Part of the army was involved. But Nebuchadnezzar succeeded in crushing the rebellion.

Jeremiah was told by the Lord to make ropes and wooden yoke-bars
and wear them about his neck to drive home the lesson that the peoples
should remain under the Babylonian yoke. He was to tell the foreign

envoys that the Lord had given to Nebuchadnezzar world sovereignty. All nations should therefore serve him and his immediate successors until Babylon's turn came to lose its preeminence to others. Addressing Zedekiah he advised him not to listen to the counsel of prophets who urged him to rebel, for he would surely perish if he followed it. To the priests and the people he declared that the hopes held out by these prophets of the return of the vessels of the temple taken away by Nebuchadnezzar were illusory. Those men should rather be warning the people lest they lose the sacred objects still left. He predicted that these objects, too, would be carried off to Babylon and remain there until it pleased the Lord to restore them to Jerusalem.

Not so long afterward a prophet from Gibeon named Hananiah encountered Jeremiah in the temple (chapter 28) and gave an oracle to the effect that within two years the Lord would bring back all the vessels of the temple and likewise king "Jeconiah" (i.e., Jehoiachin) and the exiles. The Lord, he declared, was going to break the yoke of the king of Babylon. Jeremiah agreed with the wish behind the thought but was skeptical about its realization. He noted that historically the prophets had always prophesied woe, and that the one who prophesied weal would have to be vindicated by the events. Hananiah thereupon not only reaffirmed his prediction, but broke Jeremiah's yoke-bars in a symbolical reinforcement of his declaration.

Jeremiah had no contrary message of the Lord at the moment, and went his way. But he received one subsequently, and delivered it to Hananiah.

> "Go, tell Hananiah, 'Thus says the LORD: You have broken wooden bars, but I will make in their place bars of iron." (28:13)

God will put an iron yoke on the nations through Nebuchadnezzar instead of the wooden one. And Jeremiah had a personal oracle, too, for Hananiah:

> And Jeremiah the prophet said to the prophet Hananiah, "Listen, Hananiah, the LORD has not sent you, and you have made this people trust in a lie. Therefore thus says the LORD: 'Behold, I will remove you from the face of the earth. This very year you shall die, because you have uttered rebellion against the LORD.'" (28:15–16)

The story concludes with the laconic report that two months later Hananiah died.

The Letter to the Exiles; Complaint of Shemaiah. In Babylonia, too, prophets among the exiles of Judah were agitating and predicting the end of the captivity. Presumably promises had been held out to them (and of course also to exiles from other countries) by Babylonian elements bent on overthrowing Nebuchadnezzar. When Zedekiah sent two men on a mission to Babylonia (perhaps to assure Nebuchadnezzar of his loyalty), Jeremiah gave them a letter to take along to the exiles. It seems certain that this was done with King Zedekiah's knowledge and consent, for the letter was to be circulated in all the various Jewish colonies. Its contents accorded with Zedekiah's own interests, which would certainly not have been served by a return of Jehoiachin and all those carried off with him. In the letter Jeremiah gave the following remarkable counsel:

> "Thus says the LORD of hosts, the God of Israel, to all the exiles whom I have sent into exile from Jerusalem to Babylon: Build houses and live in them; plant gardens and eat their produce. Take wives and have sons and daughters; take wives for your sons, and give your daughters in marriage, that they may bear sons and daughters; multiply there, and do not decrease. But seek the welfare of the city where I have sent you into exile, and pray to the LORD on its behalf, for in its welfare you will find your welfare."
>
> (29:4-7)

Only a man who could pray for his enemies as Jeremiah had done (18:20) could ask the exiles to pray for their Babylonian oppressors. Inhibitions about praying at all on foreign soil must still have troubled all those who thought a holy place was required for prayer, and that heathen soil was unfit for that (cf. Amos 7:17; 2 Kings 5:18). A psalmist has preserved a glimpse of the state of mind prevailing among the exiles in his question "How shall we sing the LORD's song in a foreign land?" (Ps. 137:4). But Jeremiah holds that prayer to the Lord is possible anywhere. How instrumental his letter was in preparing the way for the institution of the synagogue is unknown, but one may well believe that his words had an effect. The letter continued with warnings not to listen to the prophets among them—the Lord has not sent them. At the close Jeremiah gives a prediction concerning two prophets whom he names: They will be slain by Nebuchadnezzar and they and their fate will be used as a curse by the exiles.

The letter has undergone some expansion, and to this secondary material probably belong these words:

> "For thus says the LORD: When seventy years are completed for Babylon, I will visit you, and I will fulfil to you my promise and bring you back to this place. For I know the plans I have for you, says the LORD, plans for welfare and not for evil, to give you a future and a hope." (29:10–11)

This peculiarly precise prediction has a surprising parallel in the Assyro-Babylonian sphere. In one of his inscriptions the Assyrian king Esar-haddon relates that the god Marduk, in his anger at Babylon, had decreed that the city should be destroyed and remain desolate for seventy years, but that when eleven years had passed the god had relented and had ordered its restoration. Clearly the thought of a seventy-year desolation of Jerusalem was stimulated by knowledge of a legend of Babylon's refounding. This could well have been known to an exilic amplifier of the text of Jeremiah, but hardly to the prophet himself. The addition must have been made during the sixth century, however, since the prophet Zechariah was familiar with it (1:12).

Jeremiah's letter brought an angry protest from a prophet in Babylonia named Shemaiah to the priest Zephaniah at Jerusalem. He reminded the priest that it was his responsibility to curb disturbance in the temple precincts on the part of "every madman who prophesies, to put him in the stocks and collar"; he then asks the priest why he did not rebuke Jeremiah for writing to the exiles as he had done. He implies that Jeremiah had prophesied in a similar vein in the temple. The priest read the letter to the prophet. Thereupon Jeremiah uttered another oracle on the spot, announcing punishment for Shemaiah and his descendants. Not one of them is to see the good that the Lord will do to his people, "for he has talked rebellion against the LORD" (29:29–32). It is impossible to say whether the priest put restraints on Jeremiah's further speaking in the temple or not. The fact that so little of what Jeremiah said or thought in the next years is preserved could lend some weight to that assumption.

The Book Cast into the Euphrates. The ambassadors sent by Zedekiah to Babylon evidently were not able to convince Nebuchadnezzar that their king was not involved in treachery. Zedekiah had to appear in person before the monarch. This was still in the year 594, according to an account in the book of Jeremiah (51:59–64). Naturally the ruler was escorted by adjutants, one of whom was the quartermaster Seraiah. The prophet Jeremiah is said to have given him a "book" (or "writing") to take along, containing a prophecy against Babylon. Seraiah was to read it on arrival there, then tie a stone to it and cast in into the midst of the Euphrates (from the bridge at Babylon?). When doing so he was to utter the imprecation: "Thus shall Babylon sink, to rise no more, because of the evil that I am bringing upon her."

The story now follows a collection of oracles against Babylon (50:1-51:28) and the reader is led to think that this was the writing referred to. That view, however, must be dismissed, inasmuch as these oracles are of later origin. One may suspect that the memory of the traditioner erred in ascribing to Jeremiah the writing of any curse on Babylon. It may have been a man of Hananiah's type who gave it to Seraiah. Indeed the author may also have been mistaken about a trip to Babylon by Zedekiah in 594. From the Babylonian Chronicle texts we learn that some time after the revolt inside Babylonia had been put down, in January, 594, Nebuchadnezzar went to Syria. It was probably in March, for he returned to Babylon for the New Year's festival in April. In Syria "kings and officials came before him, and he received their heavy tribute." It seems probable that Zedekiah was among this group and likewise had to pay. This "heavy tribute," then, was the fulfillment of the prophecy of Jeremiah concerning the yoke "bars of iron" that would be imposed (28:13).

One might think that the failure of the revolution in Babylonia and its consequences for Zedekiah and for Judah would have had a dampening effect on Judah's aspirations of independence. But new circumstances must have arisen that made rebellion attractive again a few years later. Unfortunately the Chronicle text breaks off with mention of Nebuchadnezzar's mustering his army and going to Syria again in December of 594. Therewith we lose an invaluable guide to the great events of the most decisive years in Jeremiah's life and in Judah's history.

Another Slant on Conditions in Jerusalem; Judah's Rebellion

For some reason the book of Jeremiah is not particularly informative about the religious conditions in Judah for this period. But here Ezekiel, an exile of 597, who was called to be a prophet in Babylonia in 593, is of help. He followed closely the situation in Jerusalem on the basis of what was reported to him. In his account of an imaginary visit to the temple in 592, he gives a vivid picture of what was going on there (Ezek. 8:1–11:3; see pages 202–208). One must suppose that religious deterioration had taken place in a few years, as had been the case in the northern kingdom between Amos and Hosea. Jeremiah, of course, knew all about this situation, even though oracles that may have dealt with it have not been preserved.

Jeremiah's Appraisal of the Remnant. With the "disadvantaged" class of former days now in control at Jerusalem (2 Kings 24:14) the situation was evidently much worse than before. Jeremiah came to think more kindly of those who had been deported. In a vision he saw two baskets of figs placed before the temple of the Lord (chapter 24). The Lord asks him what he sees and he describes the fruit in the baskets as good in one case and bad or inedible in the other. The good figs, the Lord then tells him, are symbolic of the exiles, the bad ones of the present population headed by Zedekiah and his princes, and even including those who dwell in Egypt. The sole hope of the future depends on the exiles in Babylonia. Rejection and destruction will be the lot of this riffraff left in Judah.

Jeremiah's Counsel. While we cannot reconstruct all the circumstances that led to rebellion, it seems certain that the new interest of Egypt in the affairs of western Asia must have been a factor. Pharaoh Necho was succeeded by his son Psamtik II (593–587). It is known that this new ruler made an expedition to Phoenicia in 590. He must have persuaded Tyre to take an anti-Babylonian position, for the conquest of that city became Nebuchadnezzar's main objective after he had dealt with Judah. Whatever the coalition that Psamtik may have been able to build, Judah was persuaded to enter it and was assured of Egyptian help. The die must have been cast in 589.

Nebuchadnezzar immediately went to Syria (no doubt to Riblah, where we find him later), as so often in earlier years. His objective was not yet clear when he arrived there. Ezekiel in a vivid passage (Ezek. 21:18 ff.) sees him making his decision at the crossroads there as to which way to turn.

It was when Nebuchadnezzar's siege was developing that Zedekiah sent two emissaries to Jeremiah, asking him to inquire of the Lord whether he "will deal with us according to all his wonderful deeds, and will make him (i.e., Nebuchadnezzar) withdraw from us" (21:1 ff.). Jeremiah gave the king the oracle that the armed forces that were seeking to halt the foe would be driven back into the city, that the Lord himself would fight against it, that epidemics would destroy man and beast, that those left would be given into the hands of Nebuchadnezzar and of their enemies who would mercilessly smite them.

In an oracle given to the people in general—either at this juncture or later—Jeremiah is said to have taken a very daring stand:

> "And to this people you shall say: 'Thus says the LORD: Behold, I set before you the way of life and the way of death. He who stays in this city shall die by the sword, by famine, and by pestilence; but he who goes out and surrenders to the Chaldeans who are besieging you shall live and shall have his life as a prize of war. For I have set my face against this city for evil and not for good, says the LORD: it shall be given into the hand of the king of Babylon, and he shall burn it with fire.'" (21:8–10)

We must bear in mind that this is only a report of what Jeremiah may originally have said. One cannot be sure that he used those very words. As the text stands, however, his advice was to save oneself by quitting the city.

This shocks the modern reader. Under the impact of Greek and Roman political ethics we admire those who fight to the bitter end. The rats, we say, leave the sinking ship. But, as we will see, Jeremiah angrily rejected the charge of desertion when suspected of such an intention (37:11 ff.). Furthermore, he was not addressing the soldiers (many of whom must have deserted, 38:19), but rather the noncombatants. His wish was that the people survive. Ancient warfare knew no mercy when determined resistance had full public support.

Nebuchadnezzar did not immediately prosecute the siege with full force, as he had done in 598, when the city was in the hands of more formidable defenders. Hence the siege took much longer—a year and a half (from January 588 to August 587) instead of two months. The Babylonian now followed the strategy of Sennacherib of sending out detachments to take and destroy the other walled cities of Judah. The capture of Jerusalem itself was to be the final act of the drama.

At the time when the only outlying cities left were Lachish and Azekah, Jeremiah brought the king an oracle of the Lord, holding out hopes to him personally (34:1–7). The king may not have been alone when he received the prophet, and this may have restrained the latter from giving explicit advice. But Zedekiah must have understood what Jeremiah meant—namely that if he wanted to escape the worst consequences the thing to do was to surrender (cf. 38:17). Zedekiah had evidently been pushed into the rebellion by the people and their leaders, and that would be a mitigating circumstance for him when he stood before Nebuchadnezzar to receive his sentence.

The Slave Liberation and Its Reversal. It was while the Babylonians were subjecting the rest of Judah that Zedekiah, in a solemn covenant ceremony in the temple, set free all Hebrew slaves, male or female (ch. 34:8 ff.). But hardly had that been done when the besiegers suddenly withdrew from Jerusalem. Word had arrived that an Egyptian army was coming to do battle with the Babylonians, making it necessary for Nebuchadnezzar to concentrate his forces in the Philistine plain. At once the slave owners reclaimed their slaves. Jeremiah was incensed at this breach of a solemn covenant and proclaimed that the judgment of the Lord would be upon those who had acted so faithlessly. He predicted that the Babylonians would return and would take Jerusalem and burn it with fire.

While the outcome of the battle—on which the hope of Jerusalem's deliverance hinged—was awaited, Zedekiah sent emissaries to Jeremiah. His request was, "Pray for us to the LORD our God" (37:3 ff.). That a prophet was an effective intercessor was a belief evidently shared by the king. But Jeremiah gave the two men an oracle to the effect that the Egyptian army was about to retreat to Egypt, and that the Babylonians would surely return and destroy Jerusalem. Even if they were only a remnant of wounded men they would do it.

Jeremiah Imprisoned

It was during this same interruption of the siege that Jeremiah wanted to go forth to Anathoth "to receive his portion there among the people" (better, to deal with a matter of inheritance in the family, 37:11 ff.). He was seized at the gate by the sentry and accused of deserting. In spite of his indignant denial he was led to the officials who beat him and imprisoned him in the vaulted cistern of a house used as a prison.

Perhaps the king was not immediately aware of this, for Jeremiah was there for some time. When the ruler was anxious to have another bit of crystal gazing, he sent for Jeremiah and asked him whether there was any word from the Lord. The prophet replied that there was: Zedekiah would be given into the hands of the king of Babylon. But then the prophet pleaded not to be sent back to the prison, for he would surely die there. So Zedekiah let him stay in the court of the guard, and ordered that he be given a daily ration.

The Righteous Branch.   Under the influence of his disappointment in Zedekiah, Jeremiah may have entertained the hope for a very different ruler of the future. An oracle in prose, hence probably not giving his exact words, speaks of such a one:

> "Behold, the days are coming, says the LORD, when I will raise up for David a righteous Branch, and he shall reign as king and deal wisely, and shall execute justice and righteousness in the land. In his days Judah will be saved, and Israel will dwell securely. And this is the name by which he will be called: 'The LORD is our righteousness.' " (23:5–6)

The term "righteous branch" is found in a Phoenician inscription in the sense of "legitimate offspring." Accepting that as the real meaning we can see that the prophecy insists that a lawful descendant of David (or one acknowledged as such by the Lord) will someday reign over Judah. He will rule exercising the main regal virtues, but apparently the Lord himself will first provide the outward peace and security for a re-constituted (?) Judah and Israel. The climactic assertion is that this ruler will be called "The LORD is our righteousness." This is evidently not to be taken as the man's true name, but rather as descriptive of the realization of the ideal state that will exist under his reign. The formulation may be in contrast to the name assumed by Zedekiah which means "the LORD is my righteousness." This is a very modest kind of messianic prophecy, the more so since "righteousness" in this connection means as much as "vindication," the righteousness of God in its helpful aspect. This prophecy, too, is already referred to by Zechariah (3:8; 6:12), and so had an interest for later generations.

Jeremiah in the Court of the Guard.   While in the court of the guard Jeremiah apparently voiced defeatist sentiments in talking to men of the guard and others who passed through (38:1–13). He once was overheard by four of the leaders, who then demanded of the king that he be put to death. Zedekiah's attitude was one of helpless irony. "Behold, he is in your hands; for the king can do nothing against you." No doubt Zedekiah faced the possibility of assassination on the part of these men if he did not pursue a firm course. However, Jeremiah's accusers contented themselves with letting the prophet down into an empty cistern, where he sank into the mire. He was saved by the initiative of the Ethiopian eunuch, Ebed-melech, and allowed to remain in the court of the guard. The grateful prophet thereupon gave Ebed-melech an oracle, promising him that his life would be spared in the impending tragedy of the city (39:15–18).

It was while he was in the court of the guard, and likewise in the time of the absence of the besiegers, that the incident of the visit of Jeremiah's kinsman Hanamel occurred (32:6 ff.). The latter asked Jeremiah to buy from him his field at Anathoth, since the prophet had the right of redeeming it. With clairvoyant foreknowledge Jeremiah had anticipated this visit, and he now knew that it was the Lord's will that he should consent. The sale was made in the regular manner of the day, and the document was given to Baruch to put in a sealed jar for preservation "for a long time." This purchase is the more remarkable since Jeremiah had neither wife nor child, and since his right would pass to some kinsman of a future generation. In the words addressed to Baruch a glimmer of hope for the future appears:

'For thus says the Lord of hosts, the God of Israel: Houses and fields and vineyards shall again be bought in this land.' (32:15)

Jeremiah understood that the Lord was giving him a stake in the land for times to come, for he was not abandoning either the land or the people.

Final Phase of the Siege

As Jeremiah had foretold the Babylonians returned, presumably after defeating or driving back the Egyptian army in an unrecorded battle. The last hope of deliverance vanished and the final act of the tragedy of Jerusalem began. It must have been recognition of impending disaster which led Zedekiah to send again for the prophet (38:14 ff.).

The place where he chose to consult him was the third entrance to the temple area—presumably the most westerly and most private one of the southern approaches. It evidently was possible for the king to speak to Jeremiah there without being overheard. Jeremiah had to be persuaded of his own safety first before acceding to the king's desire for an oracle. He complained too that the king would not heed his advice in any case, so that advising him was really useless. His counsel, thus reluctantly given, was to surrender to the princes of the king of Babylon (for Nebuchadnezzar himself evidently had not returned after driving off the Egyptians). Zedekiah expressed fear of the Jewish deserters, but was reassured on that score by Jeremiah. And the prophet told him of a vision he had had. He saw the women left in the palace (presumably after the royal family had been previously extradited) mocking the king with a ditty, as they were led forth to serve new masters:

> "Your trusted friends have deceived you
> and prevailed against you;
> now that your feet are sunk in the mire,
> they turn away from you." (38:22)

As though divining the king's secret intention Jeremiah predicts that he would not escape but would be seized by the king of Babylon.

The close of the story casts a sympathetic light on the character of the king. He saw to it that the reports of the interview would agree, and that Jeremiah could not get caught in the net of cross-examination by those bent on destroying him. It is useless to criticize Jeremiah for obeying his king's order as to what to say, as some moralists have done. The Old Testament ethic is not greatly concerned about deception of the wicked.

When a breach was made in the walls of the city and the Babylonian leaders seated themselves in the middle gate (of the northern wall), so chapter 39 relates, Zedekiah and his soldiers broke out of the city by night and fled toward the plain of the Jordan. But the Babylonians (no doubt with cavalry) overtook Zedekiah and caught him near Jericho. The story neglects to report the details of how he was brought back to Jerusalem and surrendered the helpless city, his family, and possessions, and how the vision of Jeremiah was fulfilled. But it tells of

Zedekiah's subsequent appearance before Nebuchadnezzar at Riblah in Syria, and of how he was judged, and succinctly reports the deportation of the people and the destruction of the city.

Jeremiah Among the Remnant

Chapter 39 relates too of Nebuchadnezzar's previously given order that no harm be done Jeremiah and that he was taken from the court of the guard and entrusted to Gedaliah, whose father had shielded Jeremiah from the wrath of Jehoiakim (26:24). But the facts are presented somewhat differently in chapter 40. In that account we learn that Jeremiah was first carried off bound as prisoner to Ramah, along with those going into exile, and set free there. He was given his choice: to come along to Babylonia and be well provided for, to remain in the land with Gedaliah—who had been appointed governor of the population allowed to remain—or even to go wherever he liked. Jeremiah chose to stay in the land. For him to go to Babylonia and receive especially favored treatment would have exposed him to the accusation of having been a traitor.

There is no light on Jeremiah's activities while at Mizpah with Gedaliah. The narrative of the murder of Gedaliah and the flight of the people (40:7–41:18) does not pay any attention to the prophet; it is purely political in outlook. But in chapter 42 we find Jeremiah and Baruch among those who were carried off (presumably against their will) to the vicinity of Bethlehem. Here there was a road junction, where one could turn off to the coastal plain and go down to Egypt or could continue toward the south and the caves of the wilderness of Judah. Since the fugitives were without sheep or goats the latter objective would have meant a desperate struggle for existence. But there was dissention about leaving the land, and Jeremiah was asked to give them the word of God as to what they should do.

The story as related is bent on showing how little one could rely on the assurances of such leaders as Johanan, son of Kareah, who first promised to follow the Lord's advice and then, when it was given and did not please them, became insolent and assailed the prophet. Poor Baruch, the scribe, was accused of having set Jeremiah against them. His plan allegedly was to deliver them all into the hands of the

Chaldeans to be killed or exiled because of the death of Gedaliah.

In spite of Jeremiah's dire warning that they would all perish in Egypt, Johanan and his aides led the people in that direction, and compelled Jeremiah and Baruch to accompany them (43:6).

Jeremiah in Egypt

The long, weary trek to Egypt over desert sands was accomplished, and at Tahpanhes (west of el Kantara) the straggling crowd reached its goal. As though to show that the word of the Lord could be given in a foreign land Jeremiah here performed a symbolical act before a structure called "house of the king." He took stones (either pieces of the saline-gypseous crust of this region or of building stones lying about) and made a paved spot in the roadway. He did this in the sight of the men of Judah—no doubt while they were waiting for permission to stay or to pass on into the interior of Egypt. The onlookers must have been mystified until the prophet enlightened them.

> "Thus says the LORD of hosts, the God of Israel: Behold, I will send and take Nebuchadrezzar the king of Babylon, my servant, and he will set his throne above these stones which I have hid, and he will spread his royal canopy over them. He shall come and smite the land of Egypt."
>
> (43:10–11a)

The oracle is very specific in its further details. One may assume in this case, as we have done in other instances, that later knowledge of the actual course of events has colored the reporting.

Doubts have often been expressed about Nebuchadnezzar's invading Egypt. But Josephus, drawing on the fourth century Babylonian historian Berossus, reports that Nebuchadnezzar conquered Egypt in the fifth year after the destruction of Jerusalem, which was the twenty-third year of his reign (hence 582). A fragmentary Babylonian text also speaks of an invasion of Egypt in the thirty-seventh year of Nebuchadnezzar (568). We have no doubt that in one of these campaigns Nebuchadnezzar's throne was erected on the pavement made by Jeremiah at Tahpanhes. The monarch may even have judged Jewish fugitives there. Only when the facts of the reign of Nebuchadnezzar become better known through discovery of more historical inscriptions will it be possible to evaluate this prophecy of Jeremiah correctly.

Jeremiah's Swan Song

The story of Jeremiah ends with a final powerful scene (chapter 44). He has learned that the Jewish women, not only at Tahpanhes or at Migdol (a more northerly border fortress) but also those of Noph (Memphis) and Pathros (upper Egypt), were bringing sacrifice and pouring libations to the "queen of heaven." We see him addressing a group of her devotees, reminding them that it was for such heathen aberrations that the Lord had destroyed Judah and Jerusalem. The reaction of the women was that they were doing this with the knowledge of their men. And, supported by the latter, they were determined to continue it. They declared that when they had worshipped this goddess at home in Judah (i.e., before the Deuteronomic reformation) they had prospered, while since then they had lacked everything and undergone terrible misfortune.

Such defiance of the Lord led Jeremiah to utter a grim prophecy: The time would come when the Lord's name would not be invoked any more by any man of Judah in all Egypt, for they would all have been consumed by sword and famine.

Allegedly Jeremiah gave his hearers a "sign," or portent, of the fulfillment of this prediction: The Lord would hand Pharaoh Hophra over to his enemies, just as he gave Zedekiah into the hand of Nebuchadnezzar. This "sign" seems remote in time and unduly precise; for Hophra or Apries (588–568) fell into the hands of Amasis, a commander of his Egyptian troops, who were jealous of the Greek mercenaries. This revolt took place when the mercenaries were defeated in an attack on Cyrene. Amasis, after brief hesitation, executed Hophra, and so became founder of the new twenty-seventh dynasty. The narrator who added this "sign" to the story must thus have written after 568. He had evidently heard of a persecution of Jews in Egypt.

With this final address a great life fades into the mists of the past. But to the last Jeremiah manifested that uncanny feeling of power which had been his in all his ministry. He was "a wall of bronze," against which none could prevail. He proclaimed the judgments of the Lord, and history vindicated his accuracy. He was set over nations and kingdoms to pluck up and to break down, for what he spoke was the word of the Lord, of which he once said that it was like fire, and like a hammer which breaks the rock in pieces (23:29). But he also was to build and to plant through that same word. Even in this final hour, when he consigned the exiles in Egypt to extinction, his faith in the Lord's care for his people was not quenched. In distant Babylon, among the exiles, he foresaw the rebirth of his nation, which the Lord would reestablish in the land of his choice, as a people made different by the Lord's creative act.

AMONG THE MEN who had gone into exile with King Jehoiachin in 597 was one whose influence on Jewish and Christian thinking was destined to be extensive. The book bearing his name, Ezekiel, is a monumental one. Its arrangement is clearer than any other, and the materials are not so brief or fragmentary. Its repetitiousness may be due in part to careless copying and inclusion of variants from other manuscripts. But there has probably also been incorporated into the text a great deal of comment and expansion on the part of men who studied and valued it, before it was considered sacred or canonical.

The Call of Ezekiel

Ezekiel's call to the office of prophet, which came to him in a vision, is dated in 593 and localized near the exile settlement of Tel-abib at the river Chebar in Babylonia. This watercourse, as was ascertained by the Assyriologist H. V. Hilprecht, was near Nippur, a great city of ancient Babylonia lying southeast of Babylon, and is mentioned several times in fifth-century cuneiform tablets from that city. In these texts many names of Jewish persons appear. "Tel-abib" itself is probably a slightly Hebraized form of Babylonian *til-abubi*—a common term for an ancient ruin-mound—supposedly caused by the Deluge. Such a mound formed an appropriate place for resettling exiles, since it provided ground above floodwaters.

It was in the hot summertime (July 31) that Ezekiel had his bizarre vision. From the north, out of a great cloud driven by a strong wind, with brightness about it and lightning flashing forth, emerged four strange beings drawing a wagon or platform on wheels surmounted by a throne and a seated figure. In labored manner the visionary attempts to describe what he saw, indicating at the same time the utter inadequacy of human words and concepts to do justice to it. For everything is said to be "in the like of," as in the summary statement giving the clear-cut identification, "Such was the appearance of the likeness of the glory of the LORD" (1:28).

As the celestial apparition drew near Ezekiel prostrated himself. He heard a voice saying, "Son of man, stand upon your feet, and I will speak with you." The term "son of man," with which Ezekiel is so constantly addressed in revelations, emphasizes his insignificance as a mere mortal being when confronted by the immortal deity. Yet the command to stand on his feet indicates the benignity of the divine attitude toward him. It was in this manner that an Oriental king showed his gracious inclination toward one who prostrated himself before him. But so helpless was Ezekiel from the paralyzing effect of his vision that it required the aid of a supernatural agency to enable him to obey. "The Spirit," we are told, entered into him and set him on his feet. He then receives his commission: He is to go to the rebellious people of Israel (=Judah) and address them with the words: "Thus says the LORD" (and whatever particular message he may then be told to convey). "Whether they hear or refuse to hear, they will know that there is a prophet among them." He is not to be afraid of them, "though briers and thorns are with you and you sit upon scorpions"—a vivid description of the resistance he will encounter. Nor is he himself to be rebellious, like that rebellious house of Israel.

As though to test out his obedience Ezekiel is confronted with the sight of an outstretched hand holding a scroll with words of lamentation and mourning inscribed on it on obverse and reverse; it thus may have curled somewhat at one end to make the reverse visible. Lamentations were easily recognizable at a glance (especially if written in poetic lines or indented at their beginnings) from the usual introductory words such as "Woe" or "Alas." He then was commanded:

> "Son of man, eat what is offered to you; eat this scroll, and go, speak to the house of Israel." So I opened my mouth, and he gave me the scroll to eat. And he said to me, "Son of man, eat this scroll that I give you and fill your stomach with it." Then I ate it; and it was in my mouth as sweet as honey.
> (3:1-3)

He thus found himself filling his stomach with the scroll—not actually, of course, but only in his vision. But so real did the experience seem that he was conscious of a pleasurable sensation: It was sweet as honey. Parallels can be found in experiences of the mystics of the Middle Ages, but not when told to convey harsh and terrible messages. It is evident that Ezekiel's own nature was attuned to the kind of message he was to transmit. We may surmise that he derived a secret satisfaction from his role. It might have been unbearable without such a streak in his character.

After a formal dismissal (3:4–11) in which Israel is compared unfavorably with other peoples and in which the prophet is equipped for his task like Jeremiah (Jer. 1:17–19), the audience ended. As the spirit turned Ezekiel's face toward Tel-abib the newly appointed prophet heard behind him the sound of the departure of the throne-wagon of the glory of the Lord. A noise like an earthquake was caused by the flapping of wings of the four creatures and by the rumbling of the wheels as they rose to bear the conveyance aloft. If the spirit "took Ezekiel away," this remark indicates that he needed aid in walking, just as he had needed it in arising from his prostrate state. He relates:

> I went in bitterness in the heat of my spirit, the hand of the LORD being strong upon me; and I came to the exiles at Tel-abib, who dwelt by the river Chebar. And I sat there overwhelmed among them seven days.
>
> (3:14–15)

We have had to pass quickly over the background of this vision of Ezekiel, but it is one of the most colorful and intriguing elements of the book bearing his name. Jeremiah, though receiving many revelations from the Lord, records no visionary sight of him or of the heavenly beings about him. Isaiah knew only of the six winged seraphim, giving forth adulation to the enthroned king in his heavenly palace. Ezekiel's imagination was evidently stirred by what he had seen on the march into exile, which led past cities like Carchemish, where could be observed idols enthroned on platforms resting on the backs of sculptured lions, and through Assyria where one could behold in the ruins of a place like the old capital Ashur, at the entrance of palaces and temples, great winged bulls with human heads. Perhaps he had heard natives use the name "cherub" for them, for the word is a word borrowed from the Assyro-Babylonian language. On Babylonian cylinder seals he had probably seen mythological creatures pictured—some with two, three, or four heads—and men with birds' or lions' heads. Perhaps in Babylonian cities he had seen how the idols of the local deities were taken forth in a conveyance for a procession at the New Year's festival in spring time.

Out of all this material stored in his mind there evolved in the prophet's imagination his idea of the "throne-wagon," or merkabah, and of the animals drawing it. He was intrigued, too, by the idea of "doubling" and "redoubling." The throne-wagon not only had to have four wheels—one on each side suggesting that it could move in all directions in takeoff from the ground—but "wheels within the wheels." The "eyes round about" on the rims were ornamental rosettes with central eyelike circles. The deity on the throne may be imagined in the same manner as Marduk, the Babylonian creator god, was imagined in the Babylonia of Nebuchadnezzar. Coming from Babylon to Nippur he, too, would be coming from the north. When all this weird and fanciful description was regarded as revelatory of heavenly profundities it vastly enhanced mystical speculation. Thus the very entrance to the book of Ezekiel seemed to make this book, as Saint Jerome described it, "the ocean of the Scriptures and labyrinth of the mysteries of God."

The Four Symbolical Acts

The earlier phase of Ezekiel's ministry beginning in 593 is concerned chiefly with the impending fate of Judah. How intensely the nationalistic hopes and ambitions occupied the exiles at this very time we have already seen in discussing Jeremiah's letter to them (Jer. 29:1 ff., page 184). In sharp contrast to all illusory expectations Ezekiel warns of the approach of Jerusalem's doom. He set this forth in a series of symbolical acts (4:1–5:17). Such acts are always intriguing and effective—but were even more so in ancient times, when magic was believed in more widely, than they are today.

In the first act (4:1–3) to which the date of "at the end of seven days" (3:16a) originally applied, he portrayed a siege of Jerusalem by drawing a plan of the city on a mud brick before the clay was sun-dried to full hardness. The Babylonian bricks were not shaped like ours, but were about a foot square and three inches thick. Like boys building forts with the moist sand on a bathing beach, so Ezekiel proceeded to raise earthworks against the city walls as outlined on the brick. No doubt a fascinated crowd stood about him watching the performance.

The account of this act has probably been extended later with a second one (4:4–8). Here "house of Israel" is not used for Judah as in 4:3, but rather refers to the exiles of the northern kingdom. The concern of this piece is with the length of the exile of both Israel and Judah. A prediction of that length is symbolized by having Ezekiel lie first on one side for 390 days and then on the other side for forty days. This is so impossible to conceive of that it may be regarded as the brainchild of an augmenter of Ezekiel's prophecy. The basic forty days (=years) for Judah may be the counterpart of the forty-year wilderness sojourn of the Exodus period; the 390 days (=years) for Israel may be explained as the remainder of the 430 years of Exodus 12:40 when forty are deducted. The underlying theory is that history repeats itself; the length of time of the captivity of Israel and Judah will correspond to that of the Egyptian captivity of old. The figures thus are probably drawn from a biblically based speculation.

In a third act (4:9–17) Ezekiel is told to take six different varieties of grain and legumes and make bread of the mixture. He is to eat but once a day an amount of such bread corresponding to twenty shekels in weight (about a half pound) and drink water once to the amount of a *hin* (about one quart). In the end this is interpreted as signifying that the Lord will take away "the staff of bread" from Jerusalem. With such fodder—too little in quantity and too poor in quality (for the mixture indicates that it was made to stretch out the use of the good bread flours, wheat and barley)—the people will be dismayed and waste away.

In a fourth act (5:1–17) Ezekiel is commanded to use a "sharp sword" (a term that could still apply to a knife of sixteen-inch length) and cut the hair of his head and his beard. He is to divide the resultant quantity into three parts; one part he is to burn in the midst of the city (i.e., on the brick representing it?); one part he is to put round about the city and strike at it with the sword; and one part he is to scatter with the wind after reserving from it a small number of such hairs and binding them into the hem of his garment. The basic interpretation (in the midst of considerable later sermonic elaboration) is given in the prediction that a third of the people will die of pestilence or of famine in the city; a third will be cut down by the sword in the areas adjacent to the city; and the last third will be scattered by the wind with the Lord "unsheathing the sword" after them (i.e., they will be hunted down and slain by the enemy). The hairs saved, of course, are the few who will elude the pursuers.

The Visionary Visit to the Temple

One of the most impressive elements in the story of Ezekiel's ministry is that of his translation to the temple at Jerusalem. The date of the incident was September 27, 592. Ezekiel was clearly an established prophet in the community by this time, and the "elders of Judah" (i.e., those who had been leaders in Jerusalem before their exile) were in his house to consult him. What their concern was is not stated, but one may assume that some new circumstance led them to seek an oracle. In their presence Ezekiel fell into a trance and had a vision. In it a form "in the likeness of a man" came and seized him by the hair (which naturally had grown again in the year since the haircut of 5:1) and carried him off to Jerusalem. It was already believed in the time of Elijah that a prophet was sometimes transported physically by the spirit of the Lord to some place or other (2 Kings 2:16) or that his "heart" (or mind) could detach itself from the body and be present at a distant happening (2 Kings 5:26). Out of such traditional conceptions Ezekiel could readily come to believe that his inner self was actually transported to Jerusalem. He could be under no illusions as to his physical self, however, since the elders were present with him and could assure him that he had been with them in the body all the while. On his coming out of the trance he gave the elders the report of what he had seen in the temple, and in that report must lie his answer to their question.

One need not wonder greatly how Ezekiel knew about the things he saw in the temple in his mind's eye. The exiles of course were not without information about what went on in Jerusalem. Matters of property rights, leases, and rents required the going and coming of couriers. From such individuals the priest Ezekiel may have ascertained particulars about what went on in the temple. His knowledge of the worship practiced under Jehoiakim enabled him to digest the new information and reconstruct present conditions realistically.

Ezekiel tells that on arrival at the city he saw an "image of jealousy" (no doubt a sculptured figure of a deity or demon) at or near the north entrance of the temple. He speaks of seventy elders with censers, sending up incense to figures of creeping things or loathsome beasts either painted or carved in relief on a wall (clear evidence of an Egyptian-style cult); of women weeping at the gate to the inner court for the Babylonian god Tammuz; of twenty-five men, standing between the altar and the porch of the "house," facing eastward and worshiping the sun.

The moral state of affairs in the city, too, was bad. Ezekiel, standing near the house, hears the Lord saying:

> "The guilt of the house of Israel and Judah is exceedingly great; the land is full of blood, and the city full of injustice; for they say, 'The LORD has forsaken the land, and the LORD does not see.'" (9:9)

Executioners are then summoned. They come from the direction of "the upper gate" (i.e., the one of 9:1–2; Jer. 20:2), each with his destroying weapon in his hand. They were six in number, and were attended by a man clothed in linen, with a writing case at his side suggesting that he was familiar with the record of people's sins. Babylonian mythology with its seven planetary gods, one of whom was the god Nebo (Nabu), the secretary of the gods with the pen for his symbol, may have furnished Ezekiel with the idea of these seven, though he then applies it in his own way.

The Lord now instructed the man clothed in linen to put a mark on the forehead of all those men at Jerusalem who were sighing and groaning over the abominations defiling the temple. For these were to be spared when the six executioners went to work. The latter started their activity immediately by slaying the twenty-five men standing before the "house." As they were being cut down Ezekiel fell upon his face and cried out: "Ah Lord GOD! wilt thou destroy all that remains of Israel in the outpouring of thy wrath upon Jerusalem?" (9:8). Intercession was ever a function of the true prophet (cf. Amos 7:2 ff.), and Ezekiel is no exception. But the Lord was adamant in his determination to destroy.

The man in linen evidently did not have to mark very many, for he soon returned and reported his work accomplished. Thereupon he was instructed to obtain coals from a specified place under the divine throne-wagon and to strew these over the city. One of the cherubim extracted the coals for him, whereupon he departed on his errand. The latter symbolized the future burning of the city by the will of the Lord.

The killing of the twenty-five was necessary for what now follows: the exit of the glory of the Lord from the "house" and its departure to the east gate.

The Pelatiah Incident. A retarding element is brought into the vision in 11:1–12, before its logical conclusion (11:22–25). Perhaps this passage was originally told in another account of the translation of the prophet from Babylonia to the temple in Jerusalem. For Ezekiel is taken to the east gate of the outer court, where he finds twenty-five men assembled, two of them high officials. It is obvious that their presence there is inconsistent with the presence of the Lord at that same gate as related in 10:18–19 and his exit in 11:22 ff. These men, furthermore, are clearly parallel to the twenty-five that were at the door of "the house" (8:16).

Ezekiel is told that the twenty-five had given wicked counsel in the city. The words attributed to the men must be illustrative of that counsel. They are saying "The time is not near to build houses; this city is the caldron and we are the flesh" (11:3). The meaning of this is rather puzzling. Perhaps there is a rejection here of a public demand for new housing. The ruling clique sees no necessity for building, for they have been able to occupy all the fine houses left vacant by the deported aristocracy in 597. Using what may have been a proverbial phrase, they called themselves "the meat in the pot." The Lord's reply corrects this. The meat in the pot (the best people in Jerusalem) were those whom these same men have had to put to death—an allusion to proscriptions of which we have no further information. They who now consider themselves the meat shall be brought out of the pot and be executed at the border of Israel—at Riblah (cf. 6:14), or more generally speaking, at the entrance of Hamath (47:15). Ezekiel states that as he was prophesying Pelatiah, one of the two "princes," or high officials, present in the gathering, died.

What is one to think of this peculiar report? Is this an instance of clairvoyance on the part of Ezekiel? Elsewhere, too, he shows uncanny knowledge of what is going on at the moment (24:2). It may well be, however, that news of Pelatiah's death reached him later, and that on checking the date of his vision, he found that the man actually had died on that very day.

Conclusion of the Temple Tour. We must revert again to the situation preceding the incident of chapter 11:1–13. The throne-wagon, we recall, stood at the door of the east gate, as though the Lord were taking regretful leave of his temple (10:18–22). The expected continuation, the departure of the Lord from the city, now appears at the end of chapter 11 (vv. 22–25). The assumption that these verses originally followed 10:22 seems well founded. The glory of the Lord, we learn there, went up from the midst of the city, and stood upon the mountain which is on the east side of the city. This again is to be viewed sentimentally, like the stop at the east gate. The mountain is of course the Mount of Olives. Naturally the glory of the Lord did not stay there. The ancient assumption may have been that it went to a very high mountain in the north (Isa. 14:13) or even to heaven. Out of the visionary incident and the interpretation just mentioned must have come the idea of the ascension of Christ to heaven from Olivet (Acts 1:12; Luke 24:50–51).

The temple tour of Ezekiel closes with his return to Tel-abib through the agency of the spirit of God (originally the man of 8:2?), and his report to the elders of what he had seen and heard. With its report of the words of the Lord and of the acts of the six executioners and description of the departure of the glory of the Lord, any hopes the elders may have had of hearing a message of reassurance must have been disappointed.

A Portent of Exile. An undated symbolical act that is construed as a sign, or portent, supplements the message of the temple tour in an impressive manner. Ezekiel is told to prepare an exile's baggage—a bundle slung over the shoulder, such as is portrayed on some Assyrian reliefs showing prisoners of war departing from their cities. He is to go forth from one place to another in the sight of the people carrying this baggage. He is to bring it out by day (evidently letting it lie before his house) and go forth with it in the evening "as exiles do." (That this was customary is not otherwise related, but it is reasonable to suppose that much travel was done at night in the hot season of the year.) He is to cover his face "that he may not see the land." In imagination, he of course is not in Babylonia but in Judah, and the covered face is to symbolize an effort to hide the grief or dull the edge of parting by preventing a last look at the beloved home scene.

In executing the divine command Ezekiel allegedly added an extra element: He dug through the wall of the (mud-brick) house and went forth from it. He took his bundle and left the city in the sight of those gathered to observe his strange doings. No doubt he returned after a walk to the point chosen.

The prophet was importuned on returning to explain the meaning of his act. He gave no explanation until after he had received a revelation the next morning, instructing him what to say. He then told the people that the oracle concerned Jerusalem and all who were in it. Ezekiel himself in his act was a sign, or portent, of the impending exile of Judah.

The passage has probably undergone expansion to make Ezekiel prophesy what actually happened. For it reflects on Zedekiah's escape from the city (through a hole dug in or under the wall—a thing not reported in 2 Kings 25, but probably true), his capture, and even his punishment of being blinded, and the hunting down of most of those who escaped from the city with him. Such seemingly exact foreknowledge, of course, was very impressive for later readers, but in the actual situation of Ezekiel it was of no value. The portent of the exile of the people of Jerusalem was all that mattered, and that excellently supplemented the message of chapters 8–11, which had carried the prediction to the abandonment of the city by the Lord, its destruction by fire, and the death of all but very few of its inhabitants.

The Tragedy of Jerusalem

The Causes for the Coming Destruction. In his description of the temple tour Ezekiel has given ample insight into the main reason for the Lord's quitting his city: the cultic abuses being carried on in the temple precincts. In all Jerusalem there were only a few who mourned over the abominations practiced there, and who could be spared by the executioners (9:4). But in some other revelations the prophet broadens the picture into an allegorical review of Hebrew history, showing why land and city must perish. For the land this history is developed in 20:1–44. The revelation occurred on August 15, 591, hence a year after the temple tour. Not all the elders (as in 8:1) but "certain" of them came and sat before Ezekiel. Oriental politeness must have dictated their waiting for him to speak, but of course he knew what they wanted. He received a revelation on the spot declaring that the Lord would not be inquired of by them. But he was given a free hand to "judge" them (i.e., present an indictment of them). It seems probable that these men were sympathizers of the syncretistic worship revived under Jehoiakim and then continuing in Palestine.

In any case Ezekiel reviews Israel's history starting with the Egyptian sojourn—to prove that disloyalty to the Lord goes far back and is deep-seated. He dwells on Israel's sin of holding on to the idols of Egypt, even after the Lord had promised his people to search out for them and give them "the most glorious of all lands." The Lord did not punish them in Egypt, however, lest his name be profaned in the sight of the nations among whom they dwelt. They had rebelled, too, in the wilderness, but nevertheless his "eyes spared them." When he had brought them into the promised land they rebelled by sacrificing on any high hill or under any leafy tree. And they were defiling themselves in the same way to this day. Hence the Lord refuses to be inquired of by them. He vetoes their underlying intention to be like other peoples in worshiping wood and stone: "It shall never happen."

In chapter 16, in another historical review Ezekiel uses a folktale about a female infant exposed to die but rescued and brought up and later wedded by a king. Ezekiel makes it an allegory of Jerusalem and the Lord and, perhaps inspired by Hosea, introduces the idea of the harlotrous wife into the account.

An interesting survival of historical knowledge is met with at the outset. Ezekiel says to Jerusalem, "Your origin and your birth are of the land of the Canaanites; your father was an Amorite, and your mother a Hittite" (16:3). None of these names should be taken too precisely, for Amorites and Canaanites are not clearly distinguished in the historical narratives, and "Hittite" is also used very loosely for the pre-Israelitic population of the land. The Assyrians and Neo-Babylonians likewise speak of Syria and Palestine as "Hittite-land" (*Khatti*). But that there actually was a non-Semitic element in Jerusalem about 1400 B.C. is shown by the name of its king in the Amarna letters—Abdi Hepa.

For Hepa was a Mitani goddess. Another interesting historical allusion in chapter 16 is to punishment of Judah for "harlotry" in Egypt; the Lord diminished its allotted portion and delivered it to the Philistines (16:27). This is held to be a reference to Sennacherib's act of handing over much of Judah to the Philistine cities in 701.

This harlotry theme is doubled and intensified in chapter 23, for Ezekiel there relates the story of two sisters, representing Samaria (Israel) and Jerusalem (Judah). Both, figuratively speaking, were wedded by the Lord at the time of the Exodus from Egypt. Their names were Oholah and Oholibah. It seems highly probable that Ezekiel chose these names for their pleasant sound and ready pairing, rather than for their real or supposed meaning. He may have been inspired by actual names like Oholiab (Exod. 31:6) and Oholibamah (Gen. 36:41). In the story of the harlotry of the sisters much emphasis is placed on the recent Assyrian and Neo-Babylonian periods of Hebrew history. Realism is carried to an extreme here—not for a salacious purpose, but rather to bring about horror and revulsion of feeling over the depravity displayed by Israel and Judah.

The Eagle and the Cedar. To the time of the second rebellion of Judah, but before Nebuchadnezzar reacted to that challenge, belongs this undated allegory. It describes in vivid terms the historical process that has taken place, and hints at what must now come about. An eagle came to a cedar tree on Lebanon and, plucking off the topmost of its twigs, carried it to a merchant city. Lebanon here is symbolical of Jerusalem, perhaps because of all the cedar wood in its palaces (Jer. 22:14); the eagle is representative of Nebuchadnezzar and the cedar tree of the house of David. The twig carried off is Jehoiachin and the merchant city is Babylon.

Having carried off the twig the eagle took a vine seedling and planted it, so that it should become a low spreading vine, with its branches turning toward him and its roots remaining where it stood. With this seedling Zedekiah is meant; Nebuchadnezzar thought he would have him under his control.

But there was a rival eagle in the world, and the vine bent its roots and shot forth its branches in his direction, that he might water it. This second eagle is the Egyptian Pharaoh Hophra (Apries), toward whom Zedekiah leaned. What, so the prophet asks, will the first eagle do? Will he not pluck up this seedling so that it lies on the ground and withers?

In the elucidation of this allegory (17:11-20) Ezekiel restates the historical process in nonfigurative terms. A valuable bit of information comes to light in the statement that the Babylonian ruler had made a covenant with Zedekiah (apparently in Babylon) and placed him under oath (with a "vassal treaty") when appointing him king, but that the latter now had rebelled by sending ambassadors to Egypt that they might give him horses and a large army. Here Ezekiel asks:

> "Will he succeed? Can a man escape who does such things? Can he break the covenant and yet escape?" (17:15)

The continuation of the discourse presupposes knowledge of what actually happened to Zedekiah, and probably is later supplementation. A further addition is the closing prophecy of a restoration of the kingship (17:22-24).

A Fateful Decision. Late in 589 news must have reached Tel-abib that the Babylonian army, headed by the king, was about to start on a campaign from its Syrian base. No one knew what Nebuchadnezzar's objective would be. There was general anxiety about it among the exiles. Ezekiel was told by the Lord to draw a picture of a fork in a road and to mark one branch with a signpost "to the Rabbah of the Ammonites" and the other "to Judah and Jerusalem the fortified." The explanation given him was:

> For the king of Babylon stands at the parting of the way, at the head of the two ways, to use divination; he shakes the arrows, he consults the teraphim, he looks at the liver. (21:21)

Nebuchadnezzar uses three kinds of divination in deciding what to do, but only one type is made vivid: "He shakes the arrows (in the quiver)." Into his right hand comes the lot (i.e., the arrow) marked "for Jerusalem." The other two kinds of divination are not described by Ezekiel. Hepatoscopy, or divination by the sheep's liver, is well known from Babylonian sources. That with the "teraphim" (here per-

haps a mask as divine symbol, used in oracle practice; cf. Zech. 10:2)
has not yet received clarification. When the inquiries by these two
confirmed the result of the one made by the lottery-arrows, the war cry
must have been raised and the army, with its siege equipment, set in
motion to march on Jerusalem.

Ezekiel and the Beginning of the Siege. On January 15, 588, Ezekiel
received a revelation telling him to write down this day, because on it
the siege of Jerusalem was beginning (24:1–2). Since describing Nebuchadnezzar's augury at the parting of the roads, enough time may have
elapsed for news vindicating Ezekiel's prophecy to reach the exiles. His
clairvoyant knowledge of the first day of the siege need occasion no
surprise in view of his awareness of the day of the death of Pelatiah
(11:13). After making the announcement the prophet was commanded
by the Lord to perform a symbolical act with a copper cooking pot,
by stewing meat in it over a fire. The point of this has apparently been
lost from the instruction (now ending in 24:5), but may be guessed;
it was to signify that the people (or classes of people?) in the city
would be like meat being stewed in a kettle.

This original interpretation was evidently dropped when two supplementary oracles (or two versions of the same one) were added, each
beginning with "Woe to the bloody city." The first mentions that the
pot is rusty on the inside, but does not follow that up; it is chiefly concerned with the idea that no choice is to be made between the pieces
of meat that are to be taken from the pot (i.e., all the people are
equally wicked because of the bloodshed in the city). The second oracle
takes up the point of the rust in the pot; Ezekiel is to set the empty
vessel on the coals, so that the rust (or better, verdigris) may be melted
out of it. This corrosion is interpreted as the city's "filthy lewdness"
(no doubt in the figurative sense of idolatrous propensity). But the
suggested procedure cannot succeed. The point of this addition is that
the city will be burned after the people are taken out of it.

The Prophet's Tragedy. Perhaps nowhere in the book of Ezekiel does
the prophet appear as human or as great as in the personal loss that he
was called upon to bear. He was given short notice of it in a revelation:
He was to lose his wife.

Also the word of the LORD came to me: "Son of man, behold, I am about
to take the delight of your eyes away from you at a stroke; yet you shall not
mourn or weep nor shall your tears run down." (24:15–16)

He related this revelation to the people in the morning and at evening,
as he records, his wife died. The "delight of his eyes" he called her.
His sole remaining joy was taken from him. She had endured with him
the long march from Palestine to Babylonia and the hard life on the
ruin mound where mud bricks had to be made to fashion a hovel in
which to live, where toil had to be expended to put into shape old
canals and to plant seed given them by the government for the preservation of life. But Ezekiel was instructed to give no outward sign of
grief, to hold no public mourning, or follow the usual customs of
mourners. Instead he was to put on his head covering and his shoes,
as one going about his business. He records that he did this the following morning—hence, no doubt, as he went forth and buried her on
some part of the tell, after the manner of such settlers.

Those who turned out for the burial marveled at this strange disregard of the proprieties of mourning, and asked him to explain why
he was acting thus. He replied:

"Say to the house of Israel, Thus says the Lord GOD: Behold, I will profane
my sanctuary, the pride of your power, the delight of your eyes, and the
desire of your soul; and your sons and your daughters whom you left behind
shall fall by the sword. And you shall do as I have done; you shall not
cover your lips, nor eat the bread of mourners. Your turbans shall be on
your heads and your shoes on your feet; you shall not mourn or weep, but
you shall pine away in your iniquities and groan to one another. Thus shall
Ezekiel be to you a sign; according to all that he has done you shall do.
When this comes, then you will know that I am the Lord GOD." (24:21–24)

He was setting the exiles an example of how to receive the news of the
destruction of the temple, the delight of their eyes (cf. Hag. 2:3) and
likewise that of death by the sword of children left behind them. Here
was a Stoic teaching Stoicism, though without the rational justification
that a Greek would have offered for such a philosophy. It was the
product of a divine directive. He understood that not only his words
but his life was to be a sign to men. This sign of his present conduct
meant: Bury the past, and work for the future. Let not grief over what

cannot be changed overwhelm you, lest your enemies taunt you (Ps. 137:2). Prepare for the day when you will return to Zion.

Ezekiel and the Hope of Egyptian Aid. While the siege of Jerusalem was in progress, on January 7, 587, Ezekiel pronounced a poetic oracle against Egypt (29:1–5). Reliance on Egypt, Tyre, and the Transjordan states had been the very basis of Judah's rebellion. Ezekiel compares the Pharaoh (at this time Hophra) to a great dragon (crocodile?) that lies in the midst of his streams. The prophet asserts that he will be pulled out with hooks in his jaws (by Nebuchadnezzar) and his body cast on the open field.

Several prose pieces are appended to this poem, predicting sword and desolation for Egypt, and a restoration—but to very humble status—after forty years.

In a fresh series of oracles in chapter 30 Egypt's doom is elaborately described. Nebuchadnezzar and his people, "the most terrible of the nations," will destroy the land. A prose oracle (30:20–21 with later supplements appended) was delivered on April 30, 587. In it Ezekiel receives the revelation, "Son of man, I have broken the arm of Pharaoh king of Egypt." It seems certain that a battle had taken place—perhaps the one for which Nebuchadnezzar temporarily withdrew his forces from Jerusalem (cf. Jer. 37:5). The Egyptians must have been badly worsted. The damage done Hophra evidently made unlikely his being able to wield his sword again very soon.

In a fine poetic passage (31:2–9) dated at the time when Jerusalem's end was nearing, Ezekiel compared Pharaoh and his multitude to a great cedar of Lebanon that was envied by all the trees in the garden. A prose oracle (31:10–14) then describes the cutting down of this tree by the Babylonians. A further, rather artificial, supplement (31:14 ff.) describes the tree as going down to Sheol (=Hades) in imitation of 32:31 ff.

Ezekiel's Dumbness and his Release. A special but undated revelation for Ezekiel himself has been appended to chapter 24:

> "And you, son of man, on the day when I take from them their stronghold, their joy and glory, the delight of their eyes and their heart's desire, and also their sons and daughters, on that day a fugitive will come to you to

report to you the news. On that day your mouth will be opened to the fugitive, and you shall speak and be no longer dumb. So you will be a sign to them; and they will know that I am the LORD. (24:25-27)

The words presuppose that something has been related which has been lost, namely, that the prophet was told that henceforth he would be stricken with dumbness (cf. 3:22-27; 29:21) until he received the news of the fall of Jerusalem. Since it is unlikely that Ezekiel's speechlessness could have lasted the entire period of the siege (for he seems to have spoken oracles for part of that time; cf. 30:20; 31:1), one may assume that his condition befell him after June 21, 587 (the date of 31:1)—hence during the last months of the siege of Jerusalem. The speechlessness of the Lord's prophet at this stage seems a fitting accompaniment to the awesome final act of the great historical tragedy.

Release from the speechless state was to come when news of the fall of the city arrived. In chapter 33 we hear of this sequel. What is related there is somewhat surprising. In view of Ezekiel's foreknowledge of the day of the beginning of the siege one would expect him to have a similar awareness of the day of its end. However, due to his dumbness and its physical or psychiatric causes, his ability to receive revelations may have been interrupted. We have seen how Jeremiah, when carried off from Mizpah, was unable to receive a revelation until ten days after one was requested (Jer. 42:7). In his case no serious psychiatric or physical complications were involved, though the disturbance by unwelcome events may have unsettled his psychic receptivity. Ezekiel's condition evidently was such that the news had to come in the normal way.

The date and manner of the arrival of the news of the city's fall as given in 33:21 raise questions. The fifth day of the tenth month of the twelfth year of the exile would have been January 9, 585. That would be a year and a half after the actual fall of Jerusalem (August 28, 587). It seems impossible that it would have taken so long for news of this event to reach Tel-abib. A textual emendation of the "twelfth" to the "eleventh" year is imperative and widely accepted. That would bring the date back to January 19, 586, nearly five months after the fall of the city. This still seems too long, for the news must have reached Babylon by Nebuchadnezzar's mounted couriers within two weeks. The Jews at Babylon were certainly informed at once of the destruction, and word could have reached Tel-abib a day or two later. One recent commentator thinks the people at Tel-abib knew the fact of the fall earlier, but that the arrival of an escapee (Hebrew, *palit*), who could tell them the details of what had happened, was the important thing to them. However, in view of the stress laid on the date of the beginning of the siege (24:2), one would look for corresponding weight to be accorded to the one at the end of it. That weight would best be assured if Tel-abib got the first news of the fall as such from an escapee. The text certainly gives the impression that the man was fulfilling this function. Perhaps "tenth" month is an error for "seventh" month, the fifth day of which would have been September 23, 587—not quite a month after August 28. That would be fast time for the arrival of a bearer of tidings. Whether the man was a pro-Chaldean prisoner who got permission to bear tidings, or actually made his escape to the Ammonites (cf. Jer. 41:1, 10) and went by some desert route to Chaldea, is a thing one can only speculate about. In the second instance, one could assume that he had previously served as messenger from Judah, enjoyed immunity from arrest, and knew the way.

We hear nothing of whether the exiles followed the example given by the prophet at the death of his wife, and received all the sad news of the destruction of their beloved city without displaying emotion.

Ezekiel and Tyre

With his speech restored Ezekiel could renew his prophetic activity. His thoughts must have been very much concerned with the belief (and hope) that the "allies" of Judah, who had left it to perish, would share its fate. Next to Egypt Tyre was the most powerful of these states. A trilogy of prophecies against Tyre is preserved in Ezek. 26–28. They are among the most interesting and culturally informative prophecies against the nations in the Old Testament. The opening one (26:1–6) had a date, which, however, has been damaged by loss of the month-number. Since it is from the eleventh year and assumes the fall of Jerusalem, it may have been uttered in the fall of 587 or early months of 586. Tyre is described as exultant over Judah's debacle; it exclaims "Aha, the gate of the peoples (i.e., Jerusalem) is broken, it has swung open to me." Jerusalem, it seems, was the passageway to commerce with

Transjordan and Arabia. Tyre now saw an opportunity to handle this commerce directly, without paying taxes and tolls to middleman Judah. But Ezekiel predicts that the Lord is going to bring up "many nations" against Tyre, and make her a bare rock—a place on which to spread fishnets.

This first general prediction is followed by a parallel, more specific one (26:7–15). According to this passage Nebuchadnezzar, the "king of kings," will come upon Tyre from the north, no doubt with auxiliary troops under their kings. The description of the siege of the city is given in a manner ignoring its island location, and presumably was derived from some typical siege story. A third oracle sketches the effect of Tyre's fall on the princes of the sea (26:15–18), while a fourth, in more mythical terms, portrays the city's submergence under the waves and descent to Hades (26:19–21).

An elaborate lamentation on the ship Tyre in chapter 27 (heavily expanded in vv. 10–25 with prose matter highly important for ancient commercial history) dwells on the wreck of this glorious vessel in a storm and the lament of peoples of the world at the tragedy. An oracle against the "prince" (i.e., king) of Tyre (28:1–19) compares him to the first man in the garden of Eden, which is imagined as on a mountain and having trees bearing precious stones, and a cherub for a guardian. The latter casts the prince out because of his pride and iniquity. But the fate of the king passes over into that of the city at the close.

Nebuchadnezzar actually undertook a siege of Tyre soon after the fall of Jerusalem. Josephus quotes a Greek historical writer to the effect that the Babylonian besieged Tyre for thirteen years (585–573). Nebuchadnezzar apparently sought to do what Alexander accomplished centuries later—construct a causeway over to the island city. Since we have no Babylonian reports about the siege, we can get no very clear idea of what happened. A court calendar of Nebuchadnezzar lists a "King of Tyre" among the courtiers. The city must thus have come to an agreement of some sort with the Babylonian. Cuneiform texts written at Tyre lift the veil a little bit. They show that a Babylonian commissar was present there in 564 alongside of the new king Baal.

An oracle of Ezekiel in chapter 29, appended to one against Egypt already mentioned, also helps to clarify the situation. It reflects on the termination of actual operations against Tyre. It is dated April 26, 571

B.C. Matters thus came to a final decision after the death of the Tyrian king Ithobaal II:

> "Son of man, Nebuchadrezzar king of Babylon made his army labor hard against Tyre; every head was made bald and every shoulder was rubbed bare; yet neither he nor his army got anything from Tyre to pay for the labor that he had performed against it. Therefore thus says the Lord GOD: Behold, I will give the land of Egypt to Nebuchadrezzar king of Babylon; and he shall carry off its wealth and despoil it and plunder it; and it shall be the wages for his army. I have given him the land of Egypt as his recompense for which he labored, because they worked for me, says the Lord GOD."
>
> (29:18–20)

The oracle is interesting for what it reveals about the effort expended to build a causeway, and its belief that Nebuchadnezzar acted for the Lord, but got scant reward. The Lord promises Nebuchadnezzar Egypt's spoil as recompense for the labor he did for him in this siege.

Ezekiel's View of Those Left in Palestine

As the new groups of exiles came to Babylonia to be settled on the sites of other towns devastated in past wars, unfavorable reports must have come to Ezekiel about the Jews left in Judah (Jer. 39:10). There was a feeling of satisfaction among them over their prospects. This led him to denounce them (33:23–29). He quotes their boast "Abraham was only one man, yet he got possession of the land; but we are many; the land is surely given us to possess." The prophet has heard about their disregard of God's law, their idolatry, violence, and adultery. He asks "shall you then possess the land?" The new nation of the future, he declares, will not consist of them and their descendants—they will be exterminated and the mountains of Israel will become so desolate that none will pass through them.

In these predictions as now formulated there is knowledge of events otherwise unreported. This is proved sufficiently by the bare fact of Jer. 52:30 that 745 persons were deported in Nebuchadnezzar's twenty-third year (582). This is the same year in which that king is said to have made war on the Ammonites and Moabites (Josephus, *Antiquities*, 10, 9, 7). He may have taken occasion to mop up all the bandit nests that had developed in Judah after the murder of the governor Gedaliah (Jer. 41:1 ff.).

Ezekiel's oracle against the remnant in Judah may have brought him a brief moment of popularity (33:30–33). The exiles of 597 must have held themselves to be the owners of their lands, and have expected to reoccupy them at some future date. Furthermore, as a prophet whose predictions had been so fully vindicated by the events, Ezekiel's prestige must have risen enormously. People talked about him and came and sat before him to hear what he would say. But a word of the Lord taught him to evaluate this new prestige properly.

> "And, lo, you are to them like one who sings love songs with a beautiful voice and plays well on an instrument, for they hear what you say, but they will not do it." (33:32)

Isaiah had once assumed the role of a singer of love songs (Isa. 5:1–7), but Ezekiel is only compared to a popular minstrel. The Lord advises him why his sermonizing leaves men unchanged. "Their heart is set on their gain." No better diagnosis could be given of what people are like and what preaching can accomplish without aid of the Spirit. But the Lord adds a prediction to strengthen his prophet. "When this comes (i.e., the judgment over those left in Judah?)—and come it will!—then they (i.e., the exiles in Babylonia) will know that a prophet has been among them" (33:33).

The Turning Point in the Message of Ezekiel

Somewhere at the beginning of this final period of his ministry Ezekiel was given a new function—that of "watchman" (33:1–9). That this was a new development has been somewhat obscured by its anticipation in a brief summary in 3:16–21. The latter piece was evidently put in that position to give a complete picture of the prophet's functions at the outset.

The figure of the watchman is taken from that of the observer posted to report danger to his town in time of war. If such a one saw enemies approaching he had to blow the trumpet. If he failed to do so and harm resulted to anyone (e.g., a person out in the field) he was held to have incurred bloodguilt and had to pay for it with his life. But if he did his duty and gave warning he was blameless, if those who heard the trumpet did not act to save themselves.

In like manner Ezekiel is to be a moral watchman—to discern where sin is being done and to warn of the consequences. It is presupposed here that the justice of God may mete out death for sin, that God may command Ezekiel to go and tell someone that he will die unless he turns from his wicked way. If Ezekiel fails to do this and the man dies, Ezekiel will be held responsible for his life; for the warning might have saved the man from death. But if he carries out his instruction and the man fails to turn from his wicked ways and dies, Ezekiel will not be held responsible.

This new departure in Ezekiel's activities was indeed of enormous importance. Paul's concern with the individual must have been greatly influenced by Ezekiel's example. Through Paul "the care of souls" became a significant factor in theories of the Christian ministry. The prerogative assumed by the clergy to warn or reprove the individual gave it an exceptional status. However, this was only a vestigial remnant of the watchman role of Ezekiel. His ability to warn of death could not easily be imitated.

The divine purpose in assigning the watchman's function to Ezekiel was to create in the exile a disciplined people—one that would be fit to return to the land and become the beginning of a new Israel. But other things were needed to keep this people alive and intact against the day when it should play a new historical role—new doctrine, consciousness of the mistakes of the past, faith in revival, a suitable ideal, a vision of the shape of things to be. All this Ezekiel helped to provide.

The Individualistic Teaching. There was a tendency among those left in Palestine and apparently also among the exiles in Babylonia to blame the former generations for the misfortunes of the nation. It found expression in the cynical saying "The fathers have eaten sour grapes, and the children's teeth are set on edge" (18:2). (The translation "set on edge," which means "have a tingling sensation" is not the meaning of the Hebrew, which is "were blunted." Eating or chewing sour fruit was held to have the effect of blunting the teeth.) Such a proverb implied criticism of the Lord's world government as unfair. Over against this the Lord proclaims that henceforth no one in Israel is to use this proverb. All souls are his—he can take them when he chooses. But he desires to act justly. His rule is: Only the one personally guilty shall die for his sins.

What constitutes personal righteousness is then set forth, on the basis of a mixed set of rules of conduct, including cultic, ritualistic, moral, and prophetic-social elements. A man righteous in this sense will live (i.e., not die prematurely), and it will not affect his fate if a son of his is unrighteous and does all that is forbidden. Such a son will suffer the consequence of death for his own sins. Yet if that individual has begotten a son who is righteous, that son in turn will not suffer any evil consequence from having had an unrighteous father.

In a fresh approach (18:21 ff.) further consequences are drawn from this teaching. No evildoer is to be regarded as lost, nor any righteous man as saved until the final returns are in. While there is life there is opportunity for a change in either direction. The Lord, however, is not a harsh judge.

> Have I any pleasure in the death of the wicked, says the Lord GOD, and not rather that he should turn from his way and live? (18:23)

All the evil a man has done can be overlooked if he changes his ways. Ezekiel then issues the prophetic call to repentance, and urges his hearers to get themselves a new heart and a new spirit (contrast 11:19; 36:26 ff. where these must be divinely given). And he asks "Why will you die, O House of Israel?"

Set forth with all the emphasis of which Ezekiel was capable, this new dogma gradually settled itself in the Jewish mind. But human nature being what it is, the teaching was to have some unforeseen consequences. It led to scrutiny of other people's lives, and to cruel inferences if a man died prematurely or suffered illness and other afflictions. This created the problem that tortured so many afflicted psalmists—the feeling of being regarded as "sinners"—and was handled so powerfully in the book of Job. But for Ezekiel's contemporaries the teaching may have been beneficial. It must have led to a more intro-spective walk of life, and prepared the way for the compilation of the Torah, or law, setting forth God's requirements in detail. This law was the great gift of the exiles to the future of their people, when it was brought to Jerusalem by Ezra "the scribe of the God of Heaven."

The Causes of the Calamity. It was part of Ezekiel's task to draw the conclusions from the seeming end to the history of his people. The mistakes and failures had to be uncovered and their lessons heeded, if there was to be any future revival. In one oracle (22:23–31) which is much like Zeph. 3:1–5 in pattern Ezekiel gives a sweeping indictment of princes, priests, officials, prophets, and people. The Lord had sought for a man among them who would build up the wall and stand in the breach before him for the land, that he should not destroy it, but he had found none. So destruction had to take its inevitable course. There is a real understanding here of the significance of historical junctures. Where is the man who can stand in the breach in the hour of peril and hold back the foe? Ezekiel had used this figure at an earlier occasion and with prophets in mind (13:5). Here he may have thought of others as well. There are occasions when such saviors of nations appear, but if none is found, the judgment of God takes its course. That had been the case with Judah.

Ezekiel dealt with the failure of the leaders—especially "princes" and officials—to lead properly in his great indictment of the "shepherds" (34:1–24). The theme is already handled very briefly in Jer. 23:1 ff., but here is given more elaborate treatment. The Lord himself will have to assume the shepherd's role and rescue the sheep from exploitation. The beautiful added touch of the shepherd seeking out and rescuing scattered sheep has elicited a Christian counterpart in the discourse on the Good Shepherd in chapter 10 of the Gospel of John. The idea of the Lord's judging "between sheep and sheep, rams and he-goats" (34:17) evidently provided the stimulus for the powerful description of the Last Judgment in Matt. 25:31 ff.

Appended to Ezekiel's discourse is a prophecy that stands apart from the main line of thought, for it thinks of "one" future human shepherd (here figurative for "king"):

> And I will set up over them one shepherd, my servant David, and he shall feed them: he shall feed them and be their shepherd. And I, the LORD, will be their God, and my servant David shall be prince among them; I, the LORD, have spoken. (34:23–24)

The idea of a united Hebrew kingdom is thus entertained. "My servant David," however, does not mean the return of David in person any more than it does in Hos. 3:5, but rather the first king of the new kingdom, who will be of Davidic lineage—presumably a descendant of Jehoiachin. The same thought will appear again in chapter 37:22, 24 ff. (along with the "paradise" motif). In a further supplement dealing with natural conditions of those coming times (34:26 ff.), the present insecurity and desolation in Palestine are to be replaced by blessed conditions. The "covenant of peace," involving banishment of the wild beasts, is similar to Hosea 2:18, though less broadly stated. Thus supplemented the chapter became an inspiring unit for the reader. But at the time of the calamity the people were not yet ready for such hopeful thoughts. How difficult it was to rouse them to look forward to anything is shown by the next piece to be considered.

Ezekiel in the "Valley." No one can imagine what it must have meant to the survivors of the Jewish people to contemplate in all its magnitude the disaster that had taken place. Those who perished from the sword, famine, and disease in 587 must have outnumbered those who were left. The hundreds of thousands had shrunk to thousands. The prophet's belief that his people would again be reestablished in their homeland some day must have seemed utopian to the exiles of Tel-abib. Dejectedly they said, "Our bones are dried up, and our hope is lost; we are clean cut off" (37:11). But the prophet was given a revelation assuring him of God's ability to do the impossible (37:1–14). He felt himself carried out by the spirit into "the midst of the valley" or plain—presumably to a place more distant from Tel-abib than he could go to on foot. Actually he must have lain in a trance in his own house, as at the occasion of the temple tour.

The place in the plain where he imagined himself set down was one that he must have known was full of skeletons. We may assume that it was a battlefield, possibly one on which bitter fighting had taken place when the Babylonians drove back the Assyrians from this area about 622. Bones from that time would still exist, but also be "very dry." In Ezekiel's imagination this battlefield and its bones became metamorphosed into the land of Israel with its vast army of the dead. The Lord posed the question to him "Son of man, can these bones live?" The prophet answered helplessly "O Lord God, thou knowest." He then was told to prophesy to these bones that they would again be clothed with flesh and sinew and skin and be endowed with breath and come alive. From this they would know that he is the Lord—the almighty. After he had carried out the command Ezekiel in his mind's eye saw the process of resurrection take place. They "stood upon their feet, an exceedingly great host."

In the interpretation (37:11 ff.) the Lord informs Ezekiel that "these bones are the whole house of Israel" thus (secondarily?) extending the national picture to include the people of the northern kingdom that had perished in 733 and 721. As the dry bones were revived so Israel shall be revived, and brought home to its land. According to a further extension forsaking the idea of bones on the surface of the plain, the graves are to be opened and the dead of God's people raised—a significant development preparing the way for the resurrection doctrine that came up among the Palestinian Jews in the second century B.C. The promise of God, "I will place my spirit in you," hints that the restored nation will not be carnal and rebellious like the people of the past, but imbued with moral and spiritual strength through the same creative power that will call it out of death to life. This was the message that Ezekiel was able to convey to the despondent and hopeless at Tel-abib.

The Two Sticks. The remark about a restoration of the "whole house of Israel" (37:11) seemed to require further explanation, so Ezekiel was told to perform a symbolical act with two sticks (37:15 ff.). One was to be marked "For Judah, and the children of Israel associated with him," and the other "For Joseph and all the house of Israel associated with him." The fact that Judah had incorporated Israelite areas such as Benjamin, Dan, and Simeon is hinted at in the inscription on its piece. Ezekiel was to join the sticks together. (That would seem to imply that they were pieces of one stick that had been broken.) In the same manner, then, the Lord would join Israel and Judah together. In the present form of the text Ezekiel predicts that both will be under one king—the Lord's servant "David." This was similarly made the climactic prophecy in 34:23 ff.

The Prophecy of Gog of Magog. Ezekiel had the idea that history would repeat itself in another cycle, but that the outcome would be different. A new and better Israel would enter the Holy Land, and since it would enjoy the Lord's favor by avoiding the sins of the past, it would be under his protection. When a mighty onset of peoples from the north invaded the Holy Land (as it must, in order to provide a demonstration of the truth of his belief), Israel would not suffer, as it had under Tiglathpileser III, Shalmaneser V, Sennacherib, and

Nebuchadnezzar; for the Lord would destroy the foe. That day of victory corresponds to "the day of the LORD" for the coming of which the people of the past had hoped, but which they were unworthy to see (Amos 5:18). So interesting was this theme to the prophet and his amplifiers that two partially parallel prophecies are devoted to it (chapters 38 and 39).

The host that will invade the reestablished Hebrew state has for its leader "Gog, of the land of Magog, the chief prince of Meshech and Tubal." The land of Magog had best be discounted geographically, for it was probably manufactured to rhyme with Gog, and it is not to be found among the hundreds of known geographical names of the ancient Near East. Its mention in Gen. 10:2 is probably dependent on the reference in Ezekiel. Since "of the land of Magog" is not repeated between 38:3 and 39:1 the name may not even have been coined by Ezekiel himself, for whom Gog was the chief prince of Meshech and Tubal. These two names are real (cf. 27:13; 32:26; Gen. 10:2), though the late Hebrew pronunciation of them by editors (who had only the consonants Mshk and Tbl in their manuscripts) is not quite accurate; for these names appear together in the Assyrian inscriptions as Mushki and Tabali. The former is basically Phrygia; the latter is the region at the headwaters of the rivers Sarus (*Jihan*) and Pyramus (*Seihun*), north of Cilicia.

But where did Ezekiel get the name Gog? It seems certain that he did not invent it, but rather drew it from historical legend. Just as he can speak of "David" as king of the future, so he could take the name of some formidable individual named Gog and use it for an evil figure of the future. There was only one man in history with such a name. Since the Hebrew consonants (gwg) can be pronounced either as Gōg or Gūg (the former being the choice only of the Masoretes) there should be no hesitation in identifying the man with Gyges of Lydia (685–652), whose name the Assyrian inscriptions give as Gūg (u). The historical Gyges was king of Lydia (Lud in Genesis 10:22, but not mentioned here by Ezekiel). Gyges had expanded his power far to the east in Asia Minor, where he warred with the Cimmerians, who had come westward from the Caucasus. Legend may have fused him with Midas of Phrygia (who appears in the Assyrian inscriptions as Mita of Mushki). Hence the ruler of Lydia lent the personal name and the ruler of Phrygia the regional names to the imaginary figure of the future

"Gog, chief prince of Meshech and Tubal." It may be that Gyges's
return was expected, as that of Alexander or of Nero was in later
centuries. Such an expectation, we may hold, was known and utilized
by Ezekiel for his purpose.

The Lord, according to the first prophecy (chapter 38), is to turn
Gog about (into a different direction than he was bent on going),
with all his army of horsemen, and draw him toward Palestine. A later
addition expands this host to include Persia, Cush ("Ethiopia"), Put
(Libya), Gomer (the Cimmerians, the enemies of the historical Gyges)
and Beth-Togarmah (a region in eastern Asia Minor, west of the
Euphrates). Mention of African peoples seems especially strange but
exhibits the trend toward universalizing the attack.

The prophecy is repetitious, and there is no need of dwelling on
it here in detail. Suffice it to say that Gog's intent to despoil the reestablished peaceful Israel is to be thwarted by the Lord with earthquakes and other terrors of nature. The conclusion is: "So I will show
my greatness and my holiness and make myself known in the eyes of
many nations. Then they will know that I am the LORD."

The second Gog prophecy (chapter 39) dwells but briefly on Gog's
invasion and disaster. He and his host will fall on the mountains of
Israel and be a prey to birds and beasts. In this end of Gog one may
find a partial echo of the end of the Gyges of history, who met death
at the hands of the Cimmerians in 652. For the Assyrian king Ashurbanipal relates that he had prayed to his gods Ashur and Ishtar that
the corpse of Gyges (who had double-crossed him) be cast down
before his foes, and his bones carried away; and he notes with satisfaction that his prayer had been fulfilled.

This second prophecy, however, dwells more on the sequel to the
calamity than does the first. The important thing here is the burial
of Gog and his host in the Valley of the Travelers (Hebrew, Ge-ha-
'oberim) "east of the sea." This sea can hardly be the Dead Sea, or
the Mediterranean, and so must be the Sea of Galilee. According to
the Hebrew word used, the valley (Hebrew, ge) must be a narrow one.
A track known in modern times as "the road of the Hauranians," crossing the Jordan south of the Sea of Galilee and formerly much used
for travel from the Hauran to Haifa, has been suggested for it. However, it is doubtful whether Ezekiel had local knowledge of this area.
His valley may be a product of fancy, and the name "travelers" (He-

brew, '*oberim*) could be derived from the men who "pass through" (Hebrew, '*oberim*) the area subsequently searching for human bones (39:14 ff.), lest they remain unburied and defile a land that is to be holy. The valley is to be known as *Hamon-gog* "Gog's multitude." Whether the city of Hamonah, mentioned in what seems to be a gloss (39:16) as lying thereabouts, really existed is likewise uncertain.

The Gog prophecy stimulated later apocalypticists—notably the author of the book of Revelation (20:8 ff.). But there it is no longer the Lord who draws Gog to Palestine, but rather Satan. The attack takes place at the end of the millennial period and is directed at the city of the Saints of the Most High. Rabbinic texts likewise are fond of dwelling on this subject. Even Mohammed (Sura 18, 86 ff.) knows of Yajuj and Majuj, whom he imagines as two peoples behind the Iron Gate, with which Alexander the Great was said to have barred the pass through the Caucasus in the far north.

While the material in chapters 38–39 has obviously accumulated gradually as a variety of hands worked over it in the course of time, the basic conception can well have been Ezekiel's. The event it predicts will be the great vindication of the Lord in the eyes of the nations, and a demonstration to his own people that they could always have been under his protection and have been spared the travail of their history had they walked in his ways.

Ezekiel's Blueprint for the Future

In 37:15–28 the restoration of Israel is prophesied and in the Gog chapters it is presupposed. But in the final section of the book of Ezekiel (chapters 40–48) the prophet reports a grandiose vision of the restored nation given him April 19, 573. It thus antedates by two years the oracle for Nebuchadnezzar (29:17 ff.), but must synchronize rather closely with the conclusion of the siege of Tyre. It was perhaps a significant time to think about the future of the Holy Land.

As in the case of the temple tour (chapters 8–11) Ezekiel felt transported to the homeland. He was set down on a very high mountain (40:2). This seemingly presupposes the altered topography of Isa. 2:2 (=Mic. 4:1). Before him was something "like a city." A man whose appearance was "like bronze"—evidently a divine aide (cf. Zech. 2:1; Ezek. 8:2)—stood ready with flaxen line and long measuring reed to guide him through the temple, which of course was of paramount interest to the priest Ezekiel. The man instructed him to pay careful attention, so that he could report to the house of Israel what he had seen (40:3-4).

The New Temple. Beginning at the wall and eastern gate of the temple, the guide describes the outer court and inner court and their gateways, together with the side rooms. The outer court was on a platform and the inner court on a still higher platform. On the west side of the inner court stood the actual temple or "house" with its vestibule and adjacent structures. It is of interest that on the inside of the inner temple the walls and doors bore carvings of two-faced cherubim, each with a face turned Janus-like toward palm trees on the right and left. One face was human, the other that of a lion. The overall measurements of the outer court given last constituted a perfect square of 500 x 500 cubits. The cubit used was the "long" cubit, a handbreadth wider than the standard one (40:5; 43:13), about one foot eight inches long.

Returning to his starting point at the eastern gate (43:1 ff.) Ezekiel had the great experience of seeing "the glory of the God of Israel" coming from the east, as he had seen it departing in his temple tour. He fell upon his face, but the spirit lifted him up and brought him back to the inner court. Here he noted that the glory of the Lord had taken up its residence and filled the "house." He thereupon heard one speaking out of the temple (evidently the Lord himself), declaring that this was the place of his throne, where he would dwell in the midst of his people forever. Defilement of the Lord's holy name, such as had been committed in the past and had led to the people's being consumed by his anger, is henceforth to be avoided. A special new point supplements the familiar charges about past sins; kings had been buried adjacent to the temple (probably an allusion to Manasseh and Amon, 2 Kings 21:18, 26). These bodies must be removed and nothing like that must again be done. Ezekiel is then commanded to convey to the house of Israel what he has seen.

Rather surprisingly a description of the altar and regulations concerning it are injected here (43:13-27). This, one might think, would have been mentioned in the account of the inner court before dealing with the vestibule of the temple (40:48). But perhaps the altar would have blocked the way unduly for the landing of the throne-wagon. The altar was to be a staged one, like a miniature Babylonian temple tower.

Brought back to the east gate once more, Ezekiel found it shut and was informed that it should remain shut. No one should enter here because the glory of the Lord had entered by it. An appended later modification permits the "prince" to sit in the gateway and eat bread (a meal) before the Lord. But he is to enter and leave (from within) by the vestibule of the gate (44:1–3).

Ezekiel thereupon is brought back again to the upper terrace and falls upon his face before the glory of the Lord that fills the temple. Here he receives further direction to communicate to the house of Israel (44:4 ff.). No foreigner is to enter the sanctuary. The Levites are to be degraded to do menial service, while the priestly prerogatives are to belong exclusively to the house of Zadok; for both groups rules are laid down. Instruction is then given as to the land allotment and areas to be set apart—portions of the priests, of the Levites, and of the "prince" (45:1–8). This subsequently receives mention again in the larger program for the entire country, which is provided in chapter 48. But here the reference to the prince's portion is followed by rules concerning his conduct of office (45:9–17). His duty in connection with sacrifices provided the opportunity to interpolate here a whole section on feasts and sacrifices (45:18–46:15). But then we revert to a final law about what the prince may do in matters of inheritance (46:16–18).

Next Ezekiel is conducted to the chambers of the priests and the place where certain extremely sacred sacrifices were boiled; also to the outer court to see the kitchens where the sacrifices of the people were cooked (46:19–24).

The River of Life. Once more Ezekiel is brought back to the inner temple. Here, meanwhile, water has come gushing forth from the south end of the threshold of the "house." He then had to go around via the north gate to the east side of the temple, where he found the water emerging on the south side of the east gate. As the man measured off its course it became ankle-deep, knee-deep, waist-deep, and then too deep to ford. Going back upstream he noticed that it had become lined with trees. He was told by his guide that when it reached the sea (i.e., the Dead Sea) the waters of the latter would be purified and begin to swarm with fish. Fishermen would line the seashore from En-gedi (in the south) to En-eglaim (near Qumran) in the north. Wonderful trees bearing crops of fresh fruit monthly would grow along the river, and their leaves would be "for healing" (i.e., of great medicinal value). The desolate plain of the lower Jordan would again be as of old a garden of God (Gen. 13:10).

Thus the paradise motif is brought into the picture of the future, but closely tied to the temple and to the Lord, from whom all blessings flow. The author of the Revelation in his vision of the city of God (Rev. 21:10–22:5) also makes use of the river of the water of life, but has no use for the temple. The river flows from the throne of God and the Lamb.

The Boundaries. The visionary tour of Ezekiel seemingly ends in 47:12. What follows in 47:13 ff. is attached loosely as a long communication introduced by "Thus says the Lord God." It nevertheless is of great interest. Ezekiel first gives the boundaries of the Holy Land of the future (47:13–20). It should be noted that except in the northeast it is restricted to the west side of the Jordan. The northern boundary is vague as to its starting point at the Mediterranean, but is made clearer at the end. He mentions quite a few towns on the north line, perhaps because of familiarity gained with the area by sojourn in Syria, before being sent on to Babylonia. The eastern border runs from the north side of the Hauran (the only mention in the Bible of this still existing name) to Tamar (southwest of the Dead Sea). Where it crossed the rift is not stated. The southern border goes from Tamar via Kadesh to the brook of Egypt (*Wadi el Arish*). On the west the sea is the boundary, but here again the author is vague. He is including the whole Philistine country, and evidently Tyre and Sidon as well, since "the entrance to Hamath" is given as being on the same parallel with the northwest corner of the line.

A kindly gesture is made toward aliens that have established families in the midst of Israel (47:21 ff.). This seems very much of an afterthought.

The Land Division. In the land division itself (chapter 48) the tribal territories of the past are largely disregarded and a new distribution based on theoretical considerations is made. Seven tribes are on the north and five are on the south side of the sacred reservation. Judah's future possession lies north of the sacred reservation, while Benjamin borders on the latter to the south, and Reuben (originally at home in Transjordan) gets a portion north of Judah. Issachar, Zebulon, and Gad are put in the extreme south, whereas historically they were in the north and east. The sacred reservation itself consisted of the temple and the priestly portion in the center, the Levitic portion in the north, the city with city property in the south, and the Land of the Prince to the east and to the west of these.

The concluding directions (48:30–35) concern the twelve gates of the city which are to be named after the twelve tribes, with Ephraim and Manasseh combined as "Joseph" in order to make room for a Levi Gate. The circumference of the city is given, and its future name is to be "The Lord is there" (*Yahweh-shammah*). The old name, Jerusalem, the heathen origin of which was certain (16:3 ff.; 2 Sam. 5:6), must have seemed unfit for the future city of God.

Conclusion

As one contemplates the figure of Ezekiel, one sees in him a monumental greatness. He has been aptly called "a priest in the prophet's mantle." Unlike his predecessors from Amos through Jeremiah he is imbued with priestly viewpoints. The odor of sanctity pervades his thinking, and so also by contrast does the horror of the "unclean." In the final revelations of his book everything centers about the Holy Land, its holy temple and the holiness of the deity who "is there." Ezekiel has evidently seen how seriously the devotees of the Babylonian gods looked upon the temples of their deities and was impressed with the temple towers—the artificial mountains that they raised to them on their flat plain. Since a city's chief deity supposedly had a chapel with couch and table, but without an image in the topmost stage of such a tower, Ezekiel may have been stimulated to think of the residence of the Lord in a temple on a mountain top. His God is seen in the guise of an Oriental divinity with all his retinue and trappings, his prejudices and taboos. Yet he is the world-God who controls the history of nations. Here is paradox, which is just bridged over thinly by the phrase "in the likeness of," and by the "glory of the LORD" being conceived as a divine attribute—an emanation of the heavenly godhead channeled to earth, and not a complete theophany. But all the advantages of the actual personal presence of the revered divinity at a definite point are gained by this device.

But Ezekiel also wears the prophet's mantle. He can convey messages of the Lord, with the same certainty as his predecessors. He uses all their techniques such as visions, symbolical acts, and allegories to lend his message vividness and effectiveness. He has the prophetic discernment of sin, the certainty that sin must and will bring on divine judgment, the call to repentance as the only way of escaping this extreme, and the belief in a future of his people in which life would be an idyl of pacifism in a holy land and community. He continues the line of Jeremiah 31:31 ff. concerning a new order. He sees the Lord in the surgeon's role, performing an operation, whereby he will take the heart of stone out of men and put in its place a heart of flesh. This divine heart surgery is not, like ours, bent on preserving the body to live longer, but on changing human nature. This is guaranteed by the added gift of a new spirit (36:26 ff.; cf. 11:19). Ezekiel realized that without such radical measures men would remain hopelessly immersed in their evil ways, powerless to please their god and enjoy his favor. He thus wears the prophet's mantle with distinction.

But Ezekiel is not only priest and prophet. He wears the philosopher's as well as the prophet's mantle. He is the first known reflective thinker among the Jews. He can set up a constitution for a future state, as Plato did in his Republic. He has worked out a religious philosophy of history in his allegories and his Gog prophecies. He shows the ability to survey the historical process in the light of ideas. Therewith he became the father of "apocalypticism," such as we find in the book of Daniel, 2 Esdras (the little-known book in the Apocrypha often called IV Ezra after its name in the Latin Bible), and the Revelation of the New Testament. He grapples, too, with the problem of whether God punishes a man for the sins of his father (and vice versa) and comes out manfully for a liberal solution of purely individual responsibility. While he cannot be said to have solved the problem, and while his attempt to do so had some unfortunate consequences, he has revealed thereby the thoughtful bent of his mind.

In his combination of all these functions Ezekiel is the creator of the Jewish mentality that arose out of the exile—a mentality very different from the spirit of the people of preexilic times. He has thus quite properly been called "the father of Judaism." It is significant of his importance that the starting point for modern Jewish efforts to regain Palestine was a settlement named Tel Aviv, after the Tel-abib of Ezekiel.

His influence on Christianity—thanks to the adoption of the Old Testament as part of the church's sacred books—has been equally great. His thinking provided a background for Catholicism's emphasis on sacerdotalism, and was a powerful factor in leading popes to seek to reduce emperors to a role like that of "the prince" in a temple-state. His general pessimism as to human nature and his emphasis on divine discipline and his organizational ability left their mark on the mind of Calvin and on the Puritans, who gave the main moral and religious impetus to the development of our own country.

When men are measured by the influence they exert on history, the lonely exile on the Babylonian ruin-mound, gazing toward the north, whence the Lord had come with his throne-wagon and cherubim, will stand among the great religious leaders of mankind, in the row behind the founders.

11 THE PROPHET OF HOPE: DEUTERO-ISAIAH

The Man and His Primary Message

IT MAY HAVE BEEN around the time when Ezekiel dreamed of the Holy City and temple of the future that an unknown prophet whose utterances are preserved in Isaiah 40–55 was born. Modern scholars call him "Deutero-Isaiah," or the Second Isaiah. A minority believes (as the majority once did) that the same man at a later period also wrote Isaiah 56–66, but it is more widely held now that those chapters are to be attributed either to a later follower of Deutero-Isaiah, who then is called Trito-Isaiah, or to a number of such men of the same school. Our concern here is solely with the author of chapters 40–55.

Deutero-Isaiah has no vivid knowledge of the land of his fathers. He must have lived in the land of exile—perhaps at Babylon itself, where the royal family of Judah and its retainers had found a home. We can hardly think of him as a public speaker like his prophetic predecessors, though he may have spoken in "underground" gatherings. It is equally possible, however, that in his early years he circulated his oracles in writing. There may have been good reason for the young prophet to remain anonymous. Some of his sayings could readily have been regarded as seditious by the Babylonian authorities. No doubt the exiles were being watched carefully for possible involvement in revolutionary tendencies. Thrust back on himself and his world of ideas, Deutero-Isaiah generated the steam that burst forth with such power.

Judging from the bulk of his work which is in the higher key we must regard him as more poet than prophet. The actual predictive content of his utterances is not great when one discounts the imagery. He is carried away by the poetic madness, which, as noted in our introduction, Plato regarded as akin to the mania of the crystal gazer. His is not a disciplined literary art, but rather archaic art. This poet-prophet is intoxicated with his own rhetoric. "The kingly bard," says Emerson, "must smite the chords rudely and hard." Deutero-Isaiah is such a kingly bard. One can imagine him as coming out of his poet's trance to the everyday world with a sense of loss, like that when one is awakening from a beautiful dream. If the poems commonly called the Servant Songs (which we will deal with later in this chapter) were actually spoken or written by him, he could also compose in the lower key and produced new and deeper thought in it. Perhaps those sections were composed at a later juncture, when he was abused and ridiculed by dull literalists for having held expectations that ran counter to any conceivable realization.

The Historical Background. About the middle of the sixth century the great Chaldean, or Neo-Babylonian, empire erected by Nebuchadnezzar, suddenly faced internal and external crises of the greatest magnitude. King Neriglissar, the second successor of Nebuchadnezzar, died in the spring of 556. His son and successor was replaced, after a few months reign, by an Assyrian from Haran named Nabonidus, a high official of his court.

While Nabonidus in his inscriptions professed loyalty to the chief god of Babylon, the vernal sun-god Marduk, a rift soon came about between him and the powerful priesthood of the capital. It was chiefly caused by his rebuilding of the great temple of the moon-god Sin at Haran, of which his mother was high priestess. So great was the antagonism toward him that Nabonidus absented himself from Babylonia for ten years for his own safety and resided at Tema (now the oasis of *Teima*) in northern Arabia. He left the administration of Babylonia to his son Belshazzar (*Bel-shar-uṣur*). The New Year's festival, at which the king was supposed to "seize the hands of Marduk," was omitted year after year—to all true believers in Marduk a great calamity. Later Jewish legend transferred this absence of Nabonidus to Nebuchadnezzar and transformed it into a life among the beasts (Dan. 4:28 ff.).

The mood of the Hebrew exiles was one of profound discouragement. The same thing could be said of the native Babylonian population, for the Cyrus cylinder inscription, composed after Cyrus's conquest of Babylon, states that the god Marduk in conferring rule on Cyrus had mercy on all the destroyed towns and on the people of Babylonia, "who were like corpses." If the Babylonians themselves suffered under the intolerable yoke of Nabonidus's police state, how much more must that have been the case with foreign elements like the Jews, who may well have had agitators among them (Jer. 29:20 ff.) and may have suffered persecution on their account. No wonder the hated name of Belshazzar, who must have implemented whatever measures his father decreed from Tema, remained in memory for centuries to come. The author of the book of Daniel even took him to be the last king of Babylon.

Around the year 553 or soon afterward the young Jew whom we call Deutero-Isaiah may have perceived a cloud as large as a man's hand on history's horizon, and sensed that it meant something for his exiled people. He was fascinated by what was reportedly transpiring beyond those distant Zagros mountains that rimmed the Babylonian plain in the north. There another young man named Cyrus (in Old Persian, Kurash), king of the city of Anshan, had rebelled against his overlord Astyages, king of the Medes, seized his capital Ecbatana (today Hamadan), and gained control of his whole realm. Since Median power extended into Asia Minor, Cyrus's eyes were turned westward. It did not seem as though he were going to attack Babylonia, though he had good reason to do so because Nabonidus had disregarded Median rights in northern Assyria. In 547, however, Cyrus came down to Mesopotamia and crossed the Tigris near Arbela. He occupied a city (the name of which is lost from the Chronicle tablet) and put a garrison in it.

At this time, if not earlier, we suspect, Deutero-Isaiah had the experience of his call to the prophetic office. But if so, his faith was to be put to a severe test, as Isaiah's was in 713–711, for instead of turning against Babylon, Cyrus resumed his Asia Minor conquests. In 546 the Persian ruler defeated Croesus and captured Sardis, thus extending his realm to the Aegean Sea. What Cyrus did in 545–540 has been lost from the Chronicle tablet. In any case it was not until 539 that he again came down to the Tigris to settle accounts with Babylon. Jews who were familiar with the city's fortifications, and perhaps had had to labor on them for Nebuchadnezzar, were unwilling to believe that the half-nomadic Persians could take the fortified city of Babylon. It was to all such persons who could not see the footsteps of the Lord in history's onward march that Deutero-Isaiah was to address himself up almost to the very moment of the fall of the city.

The Call of the Prophet. Deutero-Isaiah seemingly had an inspirational experience in which he heard the voice of God as well as one or two other voices. In the opening words he reports God's directive to the religious leaders among the exiles, giving them their present-day task. Actually the words were intended first of all for the prophet himself:

> Comfort, comfort my people,
>> says your God.
> Speak tenderly to Jerusalem,
>> and cry to her
> that her warfare is ended,
>> that her iniquity is pardoned,
> that she has received from the LORD's hand
>> double for all her sins. (40:1-2)

The paramount need of the oppressed and weary exiles was for a message of comfort. Theirs has been a period of servitude comparable to the service of the soldier who longs for retirement. The fact that their exile was a punishment for iniquity is not forgotten, but so great has been that punishment that the Lord now regards them as having paid doubly for the sins of the past. This pronouncement is rhetorical, and not to be stressed as though God had acted unjustly; the thought is of God's great compassion.

The prophet himself hears the message that will bring comfort, spoken by a lesser voice than the Lord's but authorized by the Lord. Actually it is addressed to other invisible aides:

> "In the wilderness prepare the way of the LORD,
>> make straight in the desert a highway for our God.
> Every valley shall be lifted up,
>> and every mountain and hill be made low;
> the uneven ground shall become level,
>> and the rough places a plain.
> And the glory of the LORD shall be revealed,
>> and all flesh shall see it together,
>> for the mouth of the LORD has spoken." (40:3-5)

The words imply that preparations are now to be made for the return of the Lord to his city. This will be the revelation of his glory—a spectacle that "all flesh" shall behold. The prophet is aware that the ordinary travel route taken to Palestine—first heading north from Baby-

Ionia to Assyria, then west to Syria, then south—is unduly long and leads through territories defiled by worship of other gods. He thinks of a direct route across the desert, and thus is aware that Babylon and Jerusalem lie approximately in the same latitude. The Lord must have straight and level highway, and the agencies subject to him must and will prepare it. An underlying belief in the divine power to remove existing natural obstacles is evident. Deutero-Isaiah is an idealist, and for his God nothing is impossible.

The highway construction idea, intensified to the fantastic, rests on what the prophet had observed or heard at Babylon. For according to a Greek report (Diodorus, 2, 10) Queen Semiramis, to make an ever-lasting monument for herself as well as to shorten the way, built a road through the Zagros mountains, having the steep places lowered and the deep ones filled. But the origin of the idea is cultic. For when the idols of the gods issued forth from the temple at Babylon to go to the House of the New Year's Festival, the god Nabu was bidden to prepare the way for Marduk. "Make good his path, renew his course, make right his way, hew out for him a path." This had a practical background, for if the Babylonian king stumbled in conducting the god from his sanctuary, or if the animal drawing the ship-cart bearing his idol stumbled, or if anything happened to the cart itself, it was a bad omen for the future. Such superstition, however, was outside of Deutero-Isaiah's pale of thinking. The straight and level highway was simply the appropriate one for the deity.

Dependability of the Revelation. At this point the prophet hears a voice saying: "Cry!" and gives (or hears given?) the response "What shall I cry?" To feel what is meant by "cry" one may think of the town crier of old, who with loud, clear voice cried out the hour, news, and directives. The words that follow the question are hardly the poet's musings, but rather the answer given by the "voice":

> All flesh is grass,
>   and all its beauty is like the flower of the field.
> The grass withers, the flower fades,
>   when the breath of the LORD blows upon it . . .
> The grass withers, the flower fades;
>   but the word of our God will stand for ever. (40:6b–8)

Some later reader must have added the prosaic comment at the end of verse 7 "Surely the people is grass." But the thought must be focused on something more than the transitoriness of human life. Deutero-Isaiah was thinking of the Babylonian nation and of its mighty rulers (cf. 40:23–25). Just as it takes only the hot breath of the Lord (figurative for the parching east wind) to blow upon the flower and make it wither, so it is with national flourishing. In contrast to this evanescence of worldly power stands the permanence of the divine assurance: "The word of our God will stand forever." That, too, is not just said abstractly but refers to the specific "word" promising the revelation of the Lord's glory to all flesh. What the purpose of the implied theophany —appearance of God—is, the prophet is to disclose.

The Tidings for Jerusalem. Deutero-Isaiah himself now addresses Zion the desolate. He personifies her as a woman, as was natural since names of cities were feminine in gender. He calls her "herald of good tidings," and bids her get her up to a high mountain. Perhaps he is thinking of an increased elevation of the city (Ezek. 40:2; Isa. 2:2). Ordinarily the bearer of good tidings was a runner, who brought the report of a victory directly from the battlefield (2 Sam. 18:19 ff.). The figure of speech is applied loosely here to a person who, from a high vantage point, gives a signal message that will be relayed farther by other observers on distant summits. This was usually done by smoke, or fire, or, where the intervening distances were not too great, by trumpet. Since the message meant here would not be readily understandable by such devices, Zion is bidden to herald it by voice. Her reluctance to do so—in view of its seeming incredibility—is appreciated, but she is urged to be unafraid and raise her voice to the utmost, so that the message will be heard and carried on and on to all the cities of Judah. The message is "Behold your God"—a vivid way of saying, "Your God is arriving."

The prophet then visualizes this scene of the arrival in figurative manner, thinking of God and of his returning people in terms of shepherd and flock:

> Behold, the Lord GOD comes with might,
>   and his arm rules for him;

> behold, his reward is with him,
>   and his recompense before him.
> He will feed his flock like a shepherd,
>   he will gather the lambs in his arms,
> he will carry them in his bosom,
>   and gently lead those that are with young. (40:10–11)

The words remind hearers or readers of the power of the Lord, whose mighty acts will precede this return. His people whom he is conducting are his reward and "recompense" (cf. Ezek. 29:20) for all the exertions leading up to the victory that is assumed to have preceded. But this mighty world ruler is gracious and considerate of the returners, as a good shepherd is toward the tired lambs and the pregnant ewes. Though the shortest road through the desert has been taken, the way is still a long one. Not only for the Lord himself but for his people was the command given by the angelic voice to make it level. Of his further concern for them in connection with that road we shall hear later (43:19b–21).

God's Instrument.   The prophet's eye is fixed on the day after tomorrow. But tomorrow must come first, and he has to think of this, too; there can be no return to Zion until Babylon's might is broken. Only its military defeat can bring help. Deutero-Isaiah believes that the man who will accomplish this is already appointed.

The first allusion to this individual does not yet name him, but two subsequent poems do; it is Cyrus, the Persian. He was the Lord's chosen instrument. Deutero-Isaiah calls upon the nations to come and dispute this if they can:

> Who stirred up one from the east
>   whom victory meets at every step?
> He gives up nations before him,
>   so that he tramples kings under foot;
> he makes them like dust with his sword,
>   like driven stubble with his bow.
> He pursues them and passes on safely,
>   by paths his feet have not trod. (41:2–3)

This reflects Cyrus's victories over the Iranian tribes and his amazing takeover of the realm of Astyages.

The next allusion describes Cyrus as coming from the *north*:

> I stirred up one from the north, and he has come,
>   from the rising of the sun, and he shall call on my name;
> he shall trample on rulers as on mortar,
>   as the potter treads clay. (41:25)

That would seem to reflect a more advanced stage in Cyrus's conquests —after he had crossed the Tigris and gone on into Asia Minor in 547. His origin in the lands of the rising sun, however, is remembered in the bold poetic description of the Lord's "calling a bird of prey from the east, the man of my counsel from a far country" (46:11).

The New Situation and Its Problem

The imminence of hostilities in 539 created a new situation for Deutero-Isaiah. He had long announced that the Lord was sending Cyrus to liberate his people. But now many Babylonians, who were hoping for the defeat of their king, Nabonidus, were saying that the god of Babylon, Marduk, had called Cyrus to effect their own king's overthrow. In the Cyrus cylinder inscription a Babylonian scribe faithfully mirrors this viewpoint, when he writes how Marduk grieved for his people and sought to bring them relief:

> He mustered all lands, looking for a righteous prince according to the desire of his heart that he might seize his hands. The name of Cyrus, the king of the city of Anshan, he uttered, called him to the kingship of the whole world. He subjected to him the land of Gutium and all the Manda-people (i.e., the Medes and allied northern tribes). In justice and righteousness he (i.e., Cyrus) concerned himself about the blackheaded people whom he (the god) caused his hands to subdue. Marduk, the great lord, the protector of his people, beheld joyfully his deeds of piety and his righteous heart. To his city of Babylon he commanded him to go: yea he caused him to take the road to Babylon. Like a friend and comrade he walked at his side.

Here we find virtually the same idea attributed to Marduk on behalf of the oppressed Babylonians as, according to Deutero-Isaiah, animated the Lord in his concern for the suffering exiles of Judah.

Prophecy for Cyrus. Over against such claims the prophet had to

resort to an apologetic to maintain his position that the Lord god of
Israel was the one who had called Cyrus. One important line to take
was to address prophecy to the Persian leader:

> Thus says the LORD to his anointed, to Cyrus,
>   whose right hand I have grasped,
> to subdue nations before him
>   and ungird the loins of kings,
> to open doors before him
>   that gates may not be closed:
> "I will go before you
>   and level the mountains,
> I will break in pieces the doors of bronze
>   and cut asunder the bars of iron,
> I will give you the treasures of darkness
>   and the hoards in secret places,
> that you may know that it is I, the LORD,
>   the God of Israel, who call you by your name.
> For the sake of my servant Jacob,
>   and Israel my chosen,
> I call you by your name,
>   I surname you, though you do not know me.
> I am the LORD, and there is no other,
>   besides me there is no God;
>   I gird you, though you do not know me,
> that men may know, from the rising of the sun
>   and from the west, that there is none besides me;
> I am the LORD, and there is no other.
> I form light and create darkness,
>   I make weal and create woe,
>   I am the LORD, who do all these things. (45:1-7)

The prophet makes the admission here that Cyrus does not know the
Lord, or understand that the Lord is the one who is guiding him. But
the Lord knows Cyrus. "My anointed" (mashiah) he calls him—in the
sense in which the title, "Anointed of the LORD" was used in Israel
for the "divinely appointed ruler." The Lord assures Cyrus that he
will make level his path; he will break down the bronze doors of Babylon and give him the hidden treasures. When all this comes true as
predicted Cyrus will know that it was the Lord who called him by
name—yea, even has surnamed him, with such titles as "my anointed,"
"my shepherd" (44:28), or even with the titles "great king," "mighty

king," and "king of the entirety" that he bore before adding to them those borne by the rulers of Babylonia.

It cannot be regarded as impossible that such utterances of a prophet among the Jews were actually conveyed to Cyrus, for one must suspect in view of the liberation of Jehoiachin by Evil-merodach (2 Kings 25:27 ff.), that Jews who had been in the service of the house of Nebuchadnezzar (Dan. 1:3 ff.) were hostile to Nabonidus. Indeed, it may be that Deutero-Isaiah's prophecy brought the captive Jews to Cyrus's attention and led to his subsequent edict in their favor. Centuries later Josephus earned the gratitude of the Roman general Vespasian by prophesying that he would become emperor. Why should not a Jewish prophet's words have elicited appreciation on the part of Cyrus? All the ancient kings and captains, fearful of the uncertainties involved in battles, were constantly on the alert for favorable prophecies and auguries from any and all sources, and showed gratitude toward those who had given them support in crucial hours.

Reassurance for the Jews. Deutero-Isaiah's enthusiasm for Cyrus was not shared by all his coreligionists, any more than Jeremiah's contemporaries accepted his claim that Nebuchadnezzar was the servant of the Lord. The prophet found it necessary to rebuke those who were critical of God's way to the future, as that now was shaping up through the phenomenal rise of Cyrus:

> Thus says the LORD,
>> the Holy One of Israel, and his Maker:
> "Will you question me about my children,
>> or command me concerning the work of my hands?
> I made the earth,
>> and created man upon it;
> it was my hánds that stretched out the heavens,
>> and I commanded all their host.
> I have aroused him in righteousness,
>> and I will make straight all his ways;
> he shall build my city
>> and set my exiles free,
> not for price or reward,"
>> says the LORD of hosts. (45:11–13)

It was the Lord's righteousness—his desire to see the right thing done for his people—that led him to arouse Cyrus and give him almost un-believable success. The Jews, he then predicts, will not even have to pay their deliverer for setting them free. In continuing he declares that the Lord will give Egypt to Cyrus as their ransom, in exchange for Ethiopia (Nubia) and Seba (probably an Ethiopian district, Gen. 10:7). Deutero-Isaiah may have reasoned that a restored Jerusalem and Judah would be of advantage to Cyrus when he carried his conquest into Africa. So convinced is the prophet of such an objective on the part of the Persian that he already sees "men of stature" (cf. 18:2; Herodotus, 3, 20) from Seba coming to Jerusalem in chains, apparently as captives donated by Cyrus to the Jerusalem temple as slaves, and hailing the god of Israel (45:11–14). Perhaps it was owing to this prophecy that early Christians found the visit of a prominent Ethiopian to Jerusalem and his conversion to Christianity (Acts 8:26 ff.) so significant.

The Twilight of the Gods. Another important line of apologetic against claims made for Marduk and other gods was to assail idolatry. A specific occasion may have led Deutero-Isaiah to stress this line. For Nabonidus, on his return from Tema and in anticipation of the coming struggle, had the idols of the gods of the leading cities of Baby-lonia brought into the capital. He could have done this to have the united power of these gods behind Marduk and to make sure of the loyalty of their devotees. Deutero-Isaiah himself may have laid eyes on transports of such idols and certainly must have heard of this great assembly of the gods. No wonder, then, that with such a marshaling of the Babylonian pantheon the prophet became aware of a meta-physical background in the present decision between Nabonidus and Cyrus: a judgment of the Lord over the gods.

Deutero-Isaiah sometimes represents the idols themselves as gods, and with superior contempt insists that they are nothing but wood, stone, or metal. He describes the manufacturing process and then ridicules man for worshiping what he makes (cf. 40:18–20; 41:7; and the possibly interpolated prose section 44:9–20). The theologians of the Babylonian religion, however, viewed the idols differently. To them they were merely representations of the gods, who were imagined as moving about in freedom, like the Homeric gods. The idol was a con-cession to human need of visualizing the anthropomorphically conceived deity. Consecrated by appropriate rites, the craftsman's product took on the odor of sanctity. An idol was a guarantee of the presence of the deity represented at a temple of his choice, and of the possibility of reaching his attention by sacrifice and other means about which his priests were knowledgeable. From that standpoint Deutero-Isaiah's attack on idolatry did the gentiles an injustice. However, so far as the ignorant public was concerned god and idol may often have been identical. In any case this polemic of Deutero-Isaiah is one of the things that made the deepest impression on the Jewish mind when the book of Isaiah came to be read in the synagogue. Everywhere in Judaism we meet traces of Deutero-Isaiah's polemic against images. Even Paul is under its influence when he says of the gentiles that "they exchanged the glory of God for images resembling mortal man, or birds or animals or reptiles" (Rom. 1:23).

Deutero-Isaiah sometimes (perhaps only for the sake of argument) assumes the gods to be existing apart from their idols. This is particularly the case when he describes the future carrying off of two idols (see page 248). It is also implied when the Lord summons the gods or their worshipers as to a court of law to bring proof of the divine status claimed for them.

In connection with such polemic there sometimes is reference to "the former things" and the "new things." The Lord says of himself:

> The former things I declared of old,
>> they went forth from my mouth and I made them known;
>> then suddenly I did them and they came to pass. (48:3)

This is an allusion to the fulfillment of the word of the Lord as formerly given to his prophets. Just what prophecies Deutero-Isaiah had in mind is not made clear. Perhaps he was thinking of how Jeremiah hailed Nebuchadnezzar as servant of the Lord, just as he himself now was hailing Cyrus as the Lord's anointed. Nobody would believe Jeremiah, and Judah rebelled against Nebuchadnezzar and was destroyed. God's word as given through his prophet was vindicated. This and many other fulfilled prophecies, of which Deutero-Isaiah may have known (just as Plato knew of Delphic oracles that had been of great benefit to Greece), proved the wisdom of the Lord and his power to carry out his plans. Furthermore, he has recently shown the same capacity of foretelling what now is in process of being fulfilled (45:21b).

Deutero-Isaiah may be thinking here of prophecies of the coming destruction of Babylon such as are found in Isa. 21:1–10; 13:1 ff.; Jer. 50 ff. These are not utterances of the prophets in whose books they are found, but productions of unknown prophets who lived after the time of Ezekiel.

But the Lord is also giving further prophecy of what he is about to do:

> "From this time forth I make you hear new things,
>   hidden things which you have not known.
> They are created now, not long ago;
>   before today you have never heard of them,
>   lest you should say, 'Behold, I knew them.' " (48:6b–7)

The allusion is to what the Lord is going to do after Babylon's fall— something utterly different and unheard of, antiquating all that has preceded:

> "Remember not the former things,
>   nor consider the things of old.
> Behold, I am doing a new thing;
>   now it springs forth, do you not perceive it?
> I will make a way in the wilderness
>   and rivers in the desert.
> The wild beasts will honor me,
>   the jackals and the ostriches;
> for I give water in the wilderness,
>   rivers in the desert,
> to give drink to my chosen people,
>   the people whom I formed for myself
>   that they might declare my praise." (43:18–21)

The "new" thing is a new beginning, a re-creation, in which the defects of nature that are a hindrance for the homeward march of the Lord's people will be remedied. Rivers will spring up in the desert through the Lord's creative act. We have already heard of the highway to be built through the desert (40:3). Here the same road is meant, but the thought is centered on the Lord's provision for those whom he is going to lead. The wild creatures, even, will honor the Lord for this, and his wandering people will praise him.

The thought of such an improvement of natural conditions is extended by Deutero-Isaiah to the arid areas of the Holy Land itself:

> "For the LORD will comfort Zion;
>   he will comfort all her waste places,
> and will make her wilderness like Eden,
>   her desert like the garden of the LORD;
> joy and gladness will be found in her,
>   thanksgiving and the voice of song." (51:3)

It is the mythical idea of "paradise regained" that appears here, but broadened from a garden to a garden-like region. This is "cyclical" thinking, in which the coming cycle not only reduplicates but outstrips the past in attaining a state of affairs more satisfying to human longings. Deutero-Isaiah could scarcely have set this forth as prophecy of the Lord had he not been convinced of an idealistic dogma.

On the basis of all such prophecy—past prophecy already fulfilled, recent prophecy now being fulfilled, and new prophecy of a vast change to come but certain of fulfillment—the Lord challenges the pagan gods to bring forth proof of similar foreknowledge, or to do anything that would cause him dismay:

> Set forth your case, says the LORD;
>   bring your proofs, says the King of Jacob.
> Let them bring them, and tell us
>   what is to happen.
> Tell us the former things, what they are,
>   that we may consider them,
> that we may know their outcome;
>   or declare to us the things to come.
> Tell us what is to come hereafter,
>   that we may know that you are gods;
> do good, or do harm,
>   that we may be dismayed and terrified.
> Behold, you are nothing,
>   and your work is nought;
> an abomination is he who chooses you. (41:21–24)

The gods, of course, remain silent, unable to answer or to do anything at all, because they are devoid of reality as the closing taunt declares. The Lord alone is God.

The Omnipotent. Out of this discomfiture of the gods, taking place as the clash of arms on earth neared, arises Deutero-Isaiah's assertion of the absoluteness of the Lord. He is the world creator in whom all power is vested. Prior to Deutero-Isaiah the idea of the creator God, though present, received no particular emphasis in the religion of Israel. It led too readily to attention to pagan divinities like sun, moon, and stars, or the patrons of vegetation. All interest had centered on history, on what the Lord had done for Israel. But to outdo Marduk, whose role as world creator was the theme of the Creation Epic—the sacred book of his temple at Babylon—the Lord's role as creator now needed to be asserted. Again and again this is brought in by Deutero-Isaiah in passing clauses of praise that often retard the making of his main point. It is, however, developed more fully at times and then with great power:

> Have you not known? Have you not heard?
>   Has it not been told you from the beginning?
>   Have you not understood from the foundations of the earth?
> It is he who sits above the circle of the earth,
>   and its inhabitants are like grasshoppers;
> who stretches out the heavens like a curtain,
>   and spreads them like a tent to dwell in;
> who brings princes to nought,
>   and makes the rulers of the earth as nothing.
> Scarcely are they planted, scarcely sown,
>   scarcely has their stem taken root in the earth,
> when he blows upon them, and they wither,
>   and the tempest carries them off like stubble.
> To whom then will you compare me,
>   that I should be like him? says the Holy One.
> Lift up your eyes on high and see:
>   who created these?
> He who brings out their host by number,
>   calling them all by name;
> by the greatness of his might,
>   and because he is strong in power
>   not one is missing. (40:21–26)

The star-gods, so impressive to the Babylonians in their flat country, where the whole sweep of the north-equatorial skies is visible, do not frighten him. They are beings created by the Lord.

With the poet's love of imagery the prophet can picture the Lord in more militant terms. Thus he described him as going forth like a mighty "man of war" and working himself up into a fury after long and taxing patience (42:13–15). He can even resort to barbarous mythology in calling on the Lord to rouse himself to action:

> Awake, awake, put on strength,
> O arm of the Lord;
> awake, as in days of old,
> the generations of long ago.
> Was it not thou that didst cut Rahab in pieces,
> that didst pierce the dragon?
> Was it not thou that didst dry up the sea,
> the waters of the great deep;
> that didst make the depths of the sea a way
> for the redeemed to pass over? (51:9–10)

The allusion is to some version of a creation myth, in which the chaos monster slain by the deity was called Rahab (cf. Ps. 89:10; Job 26:12). But the myth has been "historicised" and transferred to a historical incident, namely that of the passage through the Red Sea (cf. 43:16–18). Let the Lord now show his might in bringing about a new exodus, this time from Babylonia.

Redemption Despite Unworthiness. Deutero-Isaiah speaks with the faith of the believer. But in contending with the gods he is also dealing with obstinate people among the Jews who were inclined to concede wisdom and power to these gods (48:4 ff.). On occasion he can even emphasize the bad character of Israel. The Lord still has cause to be angry with this people. He hints at their dealing treacherously and at their rebelliousness from the very beginning (48:8). But the Lord has a strong reason to subordinate these matters, and has merely subjected his people to punishment.

> "For my name's sake I defer my anger,
> for the sake of my praise I restrain it for you,
> that I may not cut you off.
> Behold, I have refined you, but not like silver;
> I have tried you in the furnace of affliction.
> For my own sake, for my own sake, I do it,
> for how should my name be profaned?
> My glory I will not give to another." (48:9–11)

Deutero-Isaiah thus reveals a belief that in redeeming Israel the Lord will be acting in the interests of justice, but for his own sake. His holy name is being profaned for having allowed his people to languish in captivity and his land to lie desolate. In the final remark the prophet may again be dismissing the Babylonian claim that it was Bel-Marduk who was bringing Cyrus to overthrow the hated king of Babylon.

The Coming Fall of Babylon.   Deutero-Isaiah revels in the thought of the fall of Babylon. He sees the idols of Bel and Nebo, the leading deities at Babylon, being loaded on weary beasts—those of their captors, which have come a long way—and being carried off into captivity. The dethroned deities themselves are powerless to prevent it and indeed must go along:

> Bel bows down, Nebo stoops,
>   their idols are on beasts and cattle;
> these things you carry are loaded
>   as burdens on weary beasts.
> They stoop, they bow down together,
>   they cannot save the burden,
>   but themselves go into captivity. (46:1-2)

He utters a lamentation over the "virgin daughter of Babylon" (chapter 47). Ironically he bids her to come down from her throne and sit in the dust and like a slave woman grind meal and tells her that she will be forced to violate modesty on the march into captivity by having to lift up her skirts in crossing streams. No longer shall Babylon be called "mistress of kingdoms." He accuses her of mistreating the Lord's people when he gave them into her hands at a time when he was angry with them. She did not think of her accountability for her cruelty toward them, since she expected to be mistress forever. But widowhood and loss of children—things which she thought would never happen to her—will now overtake her. All her wisdom, the magical texts of her sorcerers, and the predictions of her astrologers cannot save her. All will be swept away by the flames.

The Vessels of the Lord.   With inspired thought Deutero-Isaiah, even before the decisive battle, foresaw the return to the Jerusalem temple of the vessels that were carried off by Nebuchadnezzar. In calling on

Jews to leave Babylon before getting caught in the siege he says:

> Depart, depart, go out thence,
>   touch no unclean thing;
> go out from the midst of her, purify yourselves,
>   you who bear the vessels of the LORD.
> For you shall not go out in haste,
>   and you shall not go in flight,
> for the LORD will go before you,
>   and the God of Israel will be your rear guard. (52:11–12)

He here compares this hoped-for exodus with the one from Egypt, when the people went forth "in haste" (Exod. 12:11; Deut. 16:3 ff.), and when the Lord acted as vanguard or rear guard (Exod. 13:21; 14:21). The prophet cannot, however, emancipate himself from the old taboos of ritual purity in the matter of the transporting of the sacred objects. He seems to have thought, too, that these vessels could be taken away without difficulty. One cannot rule out the possibility that promises of their delivery (contingent on Nabonidus's defeat) had been made to Jewish leaders. As of that date, however, the priesthood of the Marduk temple would hardly have released these spoils of royal warfare without the consent of the king.

Renewed Consolation

Perhaps in the interval of waiting for the decisive battle in the north to develop, Deutero-Isaiah's mind became more occupied with the return and restoration. The fall of Babylon was to him a foregone conclusion, and his mind had the habit of hastening on. So we find him reverting to the themes of the beginning, and that in even more vivid colors and greater warmth.

The prophet calls on Jerusalem to awaken, shake herself from the dust, adorn herself, and loosen the bonds from her neck. The reason is that no uncircumcised or unclean person shall henceforth come into her (52:1 ff.). The remark may have been elicited by contemporary complaints emanating from Jerusalem that pagan elements and people from the northern kingdom (cf. Jer. 41:4 ff.) were coming and bringing sacrifice to the Lord, as god of the land. In the absence of priestly supervision this may have been done without due attention to matters of ritual purity. The prophet assures Zion that a new state of affairs will soon be introduced. One feels that this is a decline from his usual high level and that what he actually started out to say was that Jerusalem should adorn herself to receive the great news of her redemption. For it is this theme that is continued (after a prose interpolation, 52:3–6) in a noble saying:

> How beautiful upon the mountains
>   are the feet of him who brings good tidings,
> who publishes peace, who brings good tidings of good,
>   who publishes salvation,
>   who says to Zion, "Your God reigns."
> Hark, your watchmen lift up their voice,
>   together they sing for joy;
> for eye to eye they see
>   the return of the LORD to Zion.
> Break forth together into singing,
>   you waste places of Jerusalem;
> for the LORD has comforted his people,
>   he has redeemed Jerusalem.
> The LORD has bared his holy arm
>   before the eyes of all the nations;
> and all the ends of the earth shall see
>   the salvation of our God. (52:7–10)

Instead of Jerusalem's being bringer of good tidings to Judah's cities (40:9), she here is to be their recipient. The messenger, boldly personified as the rosy-footed dawn, is hastening from mountaintop to mountaintop with the announcement of the accession of the Lord as king of a new world order. He has "bared his arm" (in his victories over empires through his servant Cyrus) and all the world will now see the decisive act (in the return to Palestine).

Jerusalem, in particular, now like a barren woman, is called upon to sing and exult over the prospects of future expansion of population (54:1–3). Employing the marriage symbolism the prophet thinks of her as now being like a wife of youth cast off, but promises her renewal of the Lord's love in tender and comforting words. Hence she is to be unafraid of the future (54:4–8). The present historical juncture is compared in significance to that of Noah after the flood, when God made a covenant with him, reassuring mankind against another calamity of such dimensions. He now has sworn in like manner that he will never again be angry with his people. With wonderful words he emphasizes the firmness of his determination:

> For the mountains may depart
>   and the hills be removed,
>   but my steadfast love shall not depart from you,
>   and my covenant of peace shall not be removed,
>   says the LORD, who has compassion on you. (54:10)

The "covenant of peace" is here coupled with God's steadfast love (as in 1 Kings 8:23; Neh. 1:5) and hence refers in a general way to the state of grace in which his people will find itself.

The Holy City

Before Deutero-Isaiah's eyes, as before those of Ezekiel, there rises the holy city of the future. It is now the "afflicted one, storm-tossed, and not comforted," but soon is to be constructed of precious or semi-precious stones (54:11–12). The very foundations are to be set in such stones, and the pinnacles and walls are to consist of them. Deutero-Isaiah must have been impressed by reports of the stones used for adornment of the palaces and temples of Babylon. He may have seen such stones in the hands of dealers in the bazaars and have heard of those being mined in distant northern regions over which Cyrus now was ruler.

At a slightly later date the Greeks heard of the splendor of the Persian palaces at Susa and Ecbatana; these were allegedly walled off from sight and shone of gold, electrum (mixture of gold and silver), and ivory. Wonderful objects of art were being fashioned for kings. Darius received two made by a craftsman on Samos: a plane tree of gold and a vine of gold with grapes consisting of emeralds and Indian carbuncles. Fascinated by precious stones, as something "out of this world," but unfamiliar with their limitations of size, Deutero-Isaiah assumes in poetic fancy that they could be quarried as building blocks, out of which then could be constructed the outer facing of the wondrous Zion of the future. It is again his way of stretching the imagination to the utterly impossible; he believes that only the impossible would be worthy of the future city of God. This imagery (though not echoed in Isaiah 60–62) was to prove extremely stimulating to Jews of a later age, such as the authors of Tobit (13:16–17) and of Revelation (21:10 ff.).

But he does not stop with architecture. In the city shall dwell a people taught directly by the Lord (cf. Jer. 31:34), established in righteousness, without fear of oppression. No divinely caused strife will be sent, and willful attempts at strife will fail. No weapon fashioned against them will succeed and they will disprove every accusation brought against them, so wonderful will be the future people's heritage.

The Comers from Afar.   The goal is not yet reached for Deutero-Isaiah with a Jerusalem reestablished by the exiles from Babylon. Again his mind hastens on. He thinks of the land of Palestine as virtually depopulated. Since rapid restoration alone is worthy of the Lord, he sees the need for the return of those Jews dwelling in remoter lands. Already at the beginning he assured Jacob-Israel of the return of his offspring (43:5–7). Here he sees them included in a general return, for which more highways through mountain regions are needed (49:8–12):

> Lo, these shall come from afar,
>   and lo, these from the north and from the west,
>   and these from the land of Syene. (49:12)

He remains vague as to north and west, but is clear about the current southernmost habitat of Hebrew people: Syene. This is the Greek name for the place called Sewen by the ancient Egyptians and today known as Aswân. Lying below the first Nile cataract, Syene was the extreme outpost of Upper Egypt. Here, indeed, as Aramaic papyri found on Elephantine island, across from Aswân, have shown, there was a Jewish colony with its own temple of the Lord. According to one of these texts the temple was already in existence before Cambyses's invasion of Egypt (626), and hence no doubt in the time of Deutero-Isaiah. In speaking of those in the north, Deutero-Isaiah may have been thinking of the Israelite exiles in northern Mesopotamia, while in the case of the west he may have had knowledge of communities in western Asia Minor. We have no definite knowledge of Jews in Asia Minor prior to the Hellenistic era, but it is very likely that Israelite elements spread westward from Mesopotamia or were settled in Asia Minor by Assyrian or Neo-Babylonian kings. We have heard of Neriglissar's war in Cilicia

and Pamphylia. Why should Jews not have been settled there by him
at this time? Cyrus even settled "Hyrcanians" from the Caspian Sea
region in the vicinity of Sardis in Lydia.

With the difficulty in mind that many of those settled afar may not
be free to extricate themselves from their present places of settlement,
the prophet thinks of the Lord as arranging for their return to the land
of their ancestors:

> "Behold, I will lift up my hand to the nations,
>   and raise my signal to the peoples;
> and they shall bring your sons in their bosom,
>   and your daughters shall be carried on their shoulders.
> Kings shall be your foster fathers,
>   and their queens your nursing mothers.
> With their faces to the ground they shall bow down to you,
>   and lick the dust of your feet.
> Then you will know that I am the LORD;
>   those who wait for me shall not be put to shame." (49:22–23)

What a reversal for the downtrodden! What a satisfaction it will be
for Jerusalem, when pagan kings come humbly and prostrate themselves
like conquered foes, because they are impelled by the uplifted hand
of the Lord to bring home the exiles held by them.

The Missionary Idea. But Deutero-Isaiah sees more in this solicitude
of the gentile kings and their obeisance to Jerusalem than appears. He
is thinking at heart of their conversion, just as he thought of it in the
case of Cyrus's captives from Ethiopia (45:14). He has gone beyond
an earlier momentary impulse to consider the nations as accounted by
God as "less than nothing and emptiness," like their idols (40:17; cf.
41:29). Their amazement at the Lord's glorious rehabilitation of his
people (49:7) and now their obedience to his command pave the way
for larger goals. The Lord himself bids the nations come to share in
this salvation:

> "Turn to me and be saved,
>   all the ends of the earth!
> For I am God, and there is no other.
> By myself I have sworn,
>   from my mouth has gone forth in righteousness

> a word that shall not return:
> 'To me every knee shall bow,
>   every tongue shall swear.'
> "Only in the LORD, it shall be said of me,
>   are righteousness and strength;
> to him shall come and be ashamed,
>   all who were incensed against him.
> In the LORD all the offspring of Israel
>   shall triumph in glory." (45:22–25)

This is one of the great missionary utterances of the Old Testament. Paul utilized it in that sense and Christianized it in one of his finest flights of thought (Phil. 2:10 ff.).

Postlude

In his last utterances (chapter 55) Deutero-Isaiah calls upon those who thirst to come to the (newly created?) waters—apparently an invitation to come and enjoy the blessings of the Lord at Jerusalem—where wine and milk, too, can be had free of charge under paradisiacal conditions. Let them not linger in the lands of exile, where satisfaction is not to be had. And he gives them a message that will revive their souls:

> "I will make with you an everlasting covenant,
>   my steadfast, sure love for David.
> Behold, I made him a witness to the peoples,
>   a leader and commander for the peoples.
> Behold, you shall call nations that you know not,
>   and nations that knew you not shall run to you,
> because of the LORD your God, and of the Holy One of Israel,
>   for he has glorified you." (55:3b–5)

It is a question whether Deutero-Isaiah is thinking of a restoration of the monarchy, or whether he is transferring the promise made to David (2 Sam. 7:12–16) to the people. There was, we may assume, reason for cautiously stating monarchistic hopes. The role of "prince" as in Ezekiel (37:24 ff.) would seem quite compatible with Deutero-Isaiah's theocratic emphasis, for after the Lord has stabilized the situation, a continuation of government by an earthly individual would seem necessary. An inchoate mass like a people cannot govern itself without leadership.

The prophet urges his hearers to seek the Lord's mercy and forgiveness. Let those who are skeptical of the coming salvation consider the superior wisdom of God:

> For my thoughts are not your thoughts,
>   neither are your ways my ways, says the LORD.
> For as the heavens are higher than the earth,
>   so are my ways higher than your ways
>   and my thoughts than your thoughts. (55:8–9)

God's word, which the prophet had said in the beginning would stand forever (40:8), has gone forth and will accomplish his purpose.

Once more the vision of the return from exile rises before Deutero-Isaiah's eyes:

> "For you shall go out in joy,
>   and be led forth in peace;
> the mountains and the hills before you
>   shall break forth into singing,
>   and all the trees of the field shall clap their hands.
> Instead of the thorn shall come up the cypress;
>   instead of the brier shall come up the myrtle;
> and it shall be to the LORD for a memorial,
>   for an everlasting sign which shall not be cut off." (55:12–13)

The exiles will go forth from Babylon with joy and in peace, while all nature exults in sympathy. The emphasis now is not on the straight and level highway, but rather on its landscaping with ornamental trees. This contrasts markedly with Ezekiel's more utilitarian view of the kinds of verdure lining his holy river (Ezek. 47:12). Instead of the road being made for he Lord (40:3) it now is created by the Lord for his people (43:19), and its paradisiacal state will be an everlasting sign of God's power and of his care for them.

Disappointed Hopes?   History took its iron course. Cyrus crossed the Tigris in the fall of 539 and defeated the Babylonian army near Opis. On October 12 Gobryas (Gubaru), former Babylonian governor of Gutium (in the Zagros region) who had gone over to Cyrus, entered Babylon. The fleeing Nabonidus was captured. All the mighty fortifications of Nebuchadnezzar, with which a united and determined people might have prevailed over any invader, had been useless. What a lesson of the effects of disunion, of the futility of all defensive plans in certain circumstances! Cyrus himself entered the city on October 29, and was received as deliverer. The Persian paid homage to Marduk and became recognized as King of Babylon, and acknowledged as sovereign by all the vassals over whom the Chaldean kings reigned. Cyrus lost no time in speeding recovery in Babylonia. He returned the idols of the gods to the cities whence Nabonidus had brought them and he rebuilt towns Nabonidus had destroyed in quelling rebellions against his rule.

Deutero-Isaiah must have been disappointed by this lack of punishment for Babylon. Yet he had spoken under inspiration from the Lord, and must have felt that he had erred only in assuming that Cyrus was the one who would destroy the city and carry off its gods as spoils. The Lord had decided on a postponement of such drastic punishment. But the prophet must have felt that the destruction would surely happen, and in that he was correct. While the historical record is scanty it may have come partly under Darius, for Babylonia was among the provinces in which rebellions against his newly established rule were suppressed in 522–521. Later, in 482, Xerxes put down two revolts there also. Some consider him to have been the radical destroyer; in any case it was he who dismantled the great Marduk temple and its tower, the Tower of Babel, and destroyed the statue of the god Marduk. And the day was to come, long afterward, when the entire city would become uninhabited and sink into the dust, with only one of its ruin-mounds preserving to modern times its name *Babil*, in the mouth of Bedouin.

The prophet had a partial vindication a year or more after Cyrus's coming, when the conqueror gave his edict permitting the rebuilding of the Jerusalem temple, handed over the sacred vessels to a responsible Jewish group, and allowed those Jews who wished to go back to the land of their fathers to do so (Ezra 1:2–11; 6:2–5). This certainly proved that Deutero-Isaiah's hailing of Cyrus as a king who would fulfill the Lord's purpose was correct. For the reestablishment of the temple and beginning of resettlement meant the rebirth of the nation.

Deutero-Isaiah's vindication in this matter was offset to some degree by the failure of the prophesied miraculous circumstances attending the return to materialize. He had seen the coming of the Lord, and his arrival in Jerusalem along with that of the return of the golden age, as coinciding with the return of the exiles. The straight journey through the wilderness, we may be sure, was not even attempted by the returners. Practical men took the safer roundabout course. But the prophet would hardly have been disturbed by the failure of his words in this respect. He had spoken under influence of the spirit of God, but his God remained supreme—free to carry through his purposes, like a commander whose strategy is adjusted to the circumstances of the moment. Deutero-Isaiah may have concluded that the Lord did not find his people ready yet, either morally or spiritually, to experience his presence or to receive that role in the world which he planned to give to them. But he would have held to his belief that the desert would yet bloom, and that Jerusalem would be the place to which his people would return from all quarters of the earth and where the nations would acknowledge the supremacy of Israel's God. He would have said, "For the vision is for days yet to come" (Dan. 10:14).

The disappointment of Deutero-Isaiah's more boundless hopes may have had grave consequences for him. We have seen already that in a sober mood the prophet recognized the weaknesses of his own people (48:8-9). One may be sure that he was reviled, insulted, and beaten by his fellow men. When they saw him coming they, too, may have said with Joseph's brethren, "Here comes this dreamer." And one may well ask: Have we not in the prophet's personal experience the key to four poems which we have not yet considered? Do they perhaps represent a new and final stage in his message—a stage which could only be reached under the impact of disappointment and the agony of mistreatment?

The Mission of the Servant of the Lord

The Problem. The poems in question (42:1-4; 49:1-6; 50:4-9; 52:13-53:12) are of a different stamp from all the rest. A quiet, thoughtful mood pervades them, rather than that of high enthusiasm. They are like still waters between rapids of a river. They all concern a servant of the Lord. The pivotal question thus is: Who is the servant?

Here there is an endless debate between the advocates of a collective interpretation and the exponents of individual interpretations. The collectivists assert that the servant of these poems is symbolical of the Hebrew people either as a whole or in part, and they have good arguments on their side. Still an individual, Cyrus, is also called God's servant, and so one must concede that some other person could be similarly designated. The individualists who follow this line have almost unlimited possibilities for identification of the servant, ranging through the past, the author's day, and the future. We need not spread this welter of opinion before the reader, but will turn to the poems themselves and try to understand what they mean to convey.

1. The connection in which the first servant poem has been placed by the ancient editors makes it appear that the servant is introduced in contrast to Cyrus. Both are world conquerors, but while the former employs armed might, the latter uses gentler methods:

> Behold my servant, whom I uphold,
>   my chosen, in whom my soul delights;
> I have put my Spirit upon him,
>   he will bring forth justice to the nations.
> He will not cry or lift up his voice,
>   or make it heard in the street;
> a bruised reed he will not break,
>   and a dimly burning wick he will not quench;
>   he will faithfully bring forth justice.
> He will not fail or be discouraged
>   till he has established justice in the earth;
>   and the coastlands wait for his law. (42:1-4)

The vast scope of the servant's mission is here described. He is not only a proclaimer but a mediator of redemption. Through his word he will bring forth "justice" (Hebrew, *mishpat:* "judgment") to the nations. There is some vagueness as to what is meant by "justice," but since in the closing line it is paralleled with "law" (or "instruction" in what the Lord requires of man) it is a term equivalent to "religion"—in effect, religiously oriented social ethics. As the poet recognizes only one God, and hence no other law but his, he can speak of "justice" and "law" in the abstract, and hold that the nations will have to accept it.

2. The second servant poem (49:1-6) is found in a connection where the coming exodus from Babylon is the theme. That could suggest that the servant as deliverer from Babylonian exile is to be compared to Moses, the deliverer from Egyptian bondage:

Listen to me, O coastlands,
>   and harken, you peoples from afar.
The LORD called me from the womb,
>   from the body of my mother he named my name.
He made my mouth like a sharp sword,
>   in the shadow of his hand he hid me;
he made me a polished arrow,
>   in his quiver he hid me away.
And he said to me, "You are my servant,
>   Israel, in whom I will be glorified."
But I said, "I have labored in vain,
>   I have spent my strength for nothing and vanity;
yet surely my right is with the LORD,
>   and my recompense with my God."
And now the LORD says,
>   who formed me from the womb to be his servant,
to bring Jacob back to him,
>   and that Israel might be gathered to him,
for I am honored in the eyes of the LORD,
>   and my God has become my strength—
he says:
"It is too light a thing that you should be my servant
>   to raise up the tribes of Jacob
>   and to restore the preserved of Israel;
I will give you as a light to the nations,
>   that my salvation may reach to the end of the earth." (49:1–6)

The piece reminds one of the Confessions of Jeremiah. It opens with a declaration by the speaker of his election from the very womb (cf. Jer. 1:5), and quotes the commission given him of being the one through whom God will glorify himself (vv. 1–3).

In this commission, however, "Israel" is addressed and if that mention is correct, then the collective interpretation would seem to be the right one. However, this interpretation runs into grave difficulties in verses 5–6, as we shall see. The "individual" interpreters therefore eliminate the word "Israel" from this third verse as a later interpretative addition. Metrical considerations support this view.

The servant had been downhearted over the failure of his efforts, but (in recalling his commission) he braces up and relies on his vindication through the Lord (v. 4).

In this mood of faith he receives a new oracle. In the introductory praises of the Lord the author works in more detail about the servant's own task (thus expanding what was so briefly stated in the commission as quoted in v. 3). The Lord had formed him to bring Jacob home and effect the reconstitution of Israel. In applying himself to that task the servant has been feeling himself honored and strengthened by God. But, in the fresh oracle he now receives and quotes, the Lord gives him a much larger responsibility—to be a light to the nations, that God's salvation may reach to the ends of the earth (vv. 5–6).

This sounds like the prophetic consciousness of a man like Jeremiah, but on a grander scale. There is nothing to remind one of the national consciousness of Israel. If it were not for the word "Israel" in verse 3 no one would think of interpreting the servant of this poem collectively. Here speaks a prophet, and the question could only be whether he is thinking of himself or of one to come.

If the translation with a clause of purpose in verses 5 and 6 is correct then logic seems to demand the excision of the word "Israel" in verse 3. For how can Israel be the servant and at the same time have the task of restoring Israel? Some collectivists seek escape from this dilemma by translating differently. Thus for example one commentator renders in verse 6: "It is less important (literally, "lighter") to raise up the tribes of Jacob and to restore the tribes of Israel than that thou art my servant. So I make thee a light to the nations, etc." But that sort of translation is rejected by other leading collectivists. These follow instead the idea of a twofold use of "Israel." Either the ideal Israel (or a group within the people) is to restore the empirical Israel, or the thought is of a kind of mystical national personality that goes through the ages, beginning with the ancestor. But one would expect the author to have refrained from using "Israel" in two different meanings in the same breath. If one eliminates Israel in verse 3 and interprets individually, then the difficulties disappear.

3. The third poem (50:4–9) may have been put in its present place to contrast the faith of the servant with Israel's lack of faith, as expressed in the preceding context. The servant again speaks in the first person:

> The Lord God has given me
>   the tongue of those who are taught,
> that I may know how to sustain with a word
>   him that is weary.
> Morning by morning he wakens,
>   he wakens my ear
>   to hear as those who are taught.
> The Lord God has opened my ear,

> and I was not rebellious,
>> I turned not backward.
> I gave my back to the smiters,
>> and my cheeks to those who pulled out the beard;
> I hid not my face
>> from shame and spitting.
>
> For the Lord GOD helps me;
>> therefore I have not been confounded;
> therefore I have set my face like a flint,
>> and I know that I shall not be put to shame;
>> he who vindicates me is near.
> Who will contend with me?
>> Let us stand up together.
> Who is my adversary?
>> Let him come near to me.
> Behold, the Lord GOD helps me;
>> who will declare me guilty?
> Behold, all of them will wear out like a garment;
>> the moth will eat them up. (50:4–9)

The servant here dwells on his endowment with the tongue of "those who are taught" (cf. 54:13; rendered "disciples" in 8:16), thus with his speaking ability and on his receiving revelations. The latter come to him in the early morning hours. As the Lord's disciple he has persisted obediently in his task, in spite of the abuse to which he has been subjected. He feels certain of his final success, and like Job challenges his accusers to appear with him before the judgment of God. At this stage of his efforts the opposition comes entirely from his own people, who apparently do not want to follow his leadership.

4. The final, crucial problem is presented by the last and most famous of the four servant songs (52:13–53:12). It has been called the most wonderful bit of religious poetry in all literature. It is probable that this poem was not inserted here initially, because the succeeding piece 54:1 ff. (arrival at Jerusalem) continues in the vein and line of thought of the preceding one 52:7–12 (departure from Babylon).

The poem begins with a prediction of the Lord about the servant's future recognition and his past humiliation. The servant will "prosper," or be successful. Nations and kings will be amazed.

> Behold, my servant shall prosper,
>> he shall be exalted and lifted up,
>> and shall be very high.

As many were astonished at him—
    his appearance was so marred, beyond human semblance,
    and his form beyond that of the sons of men—
so shall he startle many nations;
    kings shall shut their mouths because of him;
for that which has not been told them they shall see,
    and that which they have not heard they shall understand. (52:13–15)

Here the collectivists can compare 49:7, where rather similar statements occur with reference to Israel, though the word "servant" is not used for the people in that passage. In the above rendering, however, we must be critical of the last word "understand," as it can lead to a wrong supposition about what follows in chapter 53. There is no claim of new and better insight. The word is only parallel to "see," and should be rendered "consider" (as in 43:18), or still better "behold," or "perceive."

The poem continues without interruption in chapter 53—a fact not understood when the chapter divisions were made. The transition is, indeed, not easy.

    Who has believed what we have heard?
    And to whom has the arm of the Lord been revealed? (53:1)

Who is speaking here? Most collectivists are fascinated by the idea that the kings of 52:15 are speaking about the servant. But these have just been described as speechless with astonishment—how then should they suddenly become so loquacious? The thoughts that follow in verses 2–6, furthermore, are certainly far above the heads of those pagans; here the translation "understand" in 52:15 exercises the misleading influence already mentioned.

If the kings are ruled out as speakers in 53:1 then it must be the prophetic author who is speaking. In using "we" he is uniting himself with others of similar occupation, just as in 40:1 the author and others are addressed in the plural: "Comfort (ye) my people." The phrase "what we have heard" is really a noun with possessive suffix in Hebrew and literally rendered is "our (prophetic) audition"—objectively speaking, then, "the message" (so in 28:9, 19). The second question of 53:1, about the revelation of the arm of the Lord, shows that in the first question the allusion was to the implications of the message of the coming intervention of the Lord. The questions register the prophetic author's appreciation of how unbelievable the message of 52:13 about the servant's future was, when viewed in the light of his obscurity and afflicted condition. No wonder, then, that Israel did not believe the prophecy of his coming glory:

> For he grew up before him like a young plant,
>   and like a root out of dry ground;
> he had no form or comeliness that we should look at him,
>   and no beauty that we should desire him.
> He was despised and rejected by men;
>   a man of sorrows, and acquainted with grief;
> and as one from whom men hide their faces
>   he was despised, and we esteemed him not. (53:2–3)

The servant grew up before "him" (i.e., the Lord; but perhaps to be emended to "before us," in view of the "we" that follows) like a weed out of barren soil. The author, including himself with his people in his natural state (prior to his receiving the revelation referred to in 53:1, saw no reason to regard the servant, for he lacked attractiveness. Yea more, as "man of sorrows" he became repulsive and was despised.

But through the divine revelation the prophetic speaker has received an entirely new insight into the why and wherefore of the servant's "sorrows":

> Surely he has borne our griefs
>   and carried our sorrows;
> yet we esteemed him stricken,
>   smitten by God, and afflicted.
> But he was wounded for our transgressions,
>   he was bruised for our iniquities;
> upon him was the chastisement that made us whole,
>   and with his stripes we are healed.
> All we like sheep have gone astray;
>   we have turned every one to his own way;
> and the LORD has laid on him
>   the iniquity of us all. (53:4–6)

The speaker thus joins himself with his people, as in verses 2–3. In his unenlightened state he, like all others, regarded the servant as suffering because he was a sinner, just as Job's friends cruelly inferred that his suffering was a punishment he had deserved. But through the divine revelation (53:1) the true insight has been given to the speaker: The sufferings of the servant were vicarious. "The LORD has laid on him the iniquity of us all" (the speaker again including himself with his people).

The poet then reverts again to the sufferings of the servant hinted at in verse 3, but with new detail, and gives the outcome:

> He was oppressed, and he was afflicted,
>   yet he opened not his mouth;
> like a lamb that is led to the slaughter,
>   and like a sheep that before its shearers is dumb,
>   so he opened not his mouth.
> By oppression and judgment he was taken away;
>   and as for his generation, who considered
> that he was cut off out of the land of the living,
>   stricken for the transgression of my people?
> And they made his grave with the wicked
>   and with a rich man in his death,
> although he had done no violence,
>   and there was no deceit in his mouth. (53:7-9)

There are some textual difficulties here into which we need not go. But at least one emendation that has received support from the Qumran Isaiah scroll may be mentioned. The words "and with a rich man in his death" (v. 9b), are given by the scroll as "and with rich men his tomb." "Tomb" excellently parallels "grave" in verse 9a. However, an emendation of "rich men" to "evildoers" is widely accepted, and this may have been the original reading. It is in the postexilic period of the psalmists that "rich" and "wicked" became synonymous.

Seemingly, then, the death and burial of the servant are surveyed as something that has already transpired. However, some scholars deny this and hold that we have here only the exaggerated language of the pious sufferers. Thus the psalmist can say "thou dost lay me in the dust of death" (Ps. 22:15); the drowning man in Jonah 2:6 thinks of the bars of Sheol as having closed behind him. Babylonian poems, too, use similar exaggerations. But there is a difference between saying such things in the first person and saying them in the third person.

The author then prophetically explains God's purpose and gives a prediction about the bright future of the servant:

> Yet it was the will of the LORD to bruise him;
>   he has put him to grief;
> when he makes himself an offering for sin,

> he shall see his offspring, he shall prolong his days;
> the will of the LORD shall prosper in his hand;
>   he shall see the fruit of the travail of his soul and
>   be satisfied;
> by his knowledge shall the righteous one, my servant,
>   make many to be accounted righteous;
>   and he shall bear their iniquities. (53:10–11)

The fate of the servant was God's will. A reversal in this fate will come when he has made himself an offering for sin (see the "guilt offering," Hebrew, *asham*, of Lev. 5:14–6:6) by innocent and silent suffering ending with death. Then the Lord will rehabilitate him, as he rehabilitated Job (Job 42:12 ff.). His satisfactions will include having children, living long, and seeing the success of his cause. The allusion to his having made many righteous "*by his knowledge*" seems a bit surprising, and by change of a single Hebrew letter this can be rendered "through his suffering." If "knowledge" is original, however, it can be understood in the light of the servant's prospering in 52:13 (literally "acting wisely").

The swift conclusion of the poem reverts to the standpoint of the introduction (52:13–15). The Lord now puts his seal of approval on the prophetic interpretation of the servant's ministry already given by the author:

> Therefore I will divide him a portion with the great,
>   and he shall divide the spoil with the strong;
> because he poured out his soul to death,
>   and was numbered with the transgressors;
> yet he bore the sin of many,
>   and made intercession for the transgressors. (53:12)

The Lord will divide him a portion with the great (as booty of war is divided according to rank). This will be the reward for his sacrifice, his humiliation, his vicarious bearing of sins, and his intercession for transgressors.

The Identity of the Servant. Who, we ask once more, is the servant of these poems? There are obstacles to any answer. The collective interpretation can be maintained if the servant is symbolical of the ideal Israel, or of a class of men representative of it—men who have the spirit of a Jeremiah and could be imagined by those of the same class as leading their people in the future. But this is made difficult by the fact that the four songs were evidently set down at intervals, and that the second and third, by being in the first person, reflect individual activity. The individual interpretation, insofar as it holds the servant poems to refer to a contemporary person, runs into difficulties too. It has to invent and make psychologically convincing a supposition about a person by whom Deutero-Isaiah was "taken in" to such a degree. A little more plausibility can be conceded to the theory that Deutero-Isaiah was speaking of himself. But since this theory faces objections in the case of the fourth poem, a modification becomes attractive; one may assign that piece to an admiring pupil (Trito-Isaiah?), who then was speaking of his deceased master. But it is hard to believe that any man should have such an idea of his own significance, as the first three poems display—particularly if history should prove him mistaken. Whether Deutero-Isaiah erred about another or about himself, one would have to speak of "the great illusion," and the alleged pupil who might have written the fourth piece would have been similarly mistaken. The poems would not lose their value, of course, for what was not realized in the person by or about whom they were written could be vindicated later in some future figure. The thought content would still be important.

One must wonder, then, whether it is not easier to believe that the four poems are prophecy of a future redeemer. It is certainly easier to think in vast terms about a person of the future than about one of one's own day and environment. One must assume in any case that Deutero-Isaiah was disappointed in his expectations of Cyrus and the glorious return of the Lord to Zion. He would have had to readjust his thinking. Confident of the validity of his original message of redemption he would reason that he had seen the glorious future nearer at hand than it actually was. The Lord in his wisdom had decided that other things had to happen first: the conversion of Israel through the person of some future teacher, who like Moses could be more than just a teacher—a lawgiver and national leader. One may suppose that Deutero-Isaiah had become keenly conscious of the failings of his people, of their unfitness to experience the redemption; that he foresaw that any effort to bring about the proper state of heart and mind would meet with opposition and bring martyrdom on the man who would attempt it; but that he believed that such an individual would come and was sure of his final success and vindication by the power of God.

Conclusion on Deutero-Isaiah

It is almost beyond the power of the imagination to appreciate the influence that has gone forth from the unknown prophet of the exile. But time had to march on before he was appreciated by his own people.

The first lap of the way back to national existence was long and hard for them. But after the exile, when they had become indoctrinated with the law and were being taught by a properly edited story of their national past, they realized with chagrin how ungrateful their forefathers had been to God. They now were ready to turn again to the books of the prophets. After hearing in detail the charges and threats that had been uttered by these men, they were almost unable to believe the message that they were still God's people and that he would not let them go, and that there was before them still a future of hope, when and if they became worthy of it.

In this mood of the people Deutero-Isaiah came into his own. His enthusiasm raised the prostrate; his poetic vision gave new hope. Wherever Jews listened to his words, whether in Hebrew in Palestine or in Greek translation out in the Hellenistic-Roman world, they were stirred to their innermost being. He gave them the strength to look with scorn on the idols before whom the peoples among whom they dwelt bowed down. They believed that the course of events in the world was controlled by their God—the one true God—and that the outcome of history could only be the final manifestation of his glory before all the world. Here was kindled the missionary spirit and the hope that all nations would some day come to serve him and to honor the people that they now despised. His Holy Land and his Holy City would be the theater in which that glory would be manifested. Thus, too, was nurtured the sense of "home" for a people consisting of wanderers and fugitives in the earth. It is questionable whether law and ritual alone would have given the Jews the ability to weather all the storms of history. It required the lyre of Deutero-Isaiah to give courage and hope.

But perhaps the most fateful influence exercised by Deutero-Isaiah was that on the formation of Christianity. The prophetic books at this time were being taken as full of prediction of what was to occur in the "latter days," and at any juncture that arose men would point to some prophecy as now finding its fulfillment. Thus it became possible to view John the Baptist as "the voice crying in the wilderness" to prepare the

way of the Lord. Important, too, was the idea of the servant of the
Lord, when individually interpreted. It seems probable that Jesus himself after first seeing his own ministry described in Isa. 61:1-2 (cf. Luke
4:16-21), found further light on his own path in the servant poems.
Jesus' actual ministry was that of a prophet and teacher, as is the case
with the servant, and he may have accepted the way of suffering as
foreordained for himself by God as for the servant in Isa. 53. The
messianic idea in the regal sense was relegated to the future.

Certain it is that the early Christians saw in the predicted suffering of
the servant for his people's sins, and in his restoration to life and final
exalted state, the fulfillment of this prophecy. The difficulty in verse 10
was easily met by taking "offspring" as allegorical of "followers." Thus
Isa. 53 was the trellis on which the vine of Christian dogma could
climb. And who will say that it was not the will of God that it should
do so? Where the martyred and risen Christ was experienced as "the
power of God and the wisdom of God" (1 Cor. 1:24), there was no
doubt that the spirit of God had led the prophet to prophesy of him.

When Christians adopted the Jewish scriptures and, dismissing all
national or racial limitations, considered themselves the people of God
and heirs to the promises given Israel, they took figuratively many things
that Jews valued literally. While Christians have maintained a senti-
mental interest in the Holy Land and Holy City, as the scene of events
of eternal importance, they no longer tie the idea of salvation to these
places. The basic idea of a land of God and a city of God nevertheless
remained a potent dream.

Deutero-Isaiah's lyrical assertions of God's power and of his all-
sufficiency had a more immediate value, as did his numerous beautiful
words of consolation. While the latter were addressed to the people in
general they have, when applied individually, given new comfort and
courage to untold millions of Christians in grief and sorrow. This
unknown prophet was, indeed, the evangelist of the Old Testament.

PART 3

PROPHETS OF THE PERSIAN AND GREEK ERAS

12 PROPHETS OF THE RETURN AND THE RESTORED COMMUNITY

Haggai

NO SATISFACTORY RECORDS of what happened in Judah in the years between the edict of Cyrus (538) allowing the Jews to return and the second year of Darius I (520) have come down. Such great events in the outside world as the death of Cyrus, Cambyses's campaign to Egypt and death on the way home, the seizure of power by Pseudo-Smerdis, the assassination of this imposter by Darius, must have stirred prophetic men among the Jews to give oracles, but none seem to be preserved. Darius's accession was followed by a series of revolutions that shook the Persian empire. These had been suppressed by the end of 521.

In August 520 a prophet named Haggai arose in Judah. We can gather from his words that he looked forward to more revolutions (2:6 ff.; 2:21 ff.) and hoped for a kingdom of Judah in consequence of them. There had evidently been much disillusionment with Persian rule on the part of Jews since the return.

Economic conditions must have been very depressing. There had been failure of harvests and general poverty. The ancients regarded such situations as signs that their god was displeased with them, and the question invariably was: Why? The prophet Haggai, in addressing Zerubbabel the governor and Joshua the chief priest, blamed the misfortunes on neglect of restoring the temple, the roof of which at least must have collapsed in the fire of 587. The officials were living in paneled (better, roofed?) houses, while the Lord's house lay in ruins. No wonder the deity was angry. Turning to the people Haggai urged them to go up into the hills and bring wood to start building, and predicted that if this were done the Lord would again send blessing. The man had faith, and faith is contagious.

Leaders and people were fired to undertake the task. The prophet promised that the Lord's spirit would be with them (thus giving them the power to accomplish). When they became discouraged in October, after several months of labor, he revived their flagging spirits. By the time December rolled around he foresaw a splendid harvest for the coming year. He rejected the aid of certain elements in the population that were not of the returners. Whether they were Samaritans or local residents is uncertain. To Zerubbabel, scion of the house of David, he held out the hope that the Lord would make him like a signet ring on his hand (cf. Gen. 41:42; Jer. 22:24 ff.), for the Lord had chosen him. What else could this mean but that he was the designated future king of Judah?

Zechariah and His Visions

Evidently moved by Haggai's success, a priest called Zechariah, son of Iddo, aspired to a public role. He issued a call of repentance a week after Haggai's address of October 520. In January 519 he had a series of visions of the night (1:7–6:8). In these visions, which have a title and may have been issued as a separate booklet, the Lord does not speak directly to him, but through an angelic intermediary. Perhaps the visions convinced him and others of his prophetic status, for after conclusion of the visions he gives oracles beginning in prophetic manner with "And the word of the Lord came to me."

The visions show that Zechariah, like Haggai, was expecting further turmoil in the Persian empire and hoped that the Jewish monarchy would then be restored. In the opening vision the first of four horsemen, each mounted on a horse of a different color, reports to the Lord's representative at the (western?) entrance to heaven that they have patrolled the earth in all four directions and that all the earth is quiet. This clearly means that Darius now had things firmly in hand, and that there was no immediate prospect of further revolution in Babylonia. In the closing vision Zechariah sees four chariots, drawn by horses of different colors, go forth from between two bronze mountains (in the east?). The Lord's representative acts as expediter, and then cries out to Zechariah, "Behold those who go to the north country have set my spirit at rest (better, have set down my spirit) in the north country." One can only guess what the spirit was to effect there. Some think it was to move Babylonian Jews to do more for the homeland. It seems equally possible, however, that the spirit is to cause the desired further revolutionary commotion in the heartland of the empire. The spirit works effectively (4:6), does what seems impossible. Without further rebellions in the realm there was no hope of the renewal of the Jewish monarchy.

Therewith the visions terminate. But the messianic expectation lingers, and an opportunity to voice it soon presented itself (6:9–14). Gold and silver were brought to Jerusalem by three men from Babylonia. How should it be used? Zechariah received a divine message directing that a crown be made of the gold and that he was to place it on the head of *"Joshua, the son of Jehozadak, the high priest"* (6:11). It is generally accepted that the words we have italicized are not authentic and that the text originally read "Zerubbabel, the son of Shealtiel." The symbolical coronation perhaps was intended to help bring about the realization of what was desired. Since Zerubbabel's name was dropped and Joshua's substituted for it, we must infer that the hopes placed in Zerubbabel were disappointed. The words and acts of the two prophets may have brought about his undoing.

Noteworthy too is an address made in December 518 by Zechariah. A question was raised by an outside delegation as to whether the fast on the anniversary of the destruction of the temple (2 Kings 25:8 ff.) should still be observed, now that the temple was being rebuilt (7:1–3). The address consists of retrospect (7:4–14) and prospect (8:1–23). The answer to the question of the visitors is given near the end, in 8:18–19. The day is indeed to be observed, but it, as well as two other tragic anniversaries, are to be celebrated as cheerful feasts rather than as fasts. The style of 8:1–23, with repetitions of "Thus says the Lord of Hosts" reminds one of that of Darius in the Behistun inscription. The latter, too, consists of such paragraphs (some very brief), beginning with "Says Darius the king." As the Behistun inscription was circulated in the Persian empire in Aramaic—a copy even having been found among the Elephantine papyri—it seems likely that Zechariah's style was influenced by it.

The rebuilt temple was dedicated in March 515 (Ezra 6:15–16), but Zerubbabel is not mentioned in the account. Somehow the editors neglected to delete the prediction of Zechariah that Zerubbabel's hands would complete the house (4:9). A high priestly office—of which we hear nothing in preexilic times and whose holder was privileged to wear a tiara—was allowed the Jewish community in place of a Davidic monarchy. However, another Persian governor must have succeeded Zerubbabel, whenever it was that he was recalled.

Trito-Isaiah

To the period soon after Haggai and Zechariah one may assign most of the materials in chapters 56–66 of Isaiah. A few scholars still hold that they were composed by Deutero-Isaiah himself after a (supposed) return to Palestine. Others think they are the work of an imitator or pupil of Deutero-Isaiah. But the most probable view is that this is a compilation of prophecies of this general period, spoken or written down by diverse men. One is most reminded of Deutero-Isaiah by the little booklet incorporated in chapters 60–62.

Just as Deutero-Isaiah's outburst of song was occasioned by the victories of Cyrus, so there must have been something in the world scene of the time that could lead a follower of his to become similarly enraptured, and once more foresee the day of glory arriving for Jerusalem. One might hazard the guess that it was the failure of Darius I to subdue Greece, and the formidable Ionian revolution (500–494), which raised hopes of coming redemption in the bosom of this individual.

The poet-prophet calls on Jerusalem to rouse itself in the face of this sunrise of a new day:

> Arise, shine; for your light has come,
>   and the glory of the Lord has risen upon you.
> For behold, darkness shall cover the earth,
>   and thick darkness the peoples;
> but the Lord will arise upon you,
>   and his glory will be seen upon you.
> And nations shall come to your light,
>   and kings to the brightness of your rising. (60:1–3)

In wondrous words he describes the peoples bringing their wealth and sacrifices to the city. First the Arabians come to mind: Midian and Epha, Sheba with its gold and frankincense, the Kedar and the

Nebayoth. From Tarshish, perhaps used here as a general term for the western lands visited by the big ships that went to Tarshish proper, the peoples will bring back Israel's sons. Jerusalem as yet has no walls, but the author predicts that foreigners will build them and that they will beautify the as yet unadorned temple with precious lumber from Lebanon. He revels in the self-abasement of gentile peoples and rulers.

Of particular interest is the author's declaration of his mission in chapter 61. It is apparently a counterpart to the servant songs of Deutero-Isaiah. He must have understood these as meant in the individual sense.

> The Spirit of the Lord GOD is upon me,
>   because the LORD has anointed me
> to bring good tidings to the afflicted;
>   he has sent me to bind up the brokenhearted,
> to proclaim liberty to the captives,
>   and the opening of the prison to those who are bound;
> to proclaim the year of the LORD's favor,
>   and the day of vengeance of our God;
> to comfort all who mourn ... (61:1–2)

The mourning referred to is mourning in and for Zion. The captives whose liberation is forecast are not the exiles, but those enslaved because of inability to pay debts. Jesus is said to have found in these words a prophecy of his ministry (Luke 4:16 ff.).

Of the coming redemption the author speaks vividly in chapter 62 in words heavily dependent on Deutero-Isaiah. But he coins the names Hephzibah, "My delight is in her," and Beulah, "Married," for city and land of the future. The highway-building interest of Deutero-Isaiah is narrowed down to a stretch of road near Jerusalem, and the people, instead of supernatural agencies, are to do the job.

Whether it was the same man or another of the same school who wrote the stirring poem of the judgment over Edom (63:1–6) is hard to say. It inspired Julia Ward Howe's "Battle Hymn of the Republic." This poet as hater of Edom had a rival in the author of Isaiah 34–35, who also wrote in the manner of Deutero-Isaiah. But the first to see the disaster to Edom coming was a prophet whose name is preserved— Obadiah.

Obadiah

A storm was evidently brewing for Edom when Obadiah had his "vision"; a coalition against this kingdom was being formed. Edom is a high mountain region, and Obadiah is aware of this when he says "You who live in the clefts of the rock, whose dwelling is high." Even the sages, for whom Edom was famous (e.g., Job's Eliphaz of Teman), and the leading men will be destroyed. All this is to be retribution for what the Edomites did to their brother people, Judah, on the day of their calamity in 587.

Edom must have fallen very early in the Persian period. It seems probable that Edom actually fell before an onslaught of Arab tribes c. 475. A "Geshem the Arab" was an adversary of Nehemiah (2:19) and thus must have been in a position to threaten Judah from the southeast or south. Geshem may be identical with Gashmu, the father of Qaynu (Cain) king of Kedar, who donated a silver votive bowl to an Egyptian sanctuary. The Kedar, then, would have been the leading tribe of those that destroyed the Edomite kingdom. They in turn were to be displaced about 300 by the Nabataeans.

"The vision of Obadiah," which ended in verse 15, was so short that it cried out for a continuation. This was probably supplied later, when it was decided to include this brief piece in the collection of the twelve and make a separate book of it. There are several additions; one expanded the judgment to all the nations, while retaining a special hatred for the displaced Edomites now dwelling south of Judah. Another promised territory to Israelites returning from Media and Jews from Sepharad (Sardis). The latter city had been burned in the Ionian rebellion of 498 and Jews may have wanted to get out of there. The final chord, "and the kingdom shall be the Lord's," at least ends the book on a religious note.

Malachi

Another prophet of the period was dubbed "Malachi" (my messenger), for want of a name. This designation called attention to the messenger prophecy of 3:1. He must be later than Obadiah, for he looks back on the fall of Edom. A foreign governor is in residence, evidently a Persian. The temple is standing, but the enthusiasm of the days of its renewal has waned.

Malachi is perhaps the most modern of all the prophets, because he addressed the public in discussion style. He takes up some erroneous point of view and refutes it. Whether this is a first indication of Greek influence permeating the Persian East, we cannot say. It was one world in the days of the Persian empire. There was even a trend toward universal religion. One of Malachi's finest utterances exhibits it when he says:

> . . . from the rising of the sun to its setting my name is great among the nations, and in every place incense is offered to my name, and a pure offering; for my name is great among the nations, says the LORD of hosts. (1:11)

He is apparently identifying the Lord with Ahuramazda, Zeus, and other chief gods.

Malachi is critical of the priesthood of his day. He has an ideal of the office before his mind and sees it exhibited in Levi, here viewed as ancestor of the priests (2:6-7). He has strong opinions on divorce (2:10-16). The Lord hates it, for he was a witness to the covenant when a marriage took place. The prophet is opposed to marriage with the "daughter of a foreign god" so the situation is getting like that found by Nehemiah.

There was much cynicism as to God's justice (2:17-3:5). Malachi meets this with the prediction of the sudden coming of the Lord to his temple, preceded by the messenger of the covenant. The Lord then will purge the priesthood and be a swift witness against adulterers, perjurers, and oppressors of the weak. Many who hitherto had been godfearing were backsliding (3:13-4:3). He reassures these by a revelation that the Lord was having the names of the righteous recorded in a book of remembrance before him. On the day when he acts against the evildoers their names will be found and they will be spared. This is expressed rather beautifully in the words:

> But for you who fear my name the sun of righteousness shall rise, with healing in its wings. (4:2)

Righteousness in this instance is not the moral quality but rather vindication. The figure may have been suggested by the winged solar disk—the symbol of the sun. In Persian art the god Ahuramazda was shown in the disk with his right hand extended. This may have been taken to be a gesture of healing (cf. Acts 4:30).

The concluding verses of Malachi are hardly words of the prophet himself but were added at a later time, when reading of the "former prophets" (i.e., the early historical books) in the synagogue had made people familiar with the story of ancient Israel's prophet Elijah. Since he was translated, he could conceivably return. In view of the vast amount of apostasy that arose, especially on the part of the younger generation when Greek civilization flooded the East, many hoped that Elijah might be sent again and bring about a return to the ancient faith. That seemed necessary if the Holy Land was to be spared a frightful fate when the day of the Lord arrived. The supplementer thus formulated this idea as a divine promise (4:5-6). The hope, enhanced by this prophecy, had a living influence on the minds of people in the time of Jesus.

Joel and the Locust Plague

It was apparently some time after Nehemiah, who came from Persia in 445, that Joel arose as prophet in Judah. For he refers to the walls of Jerusalem (2:9), which were built during Nehemiah's governorship. A great locust plague was the occasion of Joel's prophesying. Well may these migratory locusts be compared to an army. Joel knows that the locust has a life cycle of a number of stages; he uses special names for four of them (1:4; 2:25). (According to modern entomologists there are actually six stages.) Even the temple cult was affected by the plague. Joel mentions only the cutting off of cereal offerings and drink offerings. Perhaps bloody sacrifices were discouraged because of Persian disapproval of them. Joel calls on the priests to weep and pray in front of the temple (2:17), and demands that a public fast and assembly be held (1:14; 2:12, 15 ff.). When he says ... "rend your hearts and not your garments" (2:13) he is a worthy successor of Jeremiah (Jer. 4:4). The prophetic call to repentance (2:13b) sets forth an idea of God that is admirable: God is gracious and merciful. Joel believes so firmly in this mercy that he utters an advance song of thanksgiving (2:21-27).

It seems likely that the prophecy was made more meaningful for later readers by interpolated references to the day of the Lord (cf. 1:15; 2:1b-2a; 11b). The locusts thus came to be considered figurative for enemies or even became apocalyptic locusts (cf. Rev. 9:1-11). Some noteworthy additions were also appended at the end of the book. The first of these is the famous prophecy about eschatological portents

(2:28–32). When all the people of the Lord, down to the male and female slaves, became prophets and the Lord put his spirit upon them (Num. 11:29) or poured it out upon them (Isa. 32:15; 44:3), then the perfect society would be attained. That would be the signal for the arrival of cataclysmic events. Joel is sometimes referred to as the Prophet of the Pentecost, because of the effective use made of this passage in Peter's discourse in Acts (2:17 ff.). In another appendix (3:1–17) a judgment over the nations in the valley of Jehoshaphat is predicted. A final appendix (3:18–21) dwells on the blessed future, making reference to Ezekiel's fountain (Ezek. 47:1 ff.). All this was not in the horizon of Joel. He was concerned only with a locust plague of his own time. In calling men to repentance in the face of calamity, he did yeoman service in the true tradition of prophecy.

Ezra and the Law. When Ezra brought "the book of the law" from Babylonia (which many now believe was after the time of Nehemiah, under Artaxerxes II) and made it the very foundation of the life of the new community, prophecy began to wane. Prophets were now placed under heavy penalty (Deut. 18:20–22). We may suppose that the mistake made by Haggai and Zechariah in prophesying the kingship of Zerubbabel had much to do with the curb placed on prophets. More important in bringing about prophecy's decline was the general shift in emphasis to the study of a book. The institution of the synagogue now replaced the local sanctuaries, since only one legitimate temple, that at Jerusalem, was recognized. At Sabbath gatherings the law, soon put into a larger historical framework, was read.

But the prophetic urge did not die out entirely. It went underground. That is to say, it became literary and anonymous. Productions of this sort and of this age have been interpolated into the prophetic books in the final editing.

13 PROPHETS OF THE EARLY GREEK ERA

The Greek Era Begins

THE PERSIAN ERA ended when Alexander the Great decisively defeated Darius III in Mesopotamia in 331. He had previously taken over
Asia Minor, Syria, and Palestine—as well as Egypt—in 333–332. The
first defeat of Darius at Issus in 333 had opened the gates to Syria. The
fall of Tyre in 332 had eliminated the chief naval power aiding the
Persians. After Alexander's death at Babylon in 323 his realm soon
fell apart. The wars of the Diadochi, "successors" of Alexander, need
not detain us though they brought a major setback to Judah by a capture of Jerusalem and a deportation of many inhabitants by Ptolemy
in 321. The man who sought to preserve a unified realm, Antigonus,
was defeated at Ipsus in Phrygia in 301. The various satraps now regarded themselves as independent. Palestine came under the rule of the
Ptolemies of Egypt for a century, but was won by the Seleucids of
Syria in 198 and remained under them until Rome took over the
control of Syria in 63.

Deutero-Zechariah (Zech. 9-11)

From the early Greek era in the main may come chapters 9–11 of
the book of Zechariah, nowadays called Deutero-Zechariah. Some indeed
hold that the campaign of Alexander himself after Issus is directly

mirrored in 9:1–8. But Alexander did not come from Hadrach (near Aleppo); he came from Cilicia. A siege of Tyre is not yet an actuality, such as it so quickly became. Furthermore Gaza in Alexander's time did not have a king, as 9:5 presupposes, but was under a Persian prefect. There is thus good reason to regard this as an earlier prophecy. Whether the advent prophecy of 9:9–10 is to be considered its conclusion or is a separate entity is also a moot question. The use of this prophecy in the New Testament (Matt. 21:4 ff.) and in the religious life of the church has made it immortal:

> Rejoice greatly, O daughter of Zion!
>   Shout aloud, O daughter of Jerusalem!
> Lo, your king comes to you;
>   triumphant and victorious is he,
> humble and riding on an ass,
>   on a colt the foal of an ass.
> I will cut off the chariot from Ephraim
>   and the war horse from Jerusalem;
> and the battle bow shall be cut off,
>   and he shall command peace to the nations;
> his dominion shall be from sea to sea,
>   and from the River to the ends of the earth. (9:9–10)

The lines hail the coming of the Messiah, but he is pictured as arriving in humility, rather than in glory. Military occupation of Palestine will end; peace will prevail in the world under the Messiah's sway.

Another passage in Deutero-Zechariah that seemed prophetic to early Christians is the shepherd allegory (11:4–17) to which the misplaced "Woe to the worthless shepherd" (13:7–9) is related. The item about the thirty pieces of silver (11:13) is used for the story of Judas (Matt. 26:15; 27:9). The words, "Strike the shepherd, that the sheep may be scattered" (13:7) are quoted by Jesus as prophetic of his own death and of the desertion of the disciples (Matt. 26:31). But the passage is really an allegory dealing with persons and events in the history of the high priesthood. Since Alexander the Great, the high priest was not only the religious head, but also responsible for the civil government. Such a one, therefore, could well be called a "shepherd." It is impossible, however, to identify the persons meant, for we know too little about the internal history of Judah in the time from 330–200 B.C. It seems likely, too, that a number of hands have tampered with the original allegory.

Trito-Zechariah (Zech. 12-14)

An unknown individual, a man of priestly mentality and a pedant, put together a small eschatological section that is appended to Zechariah by a title similar to the one of 9:1. He repeatedly predicts an onslaught of the nations against Jerusalem, and their defeat by the Lord. There are some unique things in this section, notably the importance given the "house of David." It may well be that the Davidic descendants returned from exile in the Greek period and organized themselves into an important faction. Very peculiar is the great repentant mourning that is to be held by them and the inhabitants of Jerusalem for one who had been "pierced" (12:10 ff.). But how they could "look upon him" is difficult to understand, especially if this was to be an annual ritual, comparable to the Adonis ritual. The author of the fourth Gospel saw in this item a prophecy of the piercing of the side of Jesus by the Roman soldier (John 19:37). In connection with the latter day events Trito-Zehariah sees the Lord's feet standing on the Mount of Olives. Desirable changes in the local topography are to be brought about by earthquakes. The survivors of the heathen assault are to make annual pilgrimage to Jerusalem. Egyptians in particular are to be penalized if they fail to come. Everything is to be holy at Jerusalem, down to the pots and pans.

Perhaps the most surprising thing in a section that operates with prophetic oracles is the prediction of a complete elimination of prophets from the scene (13:3–6). Their own parents will disown them. They themselves will be ashamed even to admit that they are prophets. This is the sad end of the greatest religious movement of Hebrew history.

The So-called Isaiah Apocalypse (Isa. 24-27)

This is another eschatological piece, but interspersed with various other materials, such as descriptions of conditions of the time, and songs of lamentation and thanksgiving.

One of the most interesting items in the section is the echo of very ancient mythology in the punishing of Leviathan (27:1–13). Frequent allusions are made to a city that occupied a lofty position but has become desolate. Guesses as to the one meant are numerous but unconvincing. Some think the Moabite city Kir-hareseth (el- Kerak) is meant, but its destruction would seem to belong to the future (25:10–12). Samaria could be meant, now that papyri belonging to fugitives of 333 from there have been found; but that would make this a somewhat earlier production than the eschatological ideas indicate. In this section we get the first mention of the "great trumpet" (27:13; cf. Matt. 24:31), though as yet only to summon Jews from afar; allusion to an end of death (25:8; cf. 1 Cor. 15:54), to the imprisonment and punishment of the "host of heaven" (24:21; cf. Dan. 10:13; 12:1) and to the resurrection, which is to be brought about by a supernatural dew from heaven.

> Thy dead shall live, their bodies shall rise.
>   O dwellers in the dust, awake and sing for joy!
> For thy dew is a dew of light,
>   and on the land of the shades thou wilt let it fall. (26:19)

The passage comes close to Dan. 12:2 in meaning.

Jonah: Tale of an Ancient Prophet

To the Greek period one may assign the story about the ancient Israelite prophet Jonah who prophesied shortly before Amos under Jeroboam II (2 Kings 14:25). Its author must have been an urbane, broad-minded, kindly man, with a sense of humor. The story serves various useful purposes. It explains why terrible threats given by prophets were not always fulfilled and shows that this does not mean that these men were false prophets. God acts in sovereign freedom, and can adopt a different course if circumstances warrant. To bring about repentance and change of heart is the real objective of the threats made in his name, and that was achieved in this case since Nineveh did penance. The Jews, furthermore, are cautioned against hating or despising the gentiles and thinking that the Lord will annihilate all of them. Jonah, waiting on the mound opposite Nineveh to see fire and brimstone falling on it from heaven, is gently rebuked for his discontent at the nonfulfillment of his prophecy. His complaint to the Lord:

> "... for I knew that thou art a gracious God and merciful, slow to anger, and abounding in steadfast love, and repentest of evil." (4:2)

is actually and by the author's intent a supreme praise of him. After an object lesson with the castor plant or "miracle tree" the merciful Lord speaks gently with his servant, and puts him to shame because of his ill humor:

> And the LORD said, "You pity the plant, for which you did not labor, nor did you make it grow, which came into being in a night, and perished in a night. And should not I pity Nineveh, that great city, in which there are more than a hundred and twenty thousand persons who do not know their right hand from their left, and also much cattle?" (4:10–11)

Nowhere in the Old Testament have more kindly thoughts toward the gentiles been imputed to God. He cares about this great city and all that are in it. His mercy embraces all men, and he takes account of whether gentiles "know their right hand from their left" (i.e., have the insight into what God requires that the Hebrew has). Their "ignorance" (Acts 17:30) is mercifully taken into consideration. And the Lord is even reluctant to destroy all the cattle of the Ninevites which have shared in the fast, and no doubt have shown deep emotional feeling and made the welkin ring with their complaints.

It is refreshing to find among the Old Testament prophetic books one which is not centered in Jewish nationalism or views God as Israel's partisan, but rather thinks of him as the God of mankind. In the book of Jonah we thus have the afterglow of the prophetic movement, casting an effulgence once more, before it wanes. Not until Jesus raised his voice in the Sermon on the Mount and spoke of his Father in heaven, who makes the sun rise on the evil and the good, and sends rain on the just and unjust, was there a dawn of a new, more glorious day for a religion of goodwill to men.

Daniel Among the Prophets

FOR THE CHRISTIAN READER Daniel is a prophetic book. This is because he is called a prophet in the New Testament (Matt. 24:15) and because of the profound influence, especially of the visions, on Jesus and early Christianity. In our English Bible the book of Daniel follows Ezekiel. Not so in the Hebrew Bible, where it stands not among the prophets but among "the Writings." From the standpoint of the book's own suppositions the author (at any rate of the visions) was a man living in the time of the Chaldean and Persian kings. But this, in the view of all critical scholars, is a masquerade. Since prophecy, as we have seen, was virtually outlawed in the second century B.C., the idea came up to publish predictions under the name of some wise man or prophet of long ago. The pattern was provided by ancient Egyptian tales of wise men or seers who prophesied to a ruler about what would happen in the future—how his dynasty would end in social chaos and be replaced by a new one bringing blessing to the country. Jewish authors took over the pattern but gave it a new importance by providing a finale consisting of judgment over a current empire that had trodden down their people and the coming of the kingdom of God or of the Messiah. Thus was born the apocalyptic literature of which Daniel is the oldest specimen.

Much of the book of Daniel consists of narratives which were derived from older stories current in the East. They are in the Aramaic language except for 1:1–2:4a. These stories may have been written down earlier when the situation was less grave. They added spice, as well as instruction, to the book. We must forego dealing with them here. The apocalypticism really begins in the last Aramaic chapter (chapter 7), but an apocalyptic element was already injected into the story of chapter 2 over which we must briefly linger.

The Image in Nebuchadnezzar's Dream. Nebuchadnezzar saw an image which from the head down was composed of four sections consisting of different metals—gold, silver, bronze, and iron. The feet, however, though belonging to the iron section, were partly iron and partly clay. Suddenly without aid of human hands, a stone was cut from a mountain, and tumbling downhill it completely shattered the image. The stone itself then grew into a great mountain which filled all the earth.

In interpreting this dream Daniel says that the head of gold meant Nebuchadnezzar and his kingdom. The other three sections of the image are said to mean kingdoms that will follow his. The reader is left to guess what kingdoms these were. The main interest is in the fourth kingdom—the one represented by iron. It is the one near whose end the real author is living. Here the great fact is that it is a divided kingdom (as the two legs suggest) but lacks cohesion and strength (symbolized by the feet of iron and clay). Daniel's later visions will reveal that the author is thinking of the empire of Alexander the Great and its two main eastern successors, the Ptolemaic realm of Egypt and the Seleucid realm of Syria. The stone represents the kingdom of God, which will break down all these kingdoms, but itself will endure forever and be all-embracing.

It is evident that the scheme of four kingdoms is secondarily combined with that of an image. We hear of four ages represented by the same metals in other quarters. The Greek poet Hesiod (c. 700 B.C.) already has it. Ovid, who incorporated so much Oriental lore in his Metamorphoses, uses it at the beginning of that work. To apply the idea of four ages to a period starting with Nebuchadnezzar is the rather artificial device of the author of Daniel.

The Crisis. In the years preceding the issuance of the book of Daniel the Jewish people were put to a test such as had not been seen since the time of Elijah. The overlord of the Jews now was the Seleucid king Antiochus IV Epiphanes (176–164). The Seleucid empire was engaged in a desperate effort to maintain itself. Integration to form a unified people out of its diverse nationalities was the political need of the hour. The unifying factor—under Greek presuppositions—could only be a religiously oriented one. All would have to accept the imperial god. The Jews would also have to give up their ritualistic "super-stitions" that set them apart from other peoples, prevented cooperation and fellowship with the gentiles, and made impracticable any drafting of them for army service. Leading Jewish liberals encouraged Antiochus to apply the needed coercion. When Antiochus founded a Hellenistic city (which is only referred to as the "Acra" or "citadel") within Jerusalem's confines, and set up an object in the temple that was later twisted to read "the abomination that makes desolate" or the "abomin-ation of desolation" (Dan. 11:31, 12:11; cf. 9:27) this aroused horror and resentment. This event is said to have taken place on the 25th of Chislev (Dec. 17), 167. The object was evidently a symbol of the god *Baal Shamayim*, "Lord of Heaven," who was equated with the Olympian Zeus, the patron deity of the Seleucids. The Jews could, so their liberals held, simply regard Baal Shamayim as another name of their god. A sim-ilar designation, "God of heaven," had already been used for the Lord in the Persian period. But there evidently was much more that was brought into the temple by means of this Trojan horse—heathen ritual, such as had so greatly incensed Ezekiel (Ezek. 8:5 ff.). To quell opposition the high priest urged Antiochus to abolish the Mosaic law and introduce Greek law instead. Furthermore coercion was to be used and death penalties were to be meted out. Thus began the reign of terror of which 1 Maccabees 2 gives a report.

The flame of rebellion broke out in a town named Modein near the Philistine border. There a man named Mattathias slew a Jew who was bringing heathen sacrifice, along with the Greek officer supervising him. Mattathias and his sons and followers fled to a hiding place in the wilderness. After the father's death the sons under the lead of Judas Maccabaeus began a guerrilla war. It consisted first of all of killing Jews of the liberal party and then of fighting against auxiliary troops from nearby Hellenized cities sent to subdue the rebels (1 Macc. 3–4). The "regular" Seleucid troops were off with their king Antiochus, who had left Antioch probably at the end of 166, for a campaign in Persia. Judas and his followers succeeded in regaining control of the temple (though not yet of the Acra) and dedicated it anew three years after its defile-ment. This occasion was then celebrated annually. It is the festival called Hanukkah, "dedication." It was about the time of the first Ha-nukkah that the book of Daniel was issued.

The Key to Daniel's Expectations. The author of Daniel is a scripture student. The collection of the Prophets was already completed,
and men were regarding these books as not only concerned with their
own time of origin but as prophetic of the distant future. The author
was especially intrigued by Jeremiah's prophecy of the seventy years (Jer.
25:11 ff.; 29:10). He interprets this figure by mystical use of numbers,
taking each year as a week of years, hence the seventy years as 490
years. He reviews history since Jerusalem's fall to the coming "end," di-
viding 490 into three periods: 7 x 7, 62 x 7, and 1 x 7 years. He is living
in the last of these periods, and in its second half (3½ years) which,
he holds, started after the defilement of the temple by Antiochus
(9:27). He thus has a mathematical clue as to when the end will arrive.

The Vision of the Judgment over the Empires. The first vision of
Daniel is that of chapter 7. With his weird symbolism of four great
beasts that come out of the sea the author characterizes the four
empires, Chaldean, Median, Persian, and Greek, already referred to
under a different guise in chapter 2. His interest is focused on the
fourth beast, with the Seleucid kings and especially the contemporary
one, Antiochus Epiphanes, the center of interest. This is followed by
a judgment scene. The throne of flames with wheels of flame suggests
some influence derived from the Lord's throne-wagon in Ezekiel. The
deity is provided with myriads of servants—an incidental item that plays
no further role. The opening of books suggests a record of decrees or
destinies (4:17; 10:21; in Rev. 20:12 taken as record of sins).

The judgment is elicited by "the great words" the horn was speaking;
the self-vaunting pride of Antiochus thus is the intolerable thing. If
Daniel sees the (fourth) beast slain and burned, this is something yet to
come from the standpoint of the author's time. The prolongation of life
for the other three beasts, however, mirrors the standpoint of Belshazzar's time; they were already done for in the author's time.

One might think that the vision was ended therewith. But the author
adds a supplementary element:

> I saw in the night visions,
> and behold, with the clouds of heaven
> there came one like a son of man,
> and he came to the Ancient of Days
> and was presented before him.

> And to him was given dominion
>   and glory and kingdom,
> that all peoples, nations, and languages
>   should serve him;
> his dominion is an everlasting dominion,
>   which shall not pass away,
> and his kingdom one
>   that shall not be destroyed. (7:13-14)

The personage arriving from heaven was "one like a son of man." "Like" as in the case of Ezekiel's use of the word indicates the inadequacy of the comparison. "Son of man," however, is merely idiomatic Aramaic for "a man," and not as in Ezekiel's Hebrew a term reminding of the gulf between God and man. The idea thus is no different from "a form that had the appearance of a man" (Ezek. 8:2). But Daniel does not go into any description of the individual. This manlike one is presented before the ancient of days and is given lasting world dominion.

In the interpretation (7:22, 27) the manlike one is not mentioned at all—there the kingdom is to be given to the saints of the Most High, i.e., to the Jewish pious men of the day. But there can be no kingdom without a king and the interpretation cannot be regarded as excluding one. Caution and desire to avoid contention may have dictated the formulation. It is quite understandable that the figure of the "one like a son of man" was understood later as representing the Messiah. This was clearly the case in the time of Jesus when "Son of man" was used as a messianic title. Early Christians understood the scene in Daniel as predictive of the second coming of Jesus to assume the dominion.

The Course and the End of History

The last vision of Daniel (10:1–12:13) has an impressive staging. After three weeks of fasting and mourning an angel (perhaps again the Gabriel of 8:16) appears to Daniel to strengthen him. Before leaving he reveals the future to him.

A survey of history up to the time in which the author of the book is living follows (11:2–39). It passes very quickly over the Persian and early Hellenistic periods (11:2b–4), and then is concerned with the struggles between "king of the south" (the Ptolemies of Egypt) and "the king of the north" (the Seleucids of Syria, 11:5–20); it waxes most detailed when it deals with the history of Antiochus IV Epiphanes, which was still in process at the time of writing (164). From here on the author indulges in independent prediction about events to come (11:40–45) and the deliverance of the faithful (12:1–3).

He expects a new war to break out. The king of the south (Ptolemy VI) will attack, but Antiochus will rush against him and in so doing invade many lands and also the "glorious land," i.e., Palestine. The archenemies of the Jews—Edom, Moab, and the remnant of the Ammonites—will (unfortunately) go unscathed, but Egypt will be subjugated and despoiled and Lybia and Ethiopia be made tributary. Alarmed by tidings from the east and north Antiochus will retreat from Egypt and set up his tent between the sea and the "glorious holy mountain" (i.e., Zion), and there "he shall come to his end, with none to help him."

The author does not need to dilate upon the manner of the destruction of the foe, for that has been sufficiently dealt with in earlier prophecy. But he feels constrained to supplement the received picture by again bringing in the figure of the archangel "Michael," the patron angel of God's people (10:21). He will deliver all those whose names are written "in the book" (cf. Mal. 3:16; Exod. 32:32 ff.; Rev. 3:5). For there will be a time of trouble such as has never existed before. But in that book evidently were contained also the names of many who were already deceased. So the prediction continues:

> And many of those who sleep in the dust of the earth shall awake, some to everlasting life, and some to shame and everlasting contempt. And those who are wise shall shine like the brightness of the firmament; and those who turn many to righteousness, like the stars for ever and ever. (12:2–3)

A resurrection of "many" is taught here, and special glory will attend the "wise," i.e., the religious teachers of this era of martyrdom. The wicked, too, are to be raised up in order that they may receive the punishment which is due them.

The author of Daniel was mistaken in his expectations, both as to the coming events and the proximity of "the end." History took a different course. One can now be more precise about the chronology of the time. Antiochus IV died late in 164, as a new Babylonian king list has shown. News of his death reached Babylon from Persia (where he was campaigning, perhaps since the end of 166) on December 18, 164. This makes it rather certain that the desecration of the Jewish temple took place on the 25th of Chislev (December 17, 167) and its rededication on the same lunar date in 164 (December 20)—hence before the news of Antiochus's death could have reached Palestine. The author of Daniel must thus have concluded his book while Antiochus was in Persia. As the three and a half years were about up he was forced to make extensions of time to allow for a return of Antiochus and the events he had predicted. He must have been disappointed when the news of Antiochus's death came and no "end."

Actually things were not to be solved apocalyptically as the author of Daniel expected, but militarily and diplomatically through the actions of the Maccabaeans and the constant revolutions in the Seleucid royal house. The author of Daniel could go to sleep, like his ancient hero, and wait for resurrection day. The days of the kingdoms of this world were not yet over.

Conclusion

In the unrolling drama of history, Daniel's mistake in attempting to figure out the time of the end and the events preceding it by speculative means (rather than leaving God his freedom) was forgotten. The book was followed by numerous other apocalypses—all attributed to men of ancient times: Enoch, the twelve patriarchs or sons of Jacob, Moses, and others. When Greek rule was succeeded by Roman sovereignty and Roman brutality was experienced, Daniel's fourth beast was interpreted as the Roman Empire. The coming "end" of the travail of history and the arrival of the kingdom of God became a living hope, especially in times of crisis, and among the humble people who suffered helplessly from oppressors and would-be liberators alike.

But true prophecy of an earlier age than Daniel, before it expired, had foreseen its own renewal. In the synagogue, where the law and the prophets were read, the belief in the coming of another prophet like Moses (Deut. 18:18) or the return of Elijah (Mal. 4:5–6) was nurtured and was fitted into the apocalyptic expectations. The stage was thus set for new prophetic personalities to arise. John the Baptist and Jesus appeared on the scene, and each attracted attention and raised the question in the minds of the common people as to whether he was one of those expected, or even the Messiah himself.

Such public speculation was perilous, for the "end" forecast by actual arrival of the prophesied figures would imply the coming of the kingdom and the overthrow of the Roman Empire. According to Josephus, Herod Antipas put John the Baptist to death because he feared his activity would lead to a rebellion. That may be nearer to the truth than the explanation given in the Gospels. It seems certain that a similar fear was advanced in the case of Jesus by the Jewish leaders, and perhaps by Herod Antipas himself, which brought about the demand of the sentencing of the Galilean by Pilate.

The rejection of the Messiahship of Jesus by the Jews led to the one thing that was necessary to make the prophets of the past fruitful for all mankind: the rise of a new, nonnational community that regarded itself as the true Israel, and applied the ancient oracles to the story of Jesus and to its own life and conduct. Thus the prophets of the Old Testament became a bridge for the passage of multitudes into the religion of a new world.

NOTES AND REFERENCES

The following abbreviations are used for sources frequently cited in these notes and references:

Commentary, 1: Commentary on the Prophets. Vol. 1 Isaiah-Ezekiel; Commentary, 2: Commentary on the Prophets. Vol. 2 Daniel-Malachi; both by E. G. Kraeling, Thomas Nelson & Son, Camden, N.J. 1966

Bible Atlas: Rand McNally Bible Atlas, 3rd edition (revised), by E. G. Kraeling, Rand McNally & Company, Chicago, Ill. 1966

ANET: Ancient Near Eastern Texts Relating to the Old Testament, rev. ed. by James B. Pritchard, Princeton University Press, 1955

Introduction

Cf. Commentary, 1, 15–28, where matters suited to the literary-critical study, and notably to form-criticism, are dealt with; also pages 28–31 for a Bibliography on the Prophets.

PAGE 14. The reasons for the uniqueness of the Hebrew prophets were most clearly discerned by sociologist Max Weber. See his Ancient Judaism, tr. from the German work of 1923.

PAGE 18. The Egyptian tale of Wen Amon of 1100 B.C. mentions a case of prophetic seizure at Byblos in Phoenicia, but no title is used. See ANET, 26.

Chapter 1. Amos, Harbinger of Judgment

Cf. Introduction and Bibliography in Commentary, 2, 143–46.

No mention is made in this chapter of the "doxologies" (4:13; 5:8–9; 9:5–6). These are later accretions. The wisdom saying 5:13 is also an addition—perhaps a remark by a reader. The keynote saying of 1:2 is partially derived from the same quarter as Joel 3:16. It helped make Amos acceptable to those who stressed Jerusalem as the Lord's residence. The allusions to "Zion" in 6:1 and to "David" in 6:5 are likewise not original. On emendations see Commentary, 2, 166 f. The hopeful conclusion 9:8b–15 is also a later addition.

PAGE 28. The sycamore figs do not grow on outer branches or twigs like other fruits, but on short stems along the trunk and limbs. "Dressing" the fruit is called "circumcising" in Egyptian Arabic. The work is done by boys. There are three crops in Egypt—May, June and August-September. Only the first two are operated on. At the time of the third crop people are too busy with other things. For

Amos this was evidently a summer job, while others took care of the flocks in the summer pasturage.

Chapter 2. Hosea, Witness of Israel's Decline

Cf. Introduction and Bibliography in Commentary, 2, 77–85.

PAGE 52. The reader will note that some verses in 1:2–8 are not mentioned. Verses 4b–5 represent expansion of significance for the name "Jezreel." It is possible that verse 5 is an allusion to a disastrous battle fought by Israel against Tiglath-pileser III, whether when he was en route to Philistaea in 734 (see page 95 f.) or in 733 (see page 97). Verse 7 is an obvious Judean addition.

PAGE 52. The shocking announcement of the disowning of Israel was unbearable for people later. An addition amounting to a complete reversal was added in 1:10–2:1. The "one head" is presumably the future Davidic king. "They shall go up from the land" is uncertain in meaning. Perhaps one should read "the lands" (i.e. of exile). The allusion to a great day of Jezreel may be to a future Armageddon, reversing the defeat of 1:5. The chapter division was wrongly made at 2:1.

PAGE 53. The births are not apt to have taken place in quick succession, as an infant was not weaned until after three years (2 Macc. 7:27).

PAGE 53. Specific mention of the grain may well be of legal significance, as we set forth in Commentary, 2, 82 on the basis of an Assyrian law-code (see ANET, 183). A return of the slave to her owner (cf. Ex. 21:8) may have been possible by forfeiting the grain.

PAGE 54. We sided with the second theory in Commentary, 2, 80 f.

PAGE 60 f. The account of Hosea's knowledge of past history of his people and of recent or current internal affairs had to be abridged.

PAGE 63. The new Assyrian account of the campaign of 734 was published by D. J. Wiseman in Iraq, 13, 1951, 211 ff.

PAGE 58. The supplementary prophecies in 2:16–23 are of later origin. There are four of them. Verses 16–17 predict abandonment of use of the title Báal ("Lord," not to be confused with a different word so translated or with the name rendered LORD). Verse 18 predicts God will make a covenant with the wild beasts so that they will do his people no harm. The piece is extended to include the pacifistic hope of abolition of arms and warfare. Verse 19 speaks rather beautifully of a betrothal forever. Verses 21–23 deal with the future blessings of nature, and dismantle the ominous names of Hosea's children after the manner of 1:10–2:1.

PAGE 63. The theory rejected was advanced by the German scholar Alt in 1919, but has recently received renewed attention.

Chapter 3. The Early Isaiah and Micah, Judah's Warners

ISAIAH

Cf. Introduction and Bibliography in Commentary, 1, 33 f., 39–41.

Isaiah 40–66 must be cut off from 1–39. See Deutero-Isaiah. But chapters 1–39 contain much that is not by Isaiah. Chapters 36–39 are derived from 2 Kings. The real Isaiah's words must be sought in the areas of chapters 1–11, 17–18, 20, 28–32. Even here there are later pieces.

PAGE 74. That the agricultural rules were given by a deity was also believed by the ancient Sumerians. See Samuel N. Kramer, *From the Tablets of Sumer*, 1956, 61 ff. Here it was the god Ninurta.

PAGE 73. Most of those who would hold 6:13 are ready to sacrifice the words "Holy seed is its stump" as a gloss. But the clumsy and involved sentence is not in Isaiah's style. On different readings in the Qumran Isaiah Scroll see M. Burrows, *More Light on the Dead Sea Scrolls*, 1958, 147 ff.

PAGE 77. On the tomb and its inscription see *Bible Atlas*, 305 f.

MICAH

Cf. Introduction and Bibliography, *Commentary*, 2, 204 f.

Chapter 4. Isaiah and the Struggle of Nations

PAGE 89. The parenthetic remark in 7:8 probably has the resettlement of Israel's land by foreigners under Ashurbanipal (Ezra 4:10) in mind. See *Commentary*, 1, 65 f. "(Only) a remnant will return." That a battle was fought outside of the city seems clear from the very different picture of events in 2 Chron. 28:6 ff.

PAGE 90. The offer of a miraculous sign sounds legendary. The story of 38:1 ff. (see page 100) provides the kind of a sign the narrator of 7:11 had in mind.

PAGE 93. There would hardly be time enough between the birth of Shearjashub (735?) and the child of 8:1–4 (733) for the birth of the Immanuel child by the prophet's wife; see the comment to page 53.

PAGE 96. In *Commentary*, 1, 70, we regarded the Immanuel prophecy as a legendary offshoot of 8:1–4.

PAGE 97. It seems doubtful that the prediction of 9:1 was formulated in Isaiah's time or by him. The belief in a restoration of these regions could have come up in Persian or Hellenistic times. "Galilee of the nations" suggests gentile environment. The region was only Judaized in Maccabean times.

PAGE 103. For Sargon's reports see *ANET*, 285.

PAGE 109. For Sennacherib's report see *ANET*, 287 f.

Chapter 5. The Renewal of Prophecy: Zephaniah and the Young Jeremiah

ZEPHANIAH

See Introduction and Bibliography, *Commentary*, 2, 260 f.

PAGE 125. The third chapter of Zephaniah contains appended prophecies of later vintage: (1) A woe on a rebellious city (Jerusalem), 3:1–7; (2) prophecy of divine judgment over the gentiles 3:8–10, with an appended friendlier prediction of their conversion, verses 9–10; (3) description of the Jewish community at Jerusalem in the blessed future 3:11–13; (4) call to rejoicing over the sovereignty of God in the midst of his people, 3:14–15; (5) supplementary prophecies, elaborating on the divine protection and restoration.

JEREMIAH

See Introduction and Bibliography in Commentary, 1, 231–37.

Chapter 6. Prophets of the End of an Era: Jeremiah and Nahum

PAGE 152. The Babylonian Chronicle texts. An important first selection was published by C. J. Gadd, *The Fall of Nineveh*, 1923. (This text will be found translated in *ANET*.) It was republished with the rest of these materials by D. J. Wiseman, *Chronicles of Chaldaean Kings (626–556 B.C.) in the British Museum*, 1956. These texts will be referred to often.

NAHUM

Cf. Introduction and Bibliography in Commentary, 2, 229–32.
See *Bible Atlas*, 310, for plan of Nineveh and further observations.

Chapter 7. At the Beginning of the New Age: Jeremiah and Habakkuk
HABAKKUK

Cf. Introduction and Bibliography, Commentary, 2, 242–47.
PAGE 168. The name "Hatti" is used frequently for Syria and Palestine in the Assyro-Babylonian. It recalls the sovereignty that the Hittites of Anatolia had exercised there many centuries earlier. When "Heth" or "Hittite" is used for the pre-Israelite population of Palestine (e.g. Gen. 23:3; Ezek. 16:3) we have a similar usage.
PAGE 172. For the Babylonian Creation Epic see *ANET*, 60 ff. The psalm of Habakkuk was not included in the Habakkuk-Commentary from Qumran, since it furnished no material for historical comment. For this commentary, see the reference to page 266.
PAGE 188. In the Lachish Ostraca (*ANET*, 321 f.) a secret letter received from a prophet is mentioned. The man can hardly have been Jeremiah; it was probably a nationalistic prophet. On Lachish see *Bible Atlas*, 302, 315.

Chapter 10. The Warner Out of Exile: Ezekiel

Cf. Introduction and Bibliography in Commentary, 1, 401–5.

Chapter 11. The Prophet of Hope: Deutero-Isaiah

Cf. Introduction and Bibliography in Commentary, 1, 34 f. and 41–43.
PAGE 266. Those who hold that the servant poems, or at least the fourth, come from a later admirer of Deutero-Isaiah can invoke the reverence shown by the Qumran Sect for "the teacher of righteousness" (apparently the founder of the sect, who seems to have been martyred in the time of the "wicked priest"). See

the material in A. Dupont-Sommer, *The Essene Writings from Qumran*, tr. by
G. Vermes, 1962 (Meridian Books), 358 ff.

Chapter 12. Prophets of the Return and Restored Community

HAGGAI
Cf. Introduction and Bibliography in *Commentary*, 2, 273–75.
PAGE 271. The precise dates, following the Babylonian calendar, can be converted
into our calendar with the help of tables prepared by astronomers and Assyriolo-
gists. The convenient handbook for this is Richard A. Parker and Waldo Dubber-
stein, *Babylonian Chronology 626 B.C.–A.D. 75* (Brown University Studies XIX),
Brown University Press. We have omitted the days in most cases.

ZECHARIAH
Cf. Introduction and Bibliography in *Commentary*, 2, 283–87.

TRITO-ISAIAH
See note on Deutero-Isaiah.

OBADIAH
Cf. Introduction and Bibliography in *Commentary*, 2, 182–84.

MALACHI
Cf. Introduction and Bibliography in *Commentary*, 2, 324–25.

JOEL
Cf. Introduction and Bibliography in *Commentary*, 2, 124–27.
PAGE 278. Cf. the great locust plague of 1915, as described by J. D. Whiting in
National Geographic, 1915, 511–50.

Chapter 13. Prophets of the Early Greek Era

JONAH
Cf. Introduction and Bibliography in *Commentary*, 2, 191–95.

Chapter 14. Daniel and the World Empires

Cf. Introduction and Bibliography in *Commentary*, 2, 19–24.
The name Daniel was that of a much earlier wise man, Ezek. 14:14. The Ras
Shamra texts of the 15th century B.C. tell of a Phoenician Dan'el, who was a
righteous judge and probably a king. This fits Ezek. 28:3.
PAGE 291. The king list referred to was published by A. J. Sachs and D. J. Wiseman
in *Iraq*, 16, 1954, 202 ff.

INDEX